INTRODUCING FEDORA

BRIAN PROFFITT

Course Technology PTR
A part of Cengage Learning

COURSE TECHNOLOGY
CENGAGE Learning

Australia • Brazil • Japan • Korea • Mexico • Singapore • Spain • United Kingdom • United States

COURSE TECHNOLOGY
CENGAGE Learning

Introducing Fedora

Brian Proffitt

Publisher and General Manager,
Course Technology PTR:
Stacy L. Hiquet

Associate Director of Marketing:
Sarah Panella

Manager of Editorial Services:
Heather Talbot

Marketing Manager: Mark Hughes

Acquisitions Editor: Mitzi Koontz

Project and Copy Editor: Marta
Justak

Technical Reviewer: Keith
Davenport

Interior Layout Tech: MPS Limited,
A Macmillan Company

Cover Designer: Luke Fletcher

CD-ROM Producer: Brandon
Penticuff

Indexer: Chris Small

Proofreader: Sharon Hilgenberg

For product information and technology assistance, contact us at
Cengage Learning Customer & Sales Support, 1-800-354-9706

For permission to use material from this text or product, submit all requests online at **cengage.com/permissions**
Further permissions questions can be emailed to
permissionrequest@cengage.com

Library of Congress Control Number: 2010928008

ISBN-13: 978-1-4354-5778-2

ISBN-10: 1-4354-5778-1

Course Technology, a part of Cengage Learning
20 Channel Center Street
Boston, MA 02210
USA

Cengage Learning is a leading provider of customized learning solutions with office locations around the globe, including Singapore, the United Kingdom, Australia, Mexico, Brazil, and Japan. Locate your local office at: **international.cengage.com/region**

Cengage Learning products are represented in Canada by Nelson Education, Ltd.

For your lifelong learning solutions, visit **courseptr.com**

Visit our corporate website at **cengage.com**

Printed in the United States of America
1 2 3 4 5 6 7 12 11 10

For Aberash, who brings light.

ACKNOWLEDGMENTS

It goes without saying that you would not be holding this book in your hands had not some very talented and creative people lent their skills to help me get this done in what may be record time.

I can never express enough gratitude to my editors. For those of you who think this brilliant writing is the sole product of my fevered work, you would be wrong. So I thank Mitzi Koontz, Marta Justak, Chris Small, and Sharon Hilgenberg profusely for their efforts in making my stuff so much better. Marta gets an extra helping of thanks, since she has had to contend with my odd sense of humor for years.

They say no man is an island. I am fortunate enough to have four spectacular women in my life who know how to treat me right (or drive me insane, depending on the time of day). My wife and three wonderful daughters get the big thanks and smooches for putting up with me squirreled away in the basement office (a.k.a. "The Cave") for days at a stretch.

Thanks must also be extended to my friends and colleagues in the Linux community, who are always there for technical assistance, unsolicited advice, and general putting-me-in-my-place. In particular, Joe Brockmeier, Joe Eckert, and Robert Bogue—who, even though he's an avowed Microsoft consultant, has the heart of a penguin.

About the Author

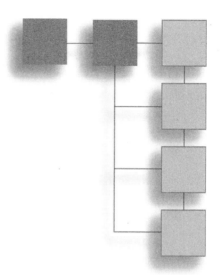

Brian Proffitt is a Linux and Open Source expert, who most recently was the Community Manager of the Linux Foundation, and part of the 2009 relaunch of Linux.com. He has also been Managing Editor of Linux Today (linuxtoday. com), a news and information site about all things Linux and Open Source, as well as four other Linux Web sites for Jupitermedia Corp. He is the author of numerous books on computer technology, mostly on Linux, but with a Mac and Windows book thrown in just for variety. He is also the author of a student guide on Plato. A black belt in taekwondo and a private pilot, he enjoys spending time with his family in his home in northern Indiana.

Contents

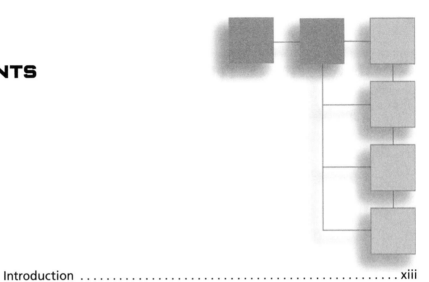

INTRODUCTION

Many people think of Fedora as an operating system that is way over their heads—that only techies can use this strange, arcane OS with the funny name.

For all of you who have been having these thoughts, this book is here to tell you that this is simply not the case. Fedora, and Linux, in general, have become very easy for everyday home and business users to install and use.

Now you can find out for yourself, in just one weekend, how easy it is to get started using Fedora and discover that there is life beyond Windows.

Is This Book for You?

Introducing Fedora is for anyone who wants to get started using Fedora, specifically Fedora 13, and only has one computer at their home or business on which to install this new operating system. Think of this book as a personal tutorial, a one-on-one class with an expert user of Fedora. You get to stay in the comfort of your own home or office and learn how to do the following things:

- Use Fedora as a sole operating system or have it happily co-exist with Windows.

- Gather information about your system to assess your system's capability to use Fedora.

- Learn about the many versions of Linux and the entire Fedora family.

- Install the Fedora operating system.

- Deal with any unusual installation issues.

- Examine the GNOME interface.

- Create a customized desktop.

- Explore the Fedora filesystem.

- Connect to the Internet.

- Add a printer to your PC.

- Add additional hardware to your PC.

- Install software using PackageKit.

- Explore some of the essential tools packaged with Fedora.

- Examine and configure Firefox to browse the Internet and use Evolution to read your email and manage your appointments

- Use OpenOffice.org 3.2 as your preferred office suite.

- Troubleshoot any installation and configuration issues that may pop up.

What's on the CD

There's not a lot you need to start using Fedora—basically, just the software and an Intel-based PC. It does not even have to be a new PC. Fedora works well on older PCs, and has much better performance on older PCs than Windows XP, and also on older machines the new Windows 7 operating system won't even touch.

Fedora is a free-of-charge distribution of Linux, which means that anyone with a broadband Internet connection (like a cable modem or DSL line) and a "write-able" CD-ROM drive can download the whole package and create his or her own CD-ROM. This is free, except for the cost of the blank disc.

For people who don't want to spend much money and don't have access to a big Internet pipe, there is a second option. A few companies download each new version as it is released, create hundreds of CD-ROMs containing the complete Fedora distribution, and then sell them for a low cost.

Much of the preparation for installation is discussed in Chapters 1 and 2. You should definitely read these chapters first so you can get ready for the rest of your exploration of Fedora.

This book details how to find and download your own copy of the Fedora operating system, which is useful for any version of Fedora. We also thought it would be a good idea to make it even easier and include a free, licensed copy of Fedora right in the back of the book. On the CD you will find a complete copy of Fedora 13, ready to install.

On that CD, besides the Fedora operating system, you will find copies of

- OpenOffice.org, a full-featured office suite for Fedora and Windows.

- Firefox, the popular browser that beats Internet Explorer on speed and reliability.

- Evolution, a robust messaging and contact management application.

CD-ROM Downloads

If you purchased an ebook version of this book, and the book had a companion CD-ROM, we will mail you a copy of the disc. Please send ptrsupplements@cengage.com the title of the book, the ISBN, your name, address, and phone number. Thank you.

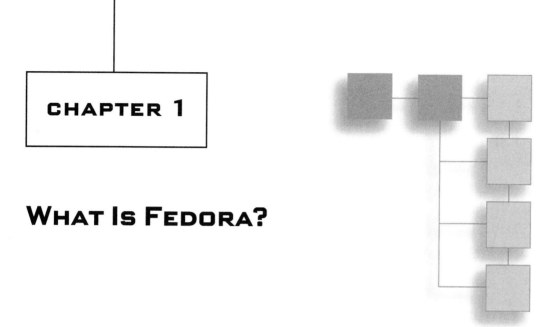

CHAPTER 1

WHAT IS FEDORA?

A fedora is typically defined as a man's hat with a low, creased crown. Popular in the mid-twentieth century, these fashion accessories have recently begun to make a comeback with urban American males.

If you think you've just picked up a book that was incorrectly shelved in the computer section rather than fashion, hold on. We're getting there.

Fedora is also the name of a popular desktop Linux distribution. Like most distributions, it's community-driven and free of charge for users.

You may be asking, what's Linux? For that matter, what's a distribution? And just how is it that an operating system that can do anything Windows can do can be offered for free?

These are common questions to those who are new to Fedora, Linux, and the whole concept of free and open source software. To really explain Fedora, we'll need to take a step back and examine the origins of the software from which Fedora sprang—GNU/Linux.

In this chapter, we'll explore the origins of Linux, learning about its many different types, of which Fedora is just one. Then we'll look into the more recent history of this branch of Linux, Fedora, which is directly descended from Red Hat Linux, and how the most successful commercial company to date can make money giving away free software.

What Is Linux?

You might be asking yourself, why bother with a history lesson? No one kicks off a book on how to use Windows or Mac OS X with a detailed biography of Bill Gates or Steve Jobs. In this case, to understand the origins of Fedora is to understand the functionality of Fedora itself.

Besides, it's a good story, which you can read while you're installing Fedora on your own PC.

A Brief History of Linux

The beginnings of Fedora actually began in Helsinki, Finland. It was there, in 1991, that a young computer science student at the University of Helsinki put the word out to an online newsgroup asking for input on a new operating system he was building for his home PC: a copy of the Minix operating system that, until then, could only be run on big, high-end machines.

That was in August. By the next month, the first version was released with no public announcement; only the group working with the student was privy to the release. On October 5, 1991, version 0.02 of the brand-new code was publicly announced. The rest, as they say, is history. The student, Linus Torvalds, based his master's thesis on the project, now dubbed *Linux*.

By the end of the decade, Linux was found on thousands of computers around the world, serving in many capacities, most notably as the operating system on which most Web site software runs. Current estimates show anywhere from 70–80 percent of the world's Web sites run on top of some version of Linux. Linus himself still serves as project manager for the Linux kernel—the very heart of the operating system—even as businesses ranging from IBM to neighborhood churches use Linux operating systems every day.

Linux has grown to a multibillion dollar a year business, which is not bad for a piece of code that is available absolutely free of charge to anyone who wants it.

You read that right: Linux is indeed free, and in more than one sense of the word. This is understandably puzzling to many new to this operating system, since the concept of making money from something that's free seems counterintuitive. How does this work? To answer, let's take a look at how Linux is put together.

How Linux and Windows Are Nothing Alike

When looking at Linux, invariably comparisons are made to its strongest competitor, Microsoft Windows. It's a fair comparison, since Windows sits on over 90 percent of desktops in the world and has made its company, Microsoft, arguably the richest company on the planet. When you look at each operating system side by side, they look quite a bit alike: there are menus, windows, icons, toolbars—all of the familiar visual cues that most people take for granted when they use a computer these days. When you crack open the hood, however, you will find that Linux and Windows are nothing alike.

Modularity

Let's revisit the work of young Linus. What he and his fellow contributors were working on was not an operating system like Windows or Mac OS X. He was working on what is known as the kernel: the tiny, but powerful, core that lies at the center of all operating systems. But an operating system is not just a kernel; there is software to talk to keyboards, mice, screens, the Internet, installed applications, not to mention the software that makes all of those pretty nifty-looking windows, icons, and menus. Underneath all of that, though, is the kernel: the piece of software that organizes all of the tasks a human being needs a computer to do and translates them into instructions the computer can understand.

Linux is not the only operating system with a kernel at its core. All operating systems have kernels, even Windows, but not all kernels are created equally.

To illustrate, think of a kernel as a child's connecting toy block. It's self-contained, and other blocks can be attached to it easily. In fact, in this example, other blocks certainly do, like the block that displays the computer's output on the screen or the block that controls the network card that lets the computer talk to the Internet. All the blocks connect rather neatly to the kernel block, which is only slightly bigger than the rest of the blocks, because it's not doing all of the work—the other blocks are. The whole thing is put together into what we know as the Linux operating system.

By contrast, the Windows kernel is also a connecting block, but it's much bigger than the blocks that connect to it. It's nearly as big as all of Linux itself, and that's just the Windows kernel. The reason for this size disparity is because the Windows kernel is so interconnected to its helper applications that essentially all the blocks are welded into one monster piece. Other blocks can connect to this kernel, but only in very specific ways. (In fact, to really play up the analogy, in Linux the blocks can be any color or shape you want; in Windows the blocks are all the same shades and very similar in shape.)

In Linux, individual "blocks" are small, and you never use them all at the same time. In Windows, however, individual "blocks" are larger and often used in groups. This difference in structure quickly reveals one of the more significant benefits of Linux over Windows: Linux doesn't need as many machine resources as Windows to run efficiently. In fact, Linux runs very well on PCs that Windows would just sputter on.

Nowhere is this difference more apparent than with the newest Windows operating system, Windows 7, which requires a lot of hardware resources. So much so that many potential Windows 7 users are looking at significant upgrade costs just to get their machines ready. Or they are looking to buy all-new machines altogether. Customers had the same problem (or worse) with the last version of Windows, Vista.

Security

Another big difference in the two operating systems' makeup is in their security. It is a documented fact that there are tens of thousands of Windows viruses, Trojans, and worms out there: a veritable zoo of malicious software designed to cause damage to your data, copy it for others to abuse, or even take over your computer so it can be used to attack other computers. On the other hand, there are only about 500 known Linux viruses, and none of them has ever been let loose in the wild on the massive scale of Windows viruses. Many Linux professionals believe that malware on Linux is so rare that antivirus protection is completely unnecessary. Your best protection is simply to never run an executable program with root, a subject that is covered in Chapter 6, "Installing and Updating Software."

Why such a big gap? One could argue that since the Windows operating system is on such a vast majority of the world's desktops, it makes them a bigger target for malicious software writers, and that's certainly a good reason. But the way Windows operating systems are constructed may also have something to do with it. Recall our analogy: the Windows connecting bricks are all basically the same shape and the same color. In real terms, that means that if one of the blocks gets affected by something bad, then it's much easier for the rest of the blocks to be affected by the same thing.

In Linux, this is not usually going to happen, because it is made up of so many different kinds of blocks. It is possible that someone could "take over" the block that runs an Internet browser on Linux, but that's all a bad coder is likely going to get. In Windows, a similar takeover of the browser could lead to total appropriation of the machine. Finally, there is one more important difference between Windows and Linux. Because of the modular nature of Linux, it can be run on pretty much any kind of computer in any kind of machine. You can find Linux running on everything from supercomputers like IBM's Big Gene/L to TiVos to Droid phones to netbooks.

This happens because Linux is modular all the way down through the kernel. Not only is the operating system made up of blocks, but the kernel itself also is modular in nature. If you want Linux to run on a smartphone like the Google Nexus One, you don't need the part of the kernel that runs a mouse, so it's just taken out. Removing the hardware that engineers don't need leaves them with a kernel that can be run just for their device, whether it's big or small.

Naturally, this doesn't matter to users of Fedora that much. They will use the "generic" version of the Linux kernel, with all of the special applications that the developers of Fedora have decided to ship. All for free.

Yes, there's that word again. Free. When you acquire Fedora, it, and most of the applications that come with it, are free of charge. You don't have to pay a cent. How does that work?

The Meaning of Free Software

Before Linus Torvalds decided to put together the school project that would eventually shake the IT world's foundations, there was a young software developer toiling away at a school a whole ocean away: the Massachusetts Institute of Technology in Cambridge, MA. The developer's name was Richard M. Stallman, and in his work at MIT's Artificial Intelligence Lab, he came up with a pretty nifty idea. Software, he reasoned, should be free for all to use. Not just free of charge, but free to share. He not only thought up this idea, but he also implemented it by creating a set of free tools perfect for the creation of a new, free operating system. Everything an infant operating system needed was included, except a kernel. He called this set of tools GNU, an acronym you will see sometimes while working with Fedora. It means, in a clever, geeky, recursive play on words, *GNU's Not UNIX.*

At the same time, beyond the wordplay, Stallman did something really radical: he created a free software license.

All software created is released under some sort of license. A license dictates how a piece of software can be sold, copied, and used. Much of the software that you have used until now, especially with Windows or OS X, has used what are known as proprietary licenses. A proprietary license states—in painfully long legal detail—that you, the user, can use one copy of the software, say, Windows. You can't copy it and sell it to anyone else. Nor are you allowed to see or otherwise manipulate the code that made Windows. To do so would bring certain doom and destruction upon you. Or worse, lawyers.

What Stallman proposed was a license that would be a mirror image of proprietary licenses. His original idea went something like this:

- You have the freedom to run the program for any purpose.

- You have the freedom to change the program to suit your needs. This means that you can have the source code—the actual human instructions used to put an application together.

- You have the freedom to redistribute copies of the program, either for free or for a fee.

- You have the freedom to redistribute changed copies of the original program.

Those are the four basic principles found in the license Stallman created: the GNU General Public License, or GPL for short. This license was written to guarantee that once software is made free under this license, it will always stay that way.

Free, in this context, means free of charge and also free of restrictions to share and change the code itself. A very common euphemism heard around the Linux community is that the GPL is "free as in 'free speech,' not as in 'free beer.'"

To break this down in nontechnical and nonlegal terms, here's what the GPL means: Here's the software. Here's the source code. Do what you want with it. If you improve it, make sure you include all of the source code with your improvements and pass it along. Don't ever try to keep other people from getting your improvements to the source code. We can tell you to do this, because we wrote the software, and these are the terms under which we're willing to let you have it.

In a less litigious society, this could be broken down even further to: "Be excellent to each other."

How the GPL became tied to Linux was really a matter of practicality. Torvalds had his kernel but none of the tools that would make that kernel into a real operating system. (Think engine without the gears, wheels, shafts, and axles that make a car.) The GNU tools were ready to go, but they had no kernel. In a classic "you've got your chocolate in my peanut butter" flash of inspiration, Torvalds modified the GNU tools so they would run with his Linux kernel, and *poof!* the Linux operating system was born.

Because of the close interplay of the GNU tools and the Linux kernel, Torvalds decided to adopt GNU's GPL for the kernel as well. This interplay is also why you will often see the operating system referred to as *GNU/Linux* and the kernel just as *Linux*. Purists, Stallman the most vocal, believe that adding GNU/ to the Linux name reflects the huge contribution the GNU tools made to the birth of the GNU/Linux operating system.

Whether people back this stance or not, the commonly accepted term for the kernel and the operating system is *Linux,* which is what this book will use unless referring to a version of Linux that specifically uses "GNU/Linux" in its official name.

Now you know how the free part of Linux works. But with all that freedom, how does anyone still make money in the Linux business? Well, if you recall from that list of principles that formed the basis of the GPL, the third item said that one could redistribute GPL software as desired, either free or for a fee. This means that companies are allowed to package Linux (or other free software) and sell it to whoever is willing to buy it.

Okay, so why would a user pay money for something that's free?

There are two reasons, actually. The first one is convenience. While Linux and all of its components are free to acquire, getting all of this software and putting it together is not always something someone wants to do. To return to our analogy, you could buy the box of connecting blocks and put Linux together on your own, but that takes a lot of time and technical expertise.

Instead, you could pay a company that has already put Linux together for you to download from the Internet or buy in a nice box, complete with instruction manuals. Whatever you prefer. Such a company or organization has created what's known as a Linux distribution. All distributions are slightly different from each other, but they're all still Linux.

The second reason someone would pay for something free is for support. After you buy software, many companies will offer free or fee-based technical support, such as a phone number or a Web site for you to use to get questions answered. Linux is no different; in fact, Linux companies depend on support fees to generate their revenue.

It should be noted at this point that Fedora isn't going to charge you money every time you need some help. Fedora doesn't ask for support fees from single users or even smaller commercial users. Instead, the commercial sponsor of Fedora, Red Hat, asks for fees from larger companies that have decided to use the more business-oriented Red Hat Enterprise Linux in their organization. For such customers, having a support contact isn't a luxury—it's a necessity.

The relationship between Fedora and Red Hat Enterprise Linux (RHEL) is relatively straightforward: Fedora is the community-based distribution that acts as a testing ground and "sandbox" for new features and software that will, once made completely secure and streamlined, end up in RHEL.

Now you know the secret to making money with Linux: don't charge for the software itself—charge for the services you can provide for the software.

So who puts all of this code together? And why do they do it? It's not always to earn a living, as you might expect.

Distributions of All Shapes and Sizes

In the very beginning, there was one distribution of Linux, known as *MCC Interim Linux*. Its singular status didn't last long. Very soon, there were a handful of distributions. Today, nearly 18 years later, there are upwards of 200 distributions. No one knows the exact number, since new ones are being created every week, and old ones are being allowed to languish into obscurity.

Watching Distributions

For an up-to-date inventory of Linux distributions, visit DistroWatch (www.distrowatch.com).

Whatever the exact number, there are a lot of distributions out there, and they all fall into one of two categories: commercial (like RHEL) or noncommercial (like Fedora).

The commercial distributions exist for a pretty self-explanatory reason: someone, either a company or a group of developers, wants to make money. These distributions tend to be the most well-known of the Linux distributions, although they are not necessarily the most influential.

Distributions in this category include RHEL, SUSE Linux Enterprise Server, Mandriva Linux, and Ubuntu Server. Those are the more commercially successful distributions; it is by no means a complete list.

Noncommercial distributions are generally run as not-for-profits, if they are well organized, or even as a hobby for one of a group of developers. The motivation for developers is varied. Some want to create something meaningful. Some do it to earn extra money. (Actually, some nonprofit distributions do receive some funding through voluntary support and donations.) Some want to have fun coding. Whatever the reason, developers have made noncommercial distributions very popular and extremely influential among all Linux developers.

Noncommercial distributions include Debian GNU/Linux, Slackware Linux, Ubuntu, openSUSE, and SimplyMEPIS. Just to give you an idea of how influential noncommercial distributions can be, know that SimplyMEPIS, Freespire, Linspire, and Xandros are among the many Linux distributions (commercial or otherwise) based on what has become the most popular noncommercial distribution today: Debian GNU/Linux.

What Fedora Is

If you were to ask under which category Fedora falls, very technically the answer would have to be commercial, if only because its development is ultimately funded by Red Hat, Inc. It's a hard thing to define, though, since community involvement in Fedora development is so intense. In fact, this involvement is a good reason why Fedora has become so popular. With so much user involvement, backed by corporate funding, Fedora has been able to become one of the most user-friendly Linux distributions available today.

There is more to it, of course.

The Red Hat Connection

Red Hat Linux is one of the earliest created Linux distributions, having been invented by Marc Ewing in 1994. Ewing actually began working on the distribution, then known as Red Hat Software Linux, in December of 1992, soon after he graduated from Carnegie Mellon University.

According to legend—because you can have legends in under 20 years on the Internet—the name "Red Hat" came from Ewing's habit of wearing a red hat while at CMU. The name stuck, even after Ewing's company was purchased by entrepreneur Bob Young in 1995.

Red Hat's initial popularity is attributed to some key technological advantages it had over other Linux distributions of the time. One such advantage was the addition of a graphical configuration system used when installing Red Hat. Primitive by today's standards, nonetheless this simple series of installation screens was hugely helpful for those early adopters who wanted to try out Linux.

Family History

Red Hat Linux is one of three major branches of Linux distributions that exist today. Many successful distributions, including Fedora, are based on Red Hat Linux, such as Red Flag, a popular Chinese distribution, and Yellow Dog, a flavor of Linux designed to run on Apple's Mac hardware.

Another advantage Red Hat had was how software applications were distributed for the Red Hat Linux platform.

Recall that while open source and free software is always available in its source code form, such a format is not easy to use. What software developers must do is deliver their application in a form that's easy to install. On Windows, this is done with a self-executing file that users can double-click and have the new program installed.

On Linux, such an approach is not a good idea. Self-executing installs can bring a host of mistakes and potentially malicious changes to a computer, and at the most fundamental level, all Linux systems resist such packages. Instead, applications are installed using packages. A Linux package can contain many of the same files as a Windows installation routine, but the control of the installation lies with the package manager—not the package itself.

Package managers will not only ensure the package is properly and safely put together, but they will also make sure that any other software the application needs will be installed as well.

Red Hat's advantage here was the introduction of the RPM package management system. RPM packages are one of two major Linux packaging systems (the other being Debian GNU/Linux's DEB package system).

Over the next nine years, Red Hat Linux would continue to capitalize on these and other advantages, devoting much of its marketing and sales efforts to getting Linux into the workplace; specifically, the enterprises which are organizations with 500 or more computer users. By targeting this market, Red Hat was essentially aiming for the low-hanging fruit; there aren't a lot of enterprise-level customers out there, but it only takes a few to really build your revenue stream.

But this approach, while commercially successful, gave Red Hat a problem. While Red Hat Linux was becoming increasingly popular in the corporate world, the community-oriented developer and user bases that had helped to bring Red Hat Linux to where it was technologically were feeling increasingly disen-franchised. What good was it to develop cutting-edge software, the community complained, when Red Hat, fearing any software instability for its well-heeled enterprise customers, would only include it after a laborious quality control process?

This issue was serious enough to prompt Red Hat to launch several community outreach programs—because if the community began to vote with their feet and walk away from Red Hat, highly valuable development resources could be lost, and Red Hat's community reputation would plummet. Some of this outreach helped, but in the end, it took the birth of a new distribution and the death of Red Hat Linux to help save Red Hat.

The Fedora Connection

Fedora actually began its existence as a simple collection of software.

One of the community outreach projects started by Red Hat as it was working to keep community interest high was the Fedora Linux project, a collection of newer and more experimental software that, when installed on Red Hat Linux, would give users a chance to enhance their computers without introducing risky software to the main Red Hat Linux distribution.

It's important to note that Fedora Linux was not a stand-alone version of Linux, like other distributions, but was actually what's known as a *repository of software*. But it would play a key role in what was to come next.

In September 2003, Red Hat made a stunning announcement: Red Hat Linux would cease to be a product. Instead, users who wanted to have commercial-grade support (such as those coveted enterprise customers) would now use and pay for Red Hat Enterprise Linux. Users who wished to continue using Red Hat Linux for free and without support would use Fedora Core, a formal merging of Red Hat Linux and the software from the Fedora Linux project.

The new Fedora Core distribution would be governed not by Red Hat, but by an independent nonprofit organization known as the Fedora Project. At the time, this was considered to be a radical move, but as Linux became more commercially viable, vendors like Red Hat were able to make the jump to a pure commercial distribution.

Initially, reaction was mixed. After all, many people wondered, what about home and small business users who wanted some level of support? In response, in 2004 Red Hat (rather quietly) released Red Hat Professional Workstation, a $100 version of Red Hat Linux that came with direct Red Hat support. It was, unfortunately, a commercial failure.

What happened next would shape the commercial/community distribution model for all future releases—not just for Red Hat, but also for other followers of the model.

Simply put, the Fedora community took care of the support problem itself.

By becoming a cohesive, flexible body, members of the Fedora Project began to fill the gaps that were once occupied by Red Hat. Documentation was created; support issues resolved; bugs tracked, identified, and removed. In short, the Fedora Core distribution became as robust and powerful as Red Hat Linux ever was and soon surpassed its parent distribution in terms of ease of use and features.

In fact, the Fedora Project became so strong that eventually Red Hat would drop its efforts for a home/small business desktop product and put time, effort, and resources back into Fedora Core.

Ultimately, this approach worked out very well for both sides. Power users and developers got a complete and robust distribution to experiment with and use, and Red Hat kept its commercial distribution solid and mature. And, as an added benefit, Fedora Core, later named just Fedora, would become a test bed for new technologies and applications, which would later be included in Red Hat Enterprise Linux.

It's a good example of a win-win situation for users, developers, and commercial vendors alike.

Conclusion

In this chapter, you learned quite a bit about the history of the operating system you are about to install. This is important, because if you understand where Fedora came from and how it is put together, you will understand the capabilities and the limitations of this popular operating system.

In Chapter 2, "Before You Install Fedora," we'll spend some very important time making a plan for your Fedora installation. Will you use it exclusively or dual boot your machine with Windows? Is your hardware going to be compatible with Fedora, or will you need to plan for some finagling to get everything to run smoothly? The beginnings of these answers will be explored in the next chapter.

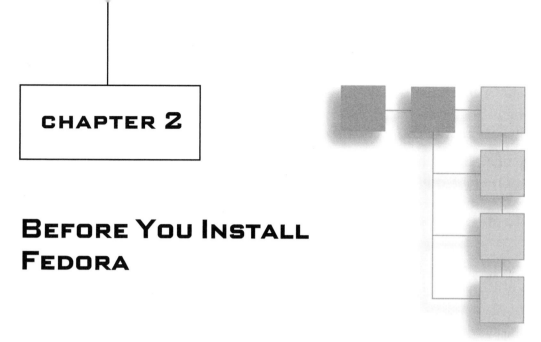

CHAPTER 2

BEFORE YOU INSTALL FEDORA

You've made the decision. After hearing about this operating system known as Fedora from friends, family, or maybe the IT staff down at the office, you are going to try it out for yourself.

But installing an operating system is not as simple as installing an application like Photoshop or Firefox. While the Fedora developers have made the process as painless as possible, there's no getting around the fact that putting a new operating system on a PC is not something that should be taken lightly. Unless you just bought the computer at the store and took it out of its box, there will be existing data on the machine that you will want to save.

Also, while Fedora is ultimately safer and faster than a Windows-based operating system, some upfront planning (discussed later in this chapter) is required to ensure that the installation process goes smoothly.

In this chapter, you'll do all the fact-finding and planning needed to successfully pull off your own installation of Fedora. Specifically, you will:

- Learn about the different versions of Fedora, called spins, and decide which is best for you.

- Discover how to obtain a copy of Fedora for yourself.

- Gather information about your computer to assess how well it will run with Fedora.

- Prepare your system for single or multiple operating systems.

Choosing the Right Fedora

After all of the discussion about all those different kinds of Linux, I'm sure you're thinking that at least it's nice there's just one Fedora.

If only. But not to worry. The differences between the versions are not so great—your choice at this point will really just come down to personal preference. And the nice thing is that you can switch to other Fedora versions if you want to try one later.

Yes, There's More Than One Way to Spin Fedora

You could almost say that Fedora is a victim of its own popularity. Because Fedora is so efficient and easy to use (even among Linux distributions), developers of all persuasions have taken a good thing and recrafted it into something they prefer even more. These variations of Fedora are known as *spins*, and they follow the same release cycle as the main version (though they might be offset by a few days here and there). Most of the differences between the flavors of Fedora are purely cosmetic: sometimes it's a different desktop environment, sometimes it's a different set of installed applications.

It is important to note that these spins are not completely different versions of Fedora; they are just Fedora pre-packaged in different ways. You can, if you wish, download and install all of the software needed to created identical versions of these spins. But having the spins already set up will save you a great deal of time and effort.

While this book will focus on the original Fedora Desktop, it won't hurt to take a quick look at the other variations, in case you see something you'd like to try later.

Desktop Environments

Before we discuss the differences between the Fedora spins, it would be a good idea to discuss *what* is different—specifically, the graphical interfaces that users work with when they work with any kind of Linux.

Most computer users are used to seeing just one graphical interface when they run their PCs. Windows 7 Home Edition users get to use the basic Windows interface, Windows 7 Premium and Ultimate Editions use the fancier Aero interface, and OS X users use Aqua. Graphical interfaces are the technical name for the windows, menus, and icons that so many computer users have grown accustomed to.

In these operating systems, you get the interface that comes with the OS. You can change the colors and the sizes of some items (bigger icons, for instance), but at the end of the day, you're still using the same interface.

In Linux, this is not the case: There are literally dozens of interfaces for you to choose from. This goes back to the whole modular nature of Linux. Unlike Windows 7, the interface applications are separate from the core operating system. So, if something creates a glitch on a Linux interface, known as a *desktop environment,* the core operating system is not affected.

These desktop environments do more than just look different; they are managed by completely different tools, and each carries its own set of specialized applications. For example, a text editor (like Windows Notepad) called *Gedit* is available for the GNOME desktop environment, and in the K Desktop Environment (KDE) the same kind of editor is known as *Kate.* (The first letter of an application is often a clue to the preferred environment for that application.)

Confusing? It shouldn't be. The good news is that applications for one desktop environment usually work in other environments without a hitch. (The author, for instance, prefers to work in KDE but won't part with the Gedit text editor. The two work together quite well.)

Fedora Desktop

The Fedora Desktop is the primary version among the Fedora "family" of spins, the one from which all the others are based.

One of Fedora's main characteristics is that it uses, by default, the GNOME desktop environment. GNOME, along with its predecessor KDE, is one of the most popular desktop environments around for Linux and other UNIX-based operating systems. It's often regarded as an easier-to-use environment, with fewer controls for users to worry about. Free software purists prefer it for the totally free nature of the code that is used to build GNOME (see Figure 2.1).

Fedora KDE

Fedora KDE is the most popular "alternate" Fedora spin, and as you might have guessed from the name, it features the KDE. The KDE environment came before GNOME, but quite a few people in the Linux community don't like it because initially it was built with the help of nonfree code. (The Debian Project, for instance, initially would not ship any release with KDE.) The GNOME Project was started as a result of this concern. Today, the code in KDE is more open, and those objections have been rendered moot.

Fedora KDE makes exclusive use of KDE and its attendant applications, as shown in Figure 2.2.

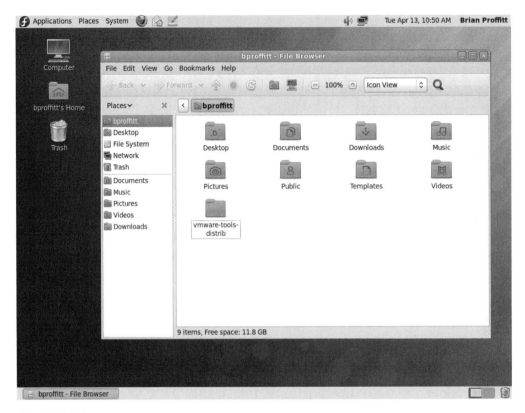

Figure 2.1
The Fedora Desktop, featuring the Nautilus file manager.

Fedora LXDE Spin

LXDE stands for "Lightweight X11 Desktop Environment," and it is designed to be very fast and light on its electronic feet. While not as popular as GNOME and KDE, the LXDE interface features multi-language support, standard keyboard shortcuts, and tabbed file browsing.

LXDE (shown in Figure 2.3) is a good environment for low-power devices such as netbooks, mobile Internet devices, or older machines.

Fedora Xfce Spin

This Fedora spin uses the Xfce environment, a simple and fast environment based on the old UNIX CDE environment. Xfce takes a bit of getting used to, because the graphic interface tools are a bit less intuitive than the more robust GNOME and KDE environments.

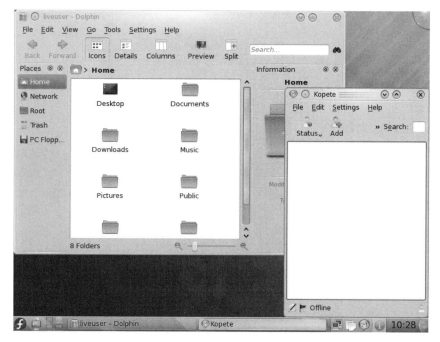

Figure 2.2
Fedora KDE, featuring the Plasma desktop components.

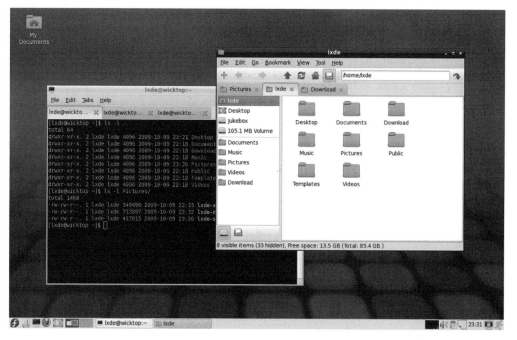

Figure 2.3
The Fedora LXDE interface.

Figure 2.4
The Fedora Xfce desktop.

But using Xfce gives this Fedora spin the added advantage of not being as resource-hungry as other Linux distributions and makes it ideal for running on slower, older PCs (see Figure 2.4).

Fedora Games Spin

Like to get your game on? The Fedora Games spin offers a great collection of games available for Fedora.

Not every Fedora game is included with this spin, but the designers have tried to put together a good representation of the different styles of games that you can get for the Fedora distribution (see Figure 2.5).

Fedora Edu Spin

Unlike the other Fedora spins, Fedora Edu is not different because of its look or feel. Rather Fedora Edu's differences lie in the content and tools it provides to users.

Fedora Edu is sometimes referred to as the "kids' Fedora," and indeed, the addition of educational and development software certainly matches that description. But the overall goal of the project is to provide an easy-to-use distribution

Figure 2.5
Games like *FlightGear* are available on the Fedora Games spin.

for all ages of students. According to the project's home page, "The purpose of this spin is to create a ready-to-go development environment for contributing to educational projects inside, but also outside of the Fedora ecosystem...."

As you can see in Figure 2.6, Edu runs a GNOME desktop, with the differences mostly in the set of educational applications that ships with the distribution. These include various language, science, and development learning tools.

Fedora BrOffice Spin

One of the interesting results of working on the international stage of the Internet is how names can be used for different things in different nations.

For instance, the office suite found in Fedora, OpenOffice.org, gets the ".org" in its official name from the fact that OpenOffice is actually a trademarked company name in the Netherlands, as well as a trademark owned by Orange UK, the British telecommunications company.

Rather than raise a ruckus, the project's organizers decided to simply tack on the ".org" to the name. But even that didn't work, as OpenOffice.org is a trademark held in Brazil.

So, OpenOffice.org users in Brazil use BrOffice. BrOffice, as you may have surmised, is the centerpiece of the Fedora BrOffice spin. But the spin's creators

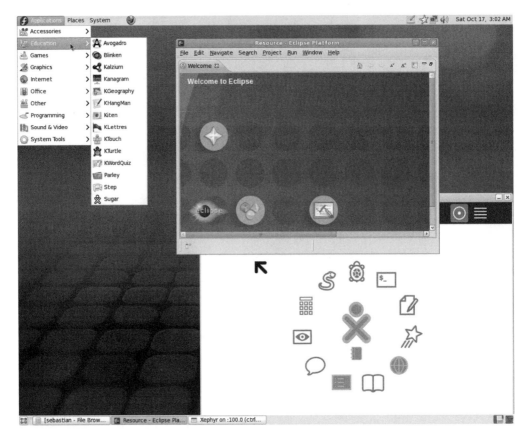

Figure 2.6
The Eclipse learning environment in Fedora Edu.

didn't stop there. This spin is loaded with language packs and applications that are well suited for Central and South American users, whether they converse in Spanish or Portuguese.

Fedora FEL Spin

Very likely the most specialized Fedora spin is the Fedora Electronic Laboratory (FEL) spin.

FEL was put together solely to provide a solid platform for the Electronic Design Automation (EDA) community. These are the people who put together things like microchips, processors, and robots. You know, easy stuff.

According to the project's Web site, FEL "provides a complete electronic laboratory setup with reliable open source design tools in order to help you keep

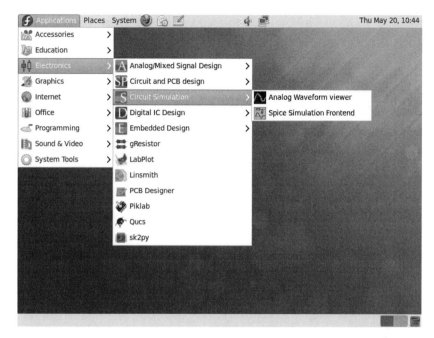

Figure 2.7
Xcircuit within the FEL spin.

in pace with the current technological race. It reduces the risk assessment of open source hardware development and enables electronic designers to create their work quickly and efficiently."

Figure 2.7 provides a look at the complexity of the tools offered in the FEL spin.

Know What You Want Your PC to Do

With all of these choices for Fedora, it's pretty easy to get hung up on which one to pick. For the purposes of this particular book, the recommended flavor is going to be the main Fedora Desktop distribution itself. Beyond simplicity, there are a couple of good reasons for going with Fedora:

- **GNOME is a good first step.** Since GNOME is the default desktop environment on Fedora, this makes Fedora a good beginner's choice. GNOME is not as robust as other desktop environments, but it is simple to configure and has some fantastic eye candy.

- **Everything is available.** Choosing Fedora will not exclude you from the features of the other flavors. You can install software, change the look and feel, whatever you'd like.

For general desktop and small business use, Fedora Desktop is the recommended version to start with—at least until you get your feet wet.

The only exception to this suggestion is for users who are interested in installing Fedora in an academic setting. In this case, you might want to check out the Fedora Edu spin first. Fedora Edu also uses GNOME, so most of the material covered in this book will apply to this flavor, if you want to look at it. The additional educational software is certainly worth exploring. Even if you choose Fedora Desktop, you can still download and install any educational software that interests you.

Getting Fedora

We've covered the menu of Fedora spins; now it's time to order.

The simplest way to acquire Fedora is to use the CD included with this book. It contains a full-featured copy of Fedora 13, no different from anything you will download from the Internet.

Of course, sometimes CDs get damaged or lost. Or you may want to download future editions of Fedora. If that's the case, then the rest of this chapter will be useful for you to learn how to acquire Fedora.

Getting your hands on Fedora is not as simple as driving down to the computer store and buying a boxed set of software. Very few Linux distributions are sold as retail offerings, and Fedora is not one of them. Nor will it come already installed on a new computer, like Windows or OS X. No, Fedora is free, but you will need to invest some time in obtaining it.

Before you begin, let's review what you will need to lay your hands on a copy of Fedora if you don't have access to the CD from this book. At a *minimum,* you will need a working CD drive capable of burning CDs and at least a dial-up connection to the Internet. This will enable you to download the software and create your own CD (or DVD if you have the right equipment). It takes a little time, but ultimately getting Fedora is pretty simple.

Download Fedora

Downloading software has become a much more common practice than it used to be. The advent of broadband, plus some technological tricks to get the software into smaller packages so downloads won't take as long, have made this practice more common. If you have fast access to the Internet, this is the way to go.

Narrowband Options

It should be noted that the converse is also true. If you don't have broadband access, you can download Fedora for installation. However, on a standard 56 K dial-up connection, it will take just over 29 hours at top speed. If you don't want to do this, see the "Getting a CD" section later in this chapter.

When you download Fedora, you are actually downloading what is known as an ISO image. A disc image (whether for CD or DVD) is analogous to a picture of all of the different 1s and 0s that will make up the contents of the disc you will eventually create. The advantage to this approach is you only have to download one (really big) file, instead of all of the hundreds of files that make up Fedora. The disadvantage is that you have to get a special application to create a CD from a disc image (which we'll discuss in the "Burning CDs/DVDs" section later).

Let's begin the acquisition process.

Via the Web

Getting Fedora from the Web is easy and (most notably) free. Except for the cost of the CD you will be burning later and your time, which won't be much, you'll soon have a full-featured operating system installed on your PC.

To begin, open your favorite Internet browser. In this book, the Firefox browser is being used, since it is free software like Linux and is a very robust application.

Where You're Coming From

As mentioned in the Introduction, it is assumed that you are using Windows Vista or 7 before you implement Fedora.

1. Surf to the Fedora Project Web site at http://fedoraproject.org/.

2. Click the Get Fedora link. The Get Fedora page will open.

3. Click the Download Now! button in the Get Fedora 13 Desktop Now section. The Opening Fedora-13-i686-Live Iso dialog box will open.

Is This Live?

"Live" refers to a form of Linux that can be run directly from your CD or DVD drive. This allows you to use Fedora without actually installing it.

4. Click the Save File radio button. (In Internet Explorer, click the Save button.)

5. Click OK. (In Internet Explorer, select a destination and again click the Save button.) The download process will begin, and the file will be saved to the default location on your Windows PC.

Via BitTorrent

Even on a broadband connection, downloading a nearly 660MB file is going to take some time. On the average day, this will be about 15 minutes, give or take. But if you are trying to get this disc image file when everyone else is trying to do the same thing, the time involved can stretch to hours as your browser patiently waits its turn to pull down the file, bit by bit.

There is a way to download the file that typically avoids the traffic jams sometimes found at central file servers, using a relatively new method known as *BitTorrent.*

You may have heard of BitTorrent in the news or technology media outlets, because it is often (and erroneously) regarded as a tool for software pirates to download and transfer their illicit wares. Actually, there are many legitimate uses for BitTorrent: Downloading a Linux distribution like Fedora is certainly one of them.

Here's how it works: Instead of downloading files from a central server, BitTorrent downloads are shared by all of the people who want to obtain those files. At least one of the users in this group (known as a *swarm*) has all of the parts of the file or files. That is the seed computer. In a BitTorrent download, all of the computers in the swarm query each other and find out what parts of the download each machine has. If my computer needs part 863 of file 42, and computer B has it, I will download it from him. If my box has part 567 of file 23 and computer B needs it, it will download the piece of the file from me. If nobody in the swarm has it yet, a computer queries the seed computer, gets the needed piece of the file, and shares it with the rest of the swarm.

In this method, known as peer-to-peer or distributed downloading, no one computer has the burden of being the source for a given file or files. The traffic load is shared among all the members of the swarm. The neat thing is that as more computers in the swarm acquire 100 percent of the files they need, those machines in turn become seeds. In this way, the process actually gets faster as time goes on.

There are many BitTorrent clients available for the three major operating systems, and you may have one already. One that can be recommended is Vuze, a robust BitTorrent client that can be used on Linux, OS X, and Windows. It's also (as a huge bonus) an open source software product.

Getting Vuze

To obtain your copy of Vuze, visit www.vuze.com with your favorite browser.

After you obtain a copy of Vuze or any other BitTorrent client, you will need to find and download what's known as a *tracker file*. A tracker file, which is very small, tells your BitTorrent application where seeds and swarms that have the files you need are located on the Internet.

Locating a BitTorrent tracker file is pretty simple, since Fedora keeps a list of them on its site. You just have to make sure you get the right one.

1. Surf to the Get Fedora page at http://fedoraproject.org/en/get-fedora.

2. Near the bottom of the page, click the See All Torrents link. A very detailed list of files will appear.

3. Click the Fedora-13-i686-Live.torrent link. Your browser will open the Opening Fedora-13-i686-Live.torrent dialog box.

The Right Stuff

Be sure "i686" appears in the name of the file, if you have a older PC. If your PC happens to be 64-bit, click Fedora-12-x86_64-Live.torrent.

4. Click the Save File radio button.

5. Click OK. The download process will begin, and the tracker file will be saved to the default location on your Windows PC.

After you have the tracker file, open your BitTorrent client and use the file to start your download of the actual image file. Using Vuze, this is a very simple process.

1. Open the Vuze application (see Figure 2.8).

2. Select the File | Open | Torrent File menu option. The Open Torrent(s) dialog will appear (see Figure 2.9).

3. Click the Add Files button. The Choose the Torrent File dialog box will open.

4. Navigate to the folder where the Fedora tracker (.torrent) file is saved.

5. Select the tracker file.

6. Click Open. The dialog box will close, and the information about the torrent contents will appear in the Open Torrents dialog box.

7. Click OK. The BitTorrent download process will begin, and the image file will be saved to the specified location on your Windows PC.

Figure 2.8
The Vuze application.

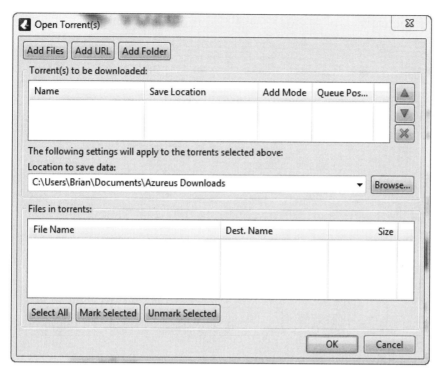

Figure 2.9
The Open Torrent(s) dialog box.

Give and Take

Don't be a leech! This is what people who just download what they need and then shut down their BitTorrent application are called. The best way for torrent downloads to work is if you continue to share the download after you acquire the files. Your client should have a notation of share ratio—the amount of torrent uploaded compared to the amount downloaded. You should not stop the torrent process until that ratio is at least greater than 1.0, meaning that you have shared your files at least one complete time. The good news is, uploading is a much slower process than downloading, so leaving it on won't affect the rest of your Internet surfing very much. If you are concerned about the bandwidth usage—for either uploads or downloads—you can adjust the maximum transfer rate in Vuze under Tools | Options.

Burning CDs

In whatever manner you get the Fedora image file to your computer, eventually you will need to create the actual CD you will use to install Fedora. Windows and

OS X each have the capability to burn .iso files onto a CD, without a separate application.

1. Insert a blank CD-R or CD-RW disc into your CD burner drive.

2. Using Windows Explorer, navigate to the Fedora .iso file you downloaded.

3. Double-click the .iso file. The Windows Disc Image Burner application will start.

4. Confirm that the correct drive where the blank CD resides is selected.

5. Click Burn. The Fedora files will be copied to the CD.

6. When finished, the new Fedora CD will eject from your drive. Click OK and remove the disc from the drive.

Getting a CD

If you don't have a broadband connection, you can obtain a copy of a Fedora CD that will be mailed right to your home or business.

There are many ways of getting CDs shipped to your door. Perhaps the most economical method is to use Fedora's FreeMedia program and request a free copy of Fedora. This method, while free, is rather slow—it can take many weeks to receive a shipped Fedora CD. That's because FreeMedia is a purely volunteer effort.

Because of this, the FreeMedia program should only be used by users who cannot download Fedora, attend an event, or get media elsewhere, such as from an Ambassador, online vendor, or local vendor.

If this meets your criteria, surf to the FreeMedia page and follow the instructions for requesting a copy of Fedora (http://fedoraproject.org/wiki/Distribution/FreeMedia). Be sure to check out the links to events, ambassadors, and vendors first, in case those options would work.

Installation Preparation

You have the CD burned and ready. Now, you can insert it into your drive and launch the installation process, right? Sure, if you're feeling invincible. But even the most avid Linux user knows that no software is perfect, and something could always go wrong.

Unless you are installing Fedora on a brand-new machine with no personal data on it, you should always back up your files so you can get to them later, whether something goes wrong or right. Even if you are installing a new machine, there are still some steps you need to take prior to installation.

Gathering Information About Your System

Fedora is a very robust operating system, and on most computers, it will install without a problem. But, if there is a problem, it will likely be because Fedora did not recognize a piece of hardware on your PC.

There are various reasons why this happens, perhaps the biggest one being that there are so many different kinds of hardware out in the world that it is impossible for even the hard-working Fedora and Linux developers to keep up with them all. Because, in a world where most hardware companies care only about working with Windows, the companies' developers generally don't spend time writing software drivers that will allow their devices to work on Linux. Fortunately, as Linux becomes more prevalent (thanks to easy-to-use distributions like Fedora), quite a few companies are seeing the error of this plan and are now working on Linux drivers.

There are still gaps in hardware coverage, unfortunately, and while most times those gaps are able to be closed with some work on the user's part, it helps if you know ahead of time.

Hardware Issues

Hardware concerns will be covered in Chapter 7, "Making Things Work."

If you're like most people, you may know the superficial information about your PC, like: "19-inch monitor, CD/DVD drive, printer, how many USB ports...," etc. To get a proper list for compatibility issues with Fedora, you will need to dig a little further. For some, this can be the most intimidating part of the installation, but really, it's not too bad.

As you begin examining your computer, you will first notice a lot of the information you need to know is right there in front of you. Your monitor, for instance, is sitting on your table or desk with its brand name and model displayed on the front or back. Likely, the same is true for your printer and any other external devices you might have. You'll want to take note of both the brand name and the model as they appear on the device.

In addition to identifying external devices, you'll need to determine what's actually inside your computer. One place to start is by displaying a list of devices as identified by your existing operating system. Windows XP, Vista, and Windows 7 use a built-in applet called the Device Manager to list known devices.

In Vista and Windows 7, open the Device Manager using the steps outlined here.

1. Click the Start button on the Windows taskbar; then select Control Panel. The Control Panel window will appear.

2. Click the Hardware and Sound link. The Hardware and Sound page will open.

3. Click the Device Manager link. The Device Manager, which lists the inner workings of your computer, will appear as shown in Figure 2.10.

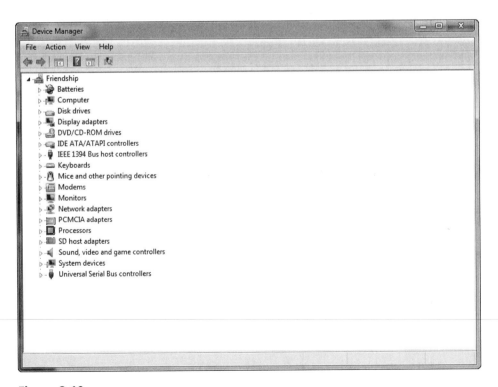

Figure 2.10
The Windows Device Manager.

Now you need to do some old-fashioned detective work. Your computer may (or may not) actually use a device for each of the device types listed in the Device Manager. For example, to determine what kind of CD-ROM drive is installed in your computer, first expand the DVD/CD-ROM drives list by clicking its expansion control (the little triangles next to each category), as shown in Figure 2.11.

As you can see in Figure 2.11, this computer has one CD-ROM drive, with a rather cryptic label. To find out more about a device, double-click the desired device. The Properties dialog box for the CD-ROM drive appears (see Figure 2.12).

This is a classic example of a device that has been made to conform to Windows' standards—so much so that Windows does not care who manufactured it. As far as Windows is concerned, this is just a standard CD-ROM drive. It is still a good

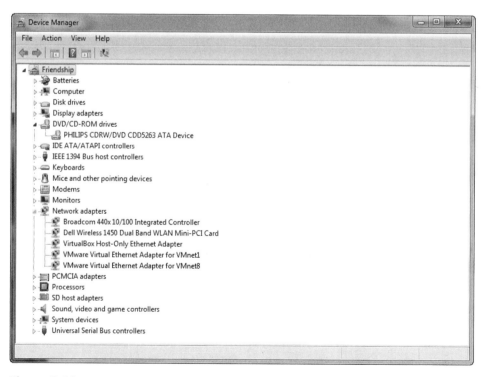

Figure 2.11
Open a list of devices by clicking the expansion box.

Figure 2.12
Not too much information here, but every little bit helps.

idea to record the non-generic information, in case there is a hiccup later with Fedora.

You may find that other books urge readers to keep a journal for tracking and recording all of their PC's hardware along with any other issues that may arise while installing Fedora. This approach has merit, but there's no need to get out the pencil and paper. In the Device Manager in Windows XP, there is a Print icon you can use to just print out all of the information Windows XP knows about the hardware on your PC.

You will find this printed document full of very technical information—most of which you will not need. Still, it saves time over writing it all down.

In newer versions of Windows, the hardware information will need to be recorded manually.

To successfully install Fedora and troubleshoot it later if problems arise, the most important information you need is for those devices that make your computer most operable, as listed in Table 2.1.

Table 2.1 Important Hardware Information Needed for Fedora Installation/Troubleshooting

Hardware	Information Needed
CPU	Manufacturer, Model, Speed
Motherboard	Manufacturer, Model
Buses	Manufacturer, Model
Memory (RAM)	Size
Video Card	Manufacturer, Model, Video RAM size, Chipset
Sound Card	Manufacturer, Model
Monitor	Manufacturer, Model, Horizontal and Vertical Synchronization Rates
Hard Drive	Manufacturer, Model, Size, Type (SCSI vs. IDE)
Network Card	Manufacturer, Model
CD-ROM Drive	Manufacturer, Model, Size
Floppy Drive	Manufacturer, Model, Size
Modem	Manufacturer, Model, Transmission Speed
Printer	Manufacturer, Model
Mouse	Manufacturer, Model, Type (PS/2 , Serial, or USB)
Keyboard	Manufacturer, Model, Number of Keys, Language
SCSI Card and Devices	Manufacturer, Model, Type of Device Controlled
IDE Adapters	Manufacturer, Model, Type of Device Controlled

Most of the information you require is included in the Device Manager output you printed, but not all. For example, you can locate information on the amount of RAM installed on your computer by clicking the General tab in the System Properties dialog box. Another option might be to right-click the hard drive icon displayed in My Computer and select the Properties option to see how large your drive space is. A little detective work will go a long way toward making your Fedora installation easier.

Backing Up Your Data

After you have ascertained your hardware setup, you will need to take the next step to get your computer ready for the installation: backing up the data on your PC.

It is always a good idea to back up your valuable data, guarding against system catastrophe. At the very least, you'll want your data protected from power surges, virus attacks, computer theft, or anything else that could affect your ability to access the data on your machine.

Installing Fedora certainly can't be classified as a catastrophic event. But depending on how you are going to be changing your hard drive's partitions or perhaps even formatting your hard drive, these events can and will erase data completely.

The first thing you should decide is what data should be backed up. That really depends on what you want to do in your Fedora installation. Especially if you plan to perform a dual boot (running Windows and Fedora on the same PC), then you will need to make sure you've safeguarded most of your Windows data.

Completely Replacing Windows

Even if you plan to completely remove Windows and install Fedora in its place, there is still merit to saving your data files. Most files created in Windows can be opened in Fedora, such as graphic files (GIFs, JPEGs, PNGs) and Adobe Acrobat (PDF) files. In addition, even Microsoft Office files can be opened, compliments of the OpenOffice.org office suite that is fully Office compatible. You'll need to save, not back up, these files if you plan to use them on your Fedora machine, though. Fedora will not be able to read a Windows backup file. If this is the case, use an external hard drive or a Flash memory stick (also known as a *thumb drive*) and directly save your data files to such a device using Windows Explorer. You will be able to use Fedora to retrieve them later.

Prepping for Dual Boot

If you are planning on dual booting your machine, a backup operating system is needed to ensure that you can still get to your Windows side in case something goes wrong with the setup. Most computer applications these days use huge amounts of disk space, primarily because today's big hard drives enable them to do so. Backing up your data and your application files is, therefore, a big job. If you have sufficient storage capacity (such as one of those external hard drives), then it is recommended that you back up your entire hard drive.

For those of you who do not have a sufficient large-capacity device to hold an entire drive's worth of data, then just back up your data files. Your data files are the documents, spreadsheets, drawings, and other files that you have created over time on your computer. If you do run into trouble, you can restore your system by first reinstalling your Windows operating system and your applications using your original discs, and then restoring your archived personal data files.

If you have never used a backup program, you will find them easy to use. Many backup programs are available, including an excellent one found with Norton System Utilities. The principles for backup utilities are pretty much the same: locate and identify the files you want to archive, specify the location of the new archive file, and then create the file. Restoration is simply the reverse of this action.

Microsoft Windows has its own utility for backup that can be used to archive your data. The next steps describe how to work with the Windows Backup utility.

1. Click Start. The Start menu will appear.

2. In the Search Programs and Files field, type Backup. The Backup and Restore link will appear in the Programs section of the menu.

3. Click the Backup and Restore link. The Backup and Restore Wizard application will open (see Figure 2.13).

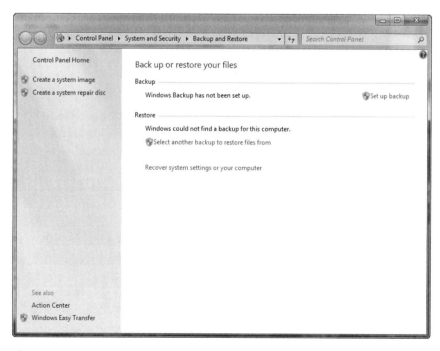

Figure 2.13
Microsoft's Backup utility.

4. Click the Set Up Backup link. The Set Up Backup dialog will appear, as shown in Figure 2.14.

5. Click the drive to save the backup files and click Next. The What Do You Want to Back Up page will appear (see Figure 2.15).

6. Here you can either choose to back up your entire set of computer files or choose to only back up selected files. If you want to back up everything, select the Let Windows Choose radio button; then click Next. The Review Your Backup Settings page will appear (see Figure 2.16).

7. Click Save Settings and Run Backup. The backup process will begin.

Make sure the backup file is stored away from your hard drive. As you will see in the next chapter, big changes are coming to your drive.

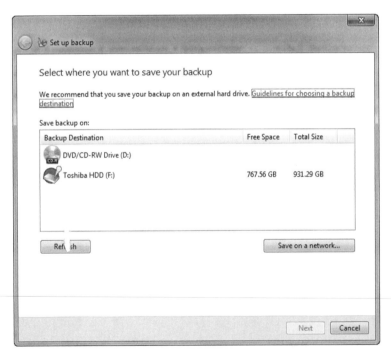

Figure 2.14
Setting up a backup job.

Figure 2.15
You can select what files you want to back up.

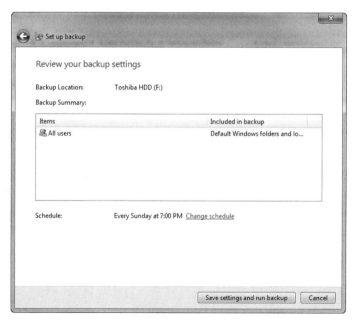

Figure 2.16
Review what you have selected.

Conclusion

In this chapter, you learned the essential steps in preparing your machine for installing Fedora, including locating and downloading Fedora, burning a CD or DVD, and prepping your computer for installation. That preparation is about to pay off, because in the next chapter, the big moment has arrived: Fedora will very shortly be running on your computer.

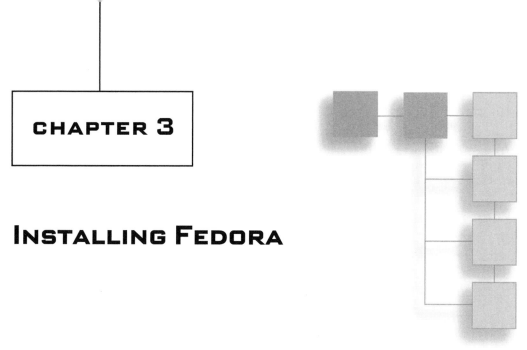

CHAPTER 3

INSTALLING FEDORA

Now comes the moment of truth. You've done the homework, figured out how you want to install your copy of Fedora, and you're ready to go.

This chapter won't disappoint you. Its sole goal is to walk you through the installation process using the Anaconda graphical installer. Along the way, you will:

- Discover how to explore Fedora—without installing it.

- Choose which option will be best for you, installing Fedora alone or alongside another operating system.

- Journey step by step through the installation process.

- Create one or more users for your Fedora machine.

Try Before You Buy

This section may leave you scratching your head and wondering why you just went through all of the preparation in Chapter 2. Be patient, there's a method to this madness.

All spins of Fedora are currently available to users as a LiveCD version. "LiveCD" is the label for operating systems that can be booted and run *right from the CD itself*—without installing on your computer's hard drive.

This means that when you insert your Fedora CD into the disc drive and restart your computer, Fedora will automatically begin running on your computer without putting on any new files or touching pre-existing data on your machine. Fedora just starts up and runs.

So why, you ask, should I bother installing Fedora at all? I can just run it from the CD. Well, this is true, and many people do—especially when they are using someone else's PC and don't want to use the pre-existing operating system. Why use Windows on your friend's computer when you can just insert your Fedora LiveCD and have a more familiar environment ready to go?

The first issue is speed: running any operating system from the CD drive means it will be a much slower process. Data has to be pumped in constantly from the drive, and only the fastest drives will give you any kind of decent user experience.

If your system is low on RAM, performance of the LiveCD will take an even bigger hit. When an operating system and its applications run, they use the RAM as a workspace to perform their operations. The more memory that's available, the more efficiently the apps will run. But once there are a lot of applications running, the RAM gets filled up. To keep up with the demand, the operating system uses space on the disk drive known as *swap space* to help fulfill memory needs. This is why you will hear your hard drive churning away when you're running a lot of stuff on your computer. Using swap space is slower, but it gets the job done.

When to Upgrade the RAM

If you hear your hard drive working a lot—even when you are using just one or two applications—it's probably time to consider getting more RAM installed on your machine. It not only speeds your operations up, but it will save a lot of wear and tear on your hard drive.

When you run a LiveCD, however, the swap space option does not apply, since Fedora from the CD won't touch your drive's data. If your system does not have a lot of RAM installed, be prepared for slow LiveCD operation.

Slow operations notwithstanding, the advantages of the LiveCD are that it lets you take your operating system with you, as mentioned before, and—something that benefits you right now—it lets you try Fedora before you "buy" it. Buy, in this case, means installation.

Everything in the LiveCD instance of Fedora matches what you would get if you installed Fedora onto your PC. All you need to do is insert the disc into your CD drive and reboot your PC.

You will see a text menu on a black screen asking you what you want to do. The preselected option is Boot or Install, so you don't have to do anything else. After a bit more of a wait (another disadvantage of using LiveCDs), Fedora will eventually come up on your screen, as shown in Figure 3.1.

If, at this point, you want to explore the Fedora operating system, you are invited to skip ahead to Chapter 4, "Desktop Basics," to begin your exploration.

If you are ready to go ahead and install Fedora, there is one more issue that needs to be addressed: whether you share your PC with Windows.

One or Two Operating Systems?

Now comes the time when you have a really important decision to make. Like all important decisions, you should weigh your options carefully. You must decide whether you are going to run Fedora alone on your PC, or whether you want to retain Windows and be able to switch back and forth between it and Fedora. This section will examine the pros and cons of each side of the decision and give you tips on what to do if you decide to dual boot your system.

Figure 3.1
The Fedora LiveCD desktop.

Making Room for Multiple Operating Systems

There are several pros and cons for using multiple operating systems on one computer. The cons include the headaches of installing two or more operating systems on a machine, resulting in more limited hard drive space available for each of the operating systems.

But the benefits of using multiple operating systems are significant. For instance, you will have the ability to run all of the programs available for each of the operating systems you'll have on your PC. You will also be able to use all of the hardware your PC has. Finally, you'll save money by not needing to buy another PC.

It is recommended that dual booting is the way you should go—especially if you have Windows applications that you just can't part with and that have no counterparts in Fedora. This option gives you the benefits of using Fedora without a lot of investment in time or money.

If you decide to include Fedora on your PC in addition to Windows, you will need to make room for it on your hard drive. But making room on your hard drive for Fedora is a far different operation than making room for the latest computer game. You will need to create a brand-new *partition* from which Fedora will operate.

Here is a crash course in disk partitions and why you can't write data to a disk without them.

Why Partition?

Imagine the bee, buzzing around your garden. If you were to follow this bee back to its home, you would find a seemingly chaotic mass of buzzing insects, each looking as if it aimlessly wanders about with nothing better to do than hang out and buzz.

But as we all know, bees all have a specific purpose, working together for the collective benefit of the hive. One group of bees has the job of taking care of all of the cute little baby bees after the queen lays her eggs. Now, think back to your science classes: Where are the baby bees raised?

If you said the honeycomb, you're right. If you're wondering what this has to do with partitions, hang on.

The honeycomb is an ingenious device composed of hexagonal cells made of beeswax, where honey and bee larvae are stored for safekeeping. Ponder this: How would the bees get by if they did not have honeycombs? The answer is they wouldn't.

Keeping the honeycombs in mind, you can apply this analogy to how data is stored on a disk drive. Data, you see, cannot be stored on a drive without some sort of structure already in place for the data to be organized.

When data is placed on a drive, it is written into this structure, called a *file system* in the Linux community. A file system is the format in which data is stored—a honeycomb of cells if you will, where each little piece of data gets placed.

Computers being computers, it's a little more complicated than that. Data for a single file, for example, does not get stored in data blocks that sit right next to each other. The data may be stored in data blocks 456, 457, and 458 and then block 6,134, then block 7,111, and so on. (This is an oversimplification, but you get the idea.) It's the job of the file system to track where each file resides so that when you send a command to work with a file, the file system knows all of the separate blocks where the file is stored.

Because of all of this file tracking and retrieving, computer engineers came up with the idea of keeping the file systems small, even on large hard drives. So the idea of partitions came into play. Basically, the partition is a virtual barrier that tells the file system: "You used to be able to write to blocks 1–25,000 all over the disk, but now you're only allowed to write to blocks 1–17,500. A second file system will write to blocks 17,501–25,000, so hands off!"

Thus, you have partitions. And each partition can use a different file system. As an analogy, honeycombs created by honeybees are different than those created by wasps—similar structure but different outcomes.

If your PC contains a typical installation of Windows, your Windows file system is contained within one big partition that covers your entire hard drive. This leaves no room for another partition and a new file system. Remember, even if you have gigabytes of empty space on your drive, this space, like files and directories, may be scattered throughout the drive and still belong to the Windows partition.

The easiest method to add a partition to your existing hard drive file system is to use the partitioning tool within Anaconda. This will shove your existing partition into a single, smaller collection of data blocks, leaving truly empty and unstructured (unformatted) space elsewhere in the drive where you can install a partition in which Fedora can reside.

Back Up Your Data

As stated in Chapter 2, before you use any tool to manipulate or create partitions, back up or save your data to an alternate physical drive. And definitely back up everything if you plan to completely replace Windows with Fedora. Please.

Partitions Fedora Will Need

When Fedora is installed, it uses an seven-step application known as *Anaconda* to accomplish the task. When Anaconda detects another operating system on your computer, it will ask you whether you will want to replace the contents of your entire hard drive or perform a partition operation.

This is the choice point that will determine if you have a single Fedora operating system on your computer or multiple ones (Fedora and Windows). The mechanics of how to go through this procedure will be outlined in the "Partition Settings" section later in this chapter. For now, there are recommendations that should be passed on to new Fedora users.

In Fedora systems, the file system is oriented toward a key root directory that is based on the drive letter of the hard drive. For most primary drives, that drive letter is "C," so the root directory in Windows is denoted as C:\. Other drives have root directories (D:\, E:\, etc.), too. The root directories are always tied to the physical drive or partition, and all the subdirectories (or subfolders as they're called in Windows) are directly descended from the root directory on the same physical drive. C:\Documents and Settings\Brian\My Documents will always be located on the primary (C:\) drive or partition.

The file systems in Fedora are a bit more flexible. For instance, the common path for a user's home directory is /home/<username>. The "home" is a subdirectory of the root folder, which is denoted in Linux-based systems as "/". So, in the author's case, the home directory might be /home/bproffitt. Here's the default directory structure for a Fedora machine.

```
/
/bin
/boot
/dev
/etc
/home
/lib
```

```
/lost+found
/media
/mnt
/opt
/proc
/root
/sbin
/selinux
/srv
/sys
/tmp
/usr
/var
```

Odd names aside, it looks similar to a set of Window folders, doesn't it? A bunch of directories in a nice tree pattern, all located on the same partition. Except, while this listing reflects the typical Fedora file system, it does not mean all of these directories are located on the same partition.

That is due to a unique UNIX file system property known as *mount points*. If you want, you can decide to put any directory on any drive or partition, and Fedora's file management will seamlessly copy, retrieve, save, or delete files wherever they are physically located.

Using the author's system as an example, the root (/) directory's mount point is located on /dev/hda2, which denotes the second partition ("2") of the primary ("a") hard drive ("dev/hd"). But the mount point for the /home directory (and all of its subdirectories) is located on /dev/hda3, a completely separate partition. The advantages to this are that the personal data that belongs to the author will always be stored on a separate partition, which means that if ever it were necessary to migrate to another Linux distribution or perform a clean installation of a future version of Fedora, that personal data would always be preserved and the files accessible though the /home directory in Fedora's file system.

You can mount different directories of the Fedora file system on any partition or drive, even different drives, if your PC is so equipped.

When you use Anaconda's partitioning tool to set up your drive, it is obvious that you will need to devote some space to your existing Windows operating system and some to Fedora. How much? The easy answer is simply to divide your drive in half, with each OS getting a fair share of the pie. Many other factors may play into making that choice different.

If, for example, you have a small drive upon which Windows is taking up a lot of space, then you will need to be conservative with your Fedora installation.

Space Available

You will need at least 4GB of disk space to handle an average Fedora installation. Figure at least two more GB of storage space, unless you have some sort of networked storage devices available.

While you are considering the amount of space you will need to set aside for Fedora, also make sure that you have enough to allocate for swap space on your drive. It is often hard to determine how much swap space to create, because different users need differing amounts based on the type of work they do. If you work with a lot of really big files (graphics, desktop publishing), you should set your swap space memory to be pretty high, such as double your system's RAM capacity. For most users, the rule of thumb is that the swap should equal 1.5 times your RAM.

Running Anaconda

For older versions of Fedora—and, indeed, for older versions of any Linux distribution—starting an installation was a matter of inserting the CD into the drive and rebooting your system. The installation application would be presented as a choice on the initial menu, and once selected, off the installation would go.

Today, with the LiveCD option for Fedora, starting the installation is even less strenuous. As you may have noticed in Figure 3.1, there is a nice little Install to Hard Drive icon on the desktop when you run the Fedora LiveCD. Now that the preliminaries are out of the way, double-click the Install to Hard Drive icon and follow this guide through the installation process.

Anaconda is a seven-step installation routine that begins with an introduction screen (called a *splash screen*). Click next to reach the Keyboard Setup screen, detailed in the next section.

Let's walk you through what happens, so you will know what to expect.

Keyboard Settings

You might think a keyboard is a keyboard, but around the world, and even within nations, there are many variations in the way people input their words into a PC. Step 1 of Anaconda, displayed in Figure 3.2, shows many of the different keyboards supported by Fedora.

The selected keyboard is the default keyboard setting based on the language selection you made when you first ran the Fedora LiveCD. If you are unsure of what kind of keyboard you are using, leave the default option selected. Otherwise, select the appropriate keyboard and then click Next to advance to Step 2.

Device Type Settings

Most Fedora users will likely be installing the Fedora operating system on a PC or PC-like device, such as a laptop or a netbook. However, advanced users and system administrators can also install Fedora on other types of machines that use storage area networks, which are a set of servers and disks designed to hold data for large organizations.

Presumably, if you have this type of project in mind, you are not going to need this book. So, we'll assume a more basic choice and leave the Basic Storage Devices option selected (shown in Figure 3.3). Click Next to continue to Step 3.

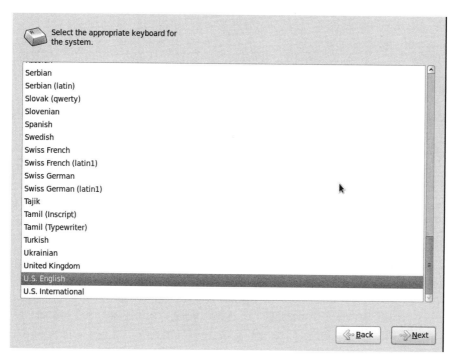

Figure 3.2
It's not just a QWERTY world out there.

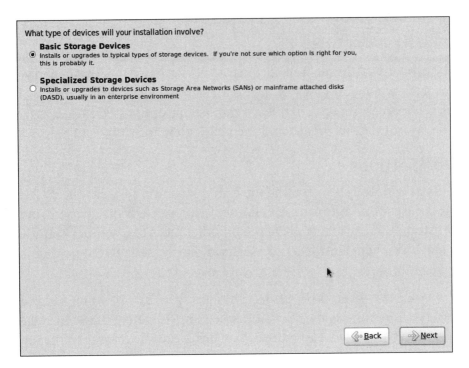

Figure 3.3
What kind of storage does your PC have?

Drive and Computer Settings

Most computers these days come with one hard drive, usually a big one. Still, there are many systems out there that come with more than one hard drive, or their users add one later.

With that in mind, Fedora lets you choose the hard drive on which you would like to install Fedora. In the example shown in Figure 3.4, there is only one drive available, so it should be clicked to select it, and then Next should be clicked to move to Step 4.

However, if you have more than one hard drive in your system, you can select the one you prefer for your Fedora installation.

In the next screen, you have the opportunity to name your computer (see Figure 3.5). Pick something simple like "Fedora" or "officepc." This name is what will identify your computer on a network, if it's connected to one.

Click Next to move to Step 5.

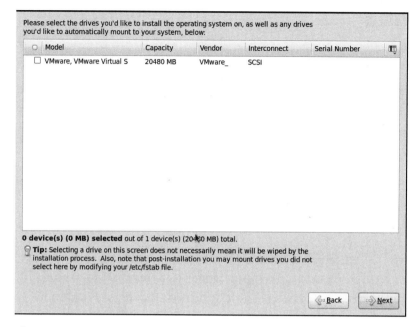

Figure 3.4
Choose the destination hard drive.

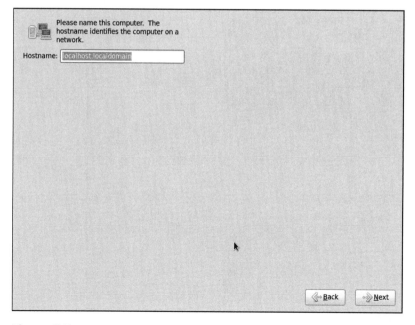

Figure 3.5
Name your computer.

Time Zone Settings

Step 5 of Anaconda displays a map of the world, with which you can determine your proper time zone settings (see Figure 3.6).

If you want to use the map, you can use the magnifying slider on the left of the map to zoom in to a specific region. Click the city closest to your location that's still in your same time zone. The city will appear in the Selected City drop-down list below the map. If you clicked on the wrong city, just try again.

Confirm that you have the correct city selected and the time zone is also correct. Click Next to proceed to Step 6.

Root Settings

On the screen shown in Figure 3.7, you will need to set your system's root password. "Root" is the name given to any Linux system's administrator account. The root user is given enormous privileges to configure a Linux system any way

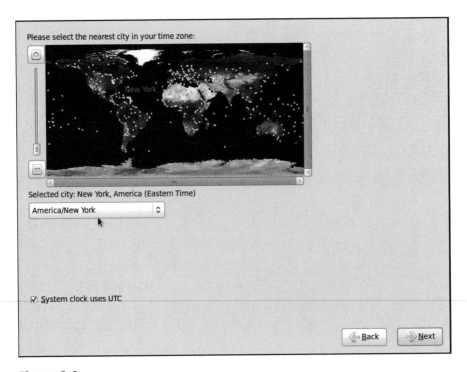

Figure 3.6
Finding yourself with Fedora.

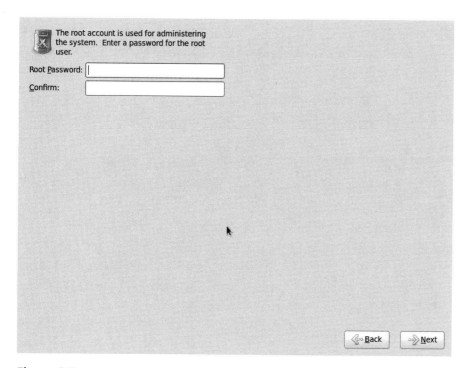

The root account is used for administering the system. Enter a password for the root user.

Root Password: |

Confirm:

Back   Next

Figure 3.7
Set the root password.

he or she can. As such, this is not a password you will use casually. Make it a good one, and don't forget it.

After entering the same password twice, click Next to move to Step 7. If Fedora detects that you have entered a weak password, such as one based on a dictionary word, it will warn you and give you the opportunity to enter a stronger password.

Partition Settings

Now comes the most important part of the Anaconda process: selecting your partition options.

By default Anaconda will select the option to Replace Existing Linux System(s). But you will need to set the option to Shrink Current System (see Figure 3.8). Before you leave that option selected and click Next, let's review what that means.

Shrink Current System means that Anaconda will attempt to reduce the size of the existing Windows system using any unused space in that file system, to make room for Fedora on a now-empty part of the disk.

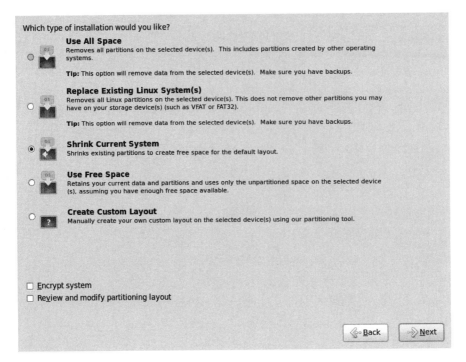

Figure 3.8
Caution: partitioning ahead.

For example, suppose you have a 200GB drive with Windows installed, and you have about 100GB of free space on the drive. Anaconda will compress the 200GB Windows file system down to 120GB, leaving 80GB of completely unused space, where it will install Fedora.

If this is the case, clicking on this option will generate the Volume to Shrink dialog box, where you can set the size for the existing Windows partition. It is recommended that you give Fedora at least 60GB of space, but you can easily manage with 20GB, especially if you have external storage available for your data.

Use All Space means that when you are finished with Anaconda, the installation process will completely format your hard drive, which means that everything that was on it (Windows and your personal data) will be gone. Forever.

If you read Chapter 2, "Before You Install Fedora," and backed up all of your system's files, then this will be only a minor headache as you restore what was overwritten by the Fedora installation process. If you did not back up your

Windows partition, and you did not want to format your entire drive, this will be akin to a major disaster.

So, and it cannot be stressed enough, be sure that you want to totally replace Windows and your personal data with Fedora before you select the Use All Space option.

Save Your Personal Files

Many new users think that somehow their personal files will be preserved and that Windows will automatically be transformed to Fedora. This is not the case. Make sure that you have your personal files safely backed up.

Choose the option you want and click Next. The Writing Storage Configuration to Disk dialog box will open (see Figure 3.9).

At this point, you are now committing yourself to installing Fedora. Clicking Write Changes to Disk will start the installation process and permanently make changes to your disk drive. It cannot be emphasized enough that all of your data should be backed up at this point.

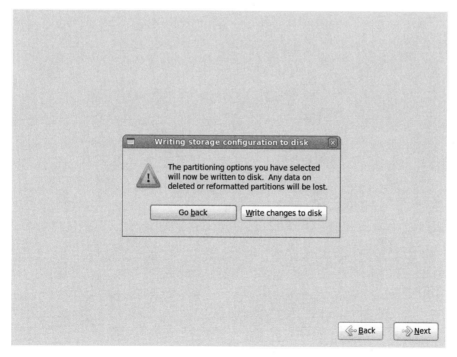

Figure 3.9
Committing to your installation.

If it is, and you are ready, click Write Changes to Disk, and the installation will begin. When Anaconda is finished (and it may take a while), the completion screen will appear (see Figure 3.10).

Click Close to exit the Anaconda installer. In the main Fedora LiveCD desktop, click the System | Shut Down menu command. Click the Restart option in the next dialog box and click OK to restart your system. You should remove the CD after the system shuts down so it doesn't reboot back to the Fedora Live system.

First Run Configuration

The very first time Fedora runs, it gives you one more set of configuration screens from the Setup Agent to finish things up.

The first Setup Agent screen you will see will be the Welcome screen, as shown in Figure 3.11. Click Forward to continue.

The second Setup Agent screen is the License screen, which briefly lets you know that the Fedora distribution is distributed as free software. This is good to know

Figure 3.10
Installation is complete.

Figure 3.11
Starting the initial configuration.

but requires little input from you (see Figure 3.12). Click Forward to move ahead.

On the third Setup Agent screen, you need to enter your personal information, including name, preferred user ID, and password (see Figure 3.13).

Most of this is straightforward information and easy to fill in. A couple of caveats for you to follow: First, never make your user ID any variation of the word "root." As mentioned earlier, logging on as the root user will give you a lot of privileges on your Fedora machine. While that may sound good, it is most assuredly not. Root, or superuser, accounts have the capability to damage many files at once, whereas regular users are not granted such access.

Superuser access is needed for some operations in Fedora, and we'll explore those later.

The second thing, and you surely will hear this a lot, is please make your password hard to guess. Use letters and numbers in combinations that don't make up words or proper names. Such passwords are easier to crack. One favorite scheme

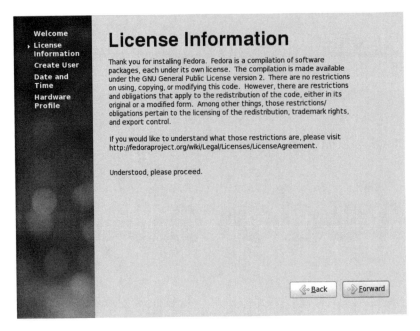

Figure 3.12
The basic Fedora license statement.

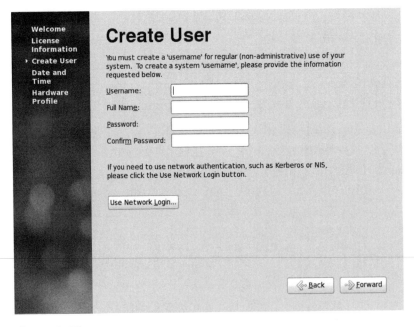

Figure 3.13
The Create User screen.

is to use the first letter of the words in a refrain from your favorite song. You should get a suitably hardened password.

Once you fill in the information, click Forward to continue.

In the Date and Time screen, shown in Figure 3.14, you can confirm the date and time information Fedora has picked up from your system and the time zone settings you made in Anaconda.

Synchronize Those Watches

If you want really accurate time, click the Synchronize Date and Time over the Network option. This will link your computer to hyper-accurate servers on the Internet that get their time settings from atomic clocks. You should never be late again.

After your time settings are confirmed, clicking Continue will bring you to the last screen of the Setup Agent: the Hardware Profile screen (see Figure 3.15).

This screen contains all of the data Anaconda and the Setup Agent gathered about your system using a tool called Smolt and presents the option to send this

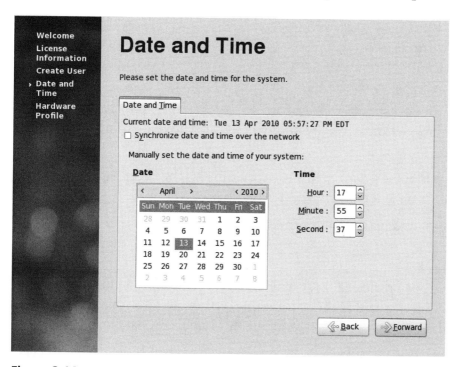

Figure 3.14
The Date and Time screen.

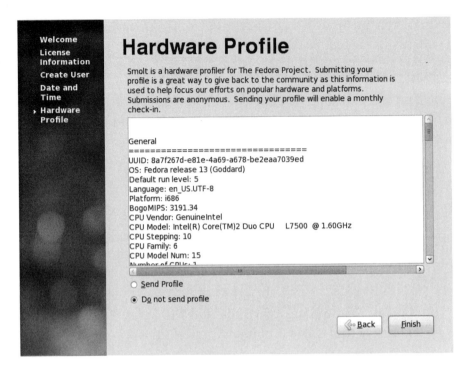

Figure 3.15
Giving back to the Fedora community.

information to Fedora. Why? Because as each system is surveyed, the Fedora developers will have a better idea of where to focus their efforts in future versions. This information is strictly anonymous, and none of your personal data will be sent.

Choose the option you want and then click Finish. The Setup Agent will close, and you will then see the main login screen.

Enter your user and password information, and enter Fedora.

Conclusion

In this chapter, you reviewed the installation steps for getting Fedora on your PC. Special attention was paid to the partitioning settings, because this is the one part of the installation where there is a potential for important data loss.

Now that Fedora is installed, it's time to take the grand tour of this excellent operating system in Chapter 4, "Desktop Basics."

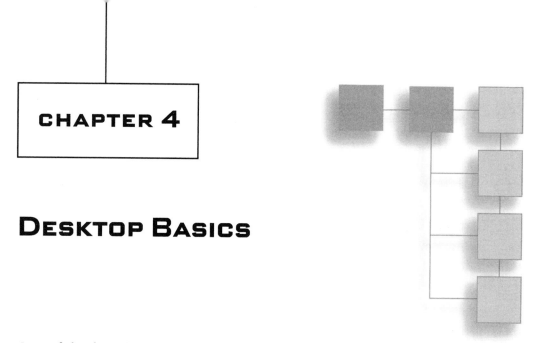

CHAPTER 4

DESKTOP BASICS

One of the first things new users notices about the Fedora desktop is its muted tones. Some users are a little more blunt: "It certainly is... blue..." they may mutter, less than enthusiastically.

Indeed, given the glitz and glam of many of today's graphic environments, the default color scheme of Fedora is rather sedated. But there is a good reason: think of a plain-ish desktop as a blank canvas upon which you can create a desktop that's purely customized to your needs. Indeed, there are so many ways to customize your desktop, and not just through color—you will hardly know where to begin.

That is what this chapter will hopefully do: provide guidance on how to begin the process of making your Fedora desktop truly your own.

In this chapter, you will:

- Learn more about the development of the GNOME desktop.

- Ensure that your monitor is set at the best resolution.

- Discover how to modify settings for various desktop elements.

- Navigate the GNOME desktop.

Understanding the GNOME Desktop

First off, it's not "gnome," like those odd little blue-coated, red-hatted critters that run around the Scandinavian countryside. It's "guh-nome," heavy on the "G" and light on the "uh."

GNOME is the brainchild of Miguel de Icaza, a Mexican computer engineering student who took one look at the KDE environment and really liked what he saw—until he discovered the non-free code sitting (at the time) within it.

De Icaza, a devoted follower of the free software ideals, decided that what was needed in Linux was a similar desktop environment that had none of the licensing limitations of KDE.

GNOME first debuted in August 1997, when de Icaza first made the announcement about the project he was working on in the comp.os.linux.announce newsgroup. By December of that same year, the first workable test version was made available to the Linux community. It would not be until March of 1999 that version 1.0 would be released to the general public, but by then the word had gotten out, and thousands of free software devotees climbed on board the GNOME bandwagon.

GNOME, like KDE, is a desktop environment. It is not a window manager, like Enlightenment or Metacity. Window managers control the look and feel of the windows, menus, and other visual components of a graphic interface. Desktop environments provide a specific platform for applications to operate within. If an application is written for a desktop environment, therefore, it can tap into a wide range of common features with other applications in that environment.

In the Linux community, GNOME is lauded for more than its free software status. It has historically been regarded as more aesthetically pleasing than KDE, as the themes available for GNOME have more of an eye-candy appeal. Recent versions of KDE would seem to dispute this, which you will learn if you should try Fedora KDE.

Beyond the look of GNOME, de Icaza has pushed new boundaries for the perception of free software in the corporate world. A year after the release of GNOME 1.0, de Icaza partnered with several major corporations to form the GNOME Foundation—a nonprofit organization dedicated to the ideal of keeping GNOME development moving forward in a rapid and open way.

The GNOME Foundation, with high-power members such as Red Hat, HP, and IBM, wants to make GNOME *the* interface for Linux and make that interface very easy for users to adapt to.

One of the major hurdles for people using Linux has been the perception that it is too hard to use, a perception the GNOME Foundation wants to change. By offering software developers a stable and communicative environment within which to create new GNOME apps, the GNOME Foundation serves as an incubator of sorts for bringing more user-friendly applications to the GNOME interface.

It is for many of these same reasons that Fedora's default desktop is GNOME. Let's take a brief tour and learn how to change the look of the desktop along the way.

Desktop Settings and Features

When you look at the GNOME desktop, you will see how simple and clean it is (see Figure 4.1). That's because the interface designers decided to present just the tools you need in as unobtrusive a way as possible. No Recycle Bins or My Documents icons will be found here—unless you want them.

Some of the elements of the desktop will be familiar in function to you, if you have used Windows or OS X in the past. Some controls and features will be less familiar, but once you get an idea of how they work, this will soon pass.

- **Applications Menu.** This menu is very similar in form and function to the Start menu in Windows. In this menu, nearly all of the graphical applications installed on your Fedora machine can be found, arranged by category (see Figure 4.2).

- **Places Menu.** This menu will allow you to navigate quickly to specific directories on your machine and others, depending on how you configure it (see Figure 4.3).

- **System Menu.** The System menu is an important component of the desktop, giving the user access to a variety of configuration settings, as well as power control and general Help access (see Figure 4.4).

- **Panels.** The Panels in Fedora are where a lot of Fedora controls (menus, launchers, switchers, etc.) reside. Panels can be customized to have different

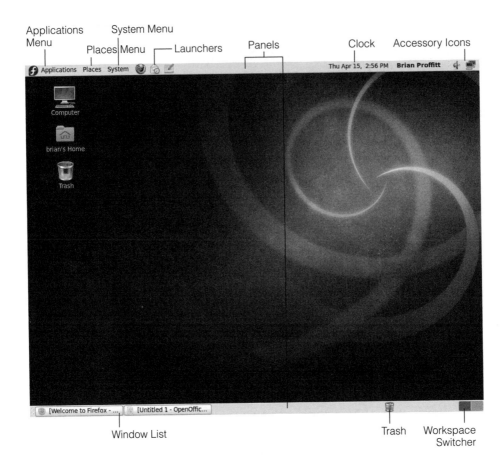

Figure 4.1
The Fedora GNOME desktop.

locations, sizes, and appearances, which will be discussed in the "Panels" section later in this chapter.

- **Trash.** The Trash icon is a placeholder for the Trash folder on your Fedora PC. When you delete files on the computer, they aren't permanently deleted; they are sent to this folder. To see the contents of Trash, click the icon (see Figure 4.5). If you want to permanently rid yourself of the files in Trash, click the Empty Trash button.

- **Workspace Switcher.** This control is unique to most distributions of Linux with robust desktop environments like GNOME. Instead of just one

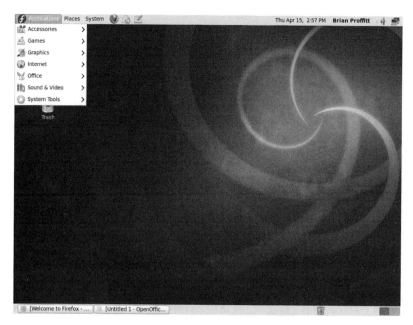

Figure 4.2
The Applications menu.

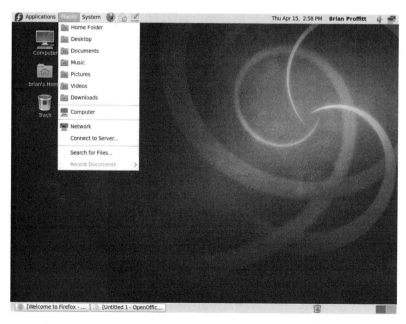

Figure 4.3
The Places menu.

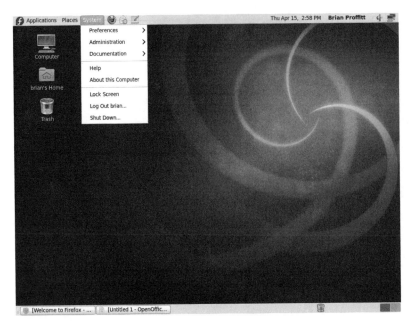

Figure 4.4
The System menu.

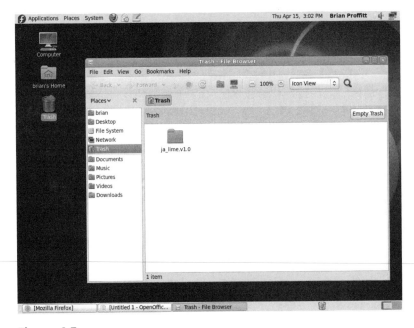

Figure 4.5
The Trash folder.

desktop, you can actually have more than one, each with its own set of open applications, icons—even looks. For further information, see the "Workspaces" section later in this chapter.

- **Window List.** Similar to the Windows taskbar or the OS X dock, the Window List will display all of the running applications and windows in Fedora (see Figure 4.6).

- **Launchers.** Icons in Fedora are still called *icons,* but if they have the assignment of launching something, such as an application, file, or folder, then they are called *launchers.* Launchers can appear on the desktop or in desktop panels.

- **Accessory Icons.** Some icons don't just launch something; they're there to tell the user something, too, such as whether the computer is connected to a network.

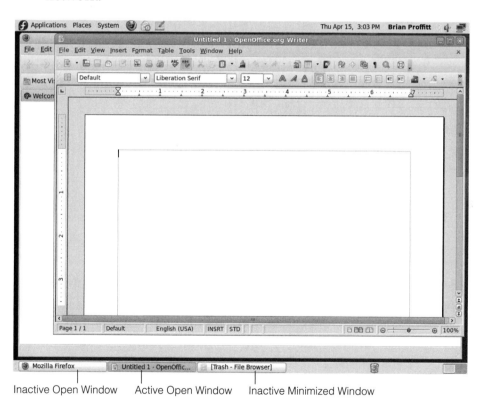

Figure 4.6
An active Window List.

- **Clock.** The name pretty much says it all—a panel accessory that informs users of the time and date. It does more, such as tap into Evolution, Fedora's personal information management application, for access to current appointments and tasks. It will even tell you the weather forecast.

There's more, much more to the GNOME desktop than just these features listed here. But these are the basics you will need to know first, as you continue your exploration of this new interface. Now it's time to learn how to customize the desktop and make it more your own.

Resolution

The screen resolution in Fedora is not strictly a desktop function, since changing the size of the screen resolution actually affects everything in Fedora, not just the desktop. Still, before you do anything else, let's see if we can make your viewing experience better.

Screen resolution is tech shorthand for the number of pixels displayed on the screen at any one time. It is usually denoted as width × height, in pixels. So, a common resolution of 800×600 displays 800 pixels of graphic information across your monitor screen and 600 pixels down (for a total of 480,000 pixels on the whole screen). That's a lot of pixels, but, truth be told, 800×600 is a bit below average in terms of today's powerful graphics cards and monitors.

These days, 1280×1024 is a good resolution, and resolutions of 1600×1200 and more are becoming popular as well.

The net effect of these resolutions settings is, the higher the resolution, the more pixels can fit on a screen. The more pixels, the smaller the objects on the screen will look. Thus, with a higher resolution, you can fit more information and windows on your screen.

When Fedora is first installed, it typically does a good job of probing your monitor and graphics card and figuring out which resolution is the best fit for your hardware's capabilities. There is a lot of hardware out there, though, and sometimes Fedora misses the mark. Before moving on to specific desktop settings, let's check the resolution.

As you can see in Figure 4.7, the resolution for the desktop shown is a bit low—objects are very large, and there's not a lot of screen "real estate" available. Your monitor may be able to handle something larger.

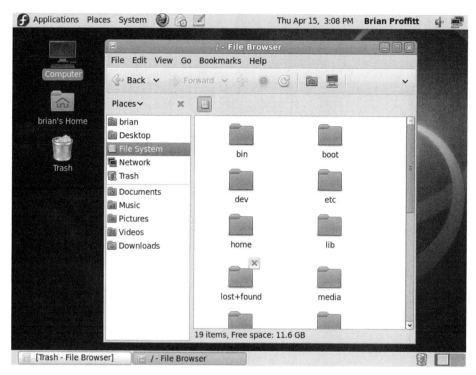

Figure 4.7
An 800×600 desktop resolution.

Changing this is easy; just use the steps outlined below.

1. Click the System | Preferences | Monitors menu command. The Monitor Preferences dialog box will open (see Figure 4.8).

2. Click the Resolution drop-down list and select a resolution value higher than the current one.

3. Click Apply. The desktop resolution will be changed, and a confirmation dialog will open.

4. Click Keep This Configuration. The confirmation dialog will close.

5. Click Close. The Monitor Preferences dialog box will close.

Picky Monitors

Some LCD monitors have what are known as native resolutions, which are resolutions at which they function best. Your monitor's reference guide should have more information, and newer monitors will actually alert you via a message if an attempted resolution is not a good fit.

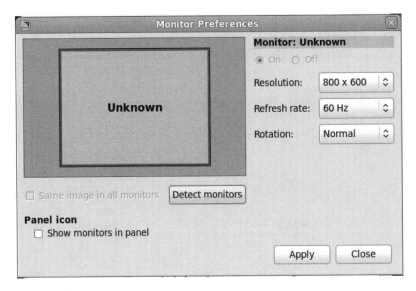

Figure 4.8
You say you want a resolution.

Menus

One of the nicer features of Fedora is the ready capability of editing the contents of menus to include exactly what you want. Fedora does a good job of including the most used applications in its menus, but there may be some that you would like to have in the menus for more ready access.

Configuring Fedora's menus is relatively simple. And, while you're doing so, you may learn about even more applications you didn't know that Fedora had.

1. Click the System | Preferences | Main Menu menu command. The Main Menu dialog box will open (see Figure 4.9).

2. Click a submenu item in the Menus column. Items in italic print are currently not visible on any menu. The contents of that submenu will be displayed in the Items column.

3. To add an item to a menu, click the check box next to that item in the Items column. The item will be selected (see Figure 4.10).

4. To move an item, click the item you want to move. The Move Up and/or the Move Down buttons will become active.

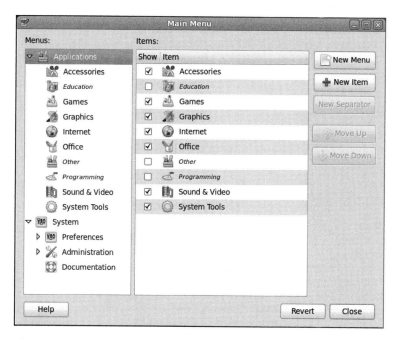

Figure 4.9
Configuring menu contents.

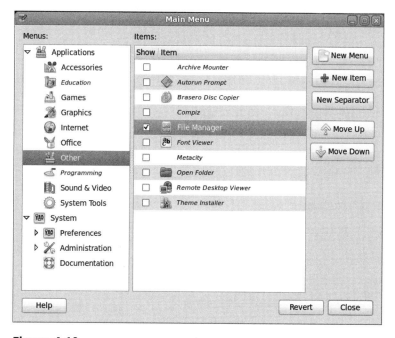

Figure 4.10
Adding menu items.

5. Click Move Up. The menu item will move one place up in its list.

6. Click Close. The menus will reflect your changes.

Not only can you make items visible and move them around, but you can also add items to menus.

1. To add a new item, navigate to the submenu where you want the item to be and click New Item. The Create Launcher dialog box will open (see Figure 4.11).

2. Type the name of the application you want to add in the Name field.

3. Type the command used to start the program in the Command field.

Choosing Helper Applications

You can use the Browse button to open the Choose an Application dialog box and navigate to the appropriate command. Many applications are found in the /usr/bin or /usr/sbin directory.

4. To add an icon, click the Launcher button. The Choose an Icon dialog box will open (see Figure 4.12).

5. Click a desired icon and then click Open. The selected icon will appear in the Create Launcher dialog box.

6. Click OK. The Create Launcher dialog box will close, and the new menu item will appear in the Item column of the Main Menu dialog.

7. Click Close. The menus will reflect your changes.

Figure 4.11
Creating menu items.

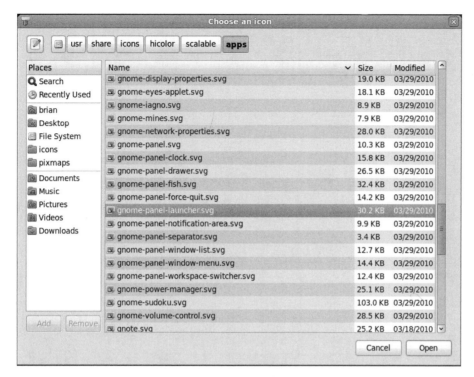

Figure 4.12
Looking for icons.

To add a new submenu to your menu selection, proceed with these steps:

1. Click the top-level menu where you want your new submenu to be.

2. Click New Menu. The Directory Properties dialog box will open (see Figure 4.13).

3. Type the name of the application you want to add in the Name field.

4. To add an icon, click the Folder button. The Choose an Icon dialog box will open.

5. Click a desired icon and then click OK. The selected icon will appear in the Directory Properties dialog box.

6. Click Close. The Directory Properties dialog box will close, and the new submenu item will appear in the Menu column of the Main Menu dialog.

7. Click Close. The menus will reflect your changes.

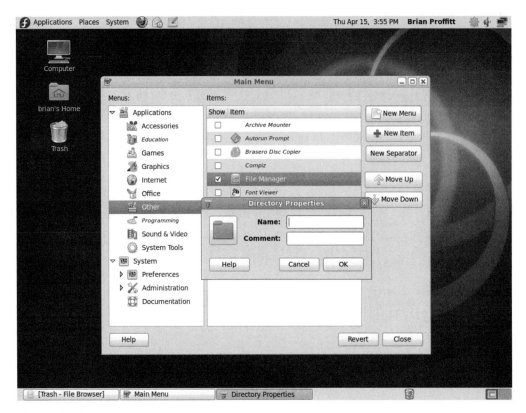

Figure 4.13
Creating a new submenu.

Panels

Menus aren't the only thing that can be customized in Fedora. In fact, when you come right down to it, it's a lot easier to list the elements in Fedora that aren't customizable in some way.

Panels are no exception. The panels are the gray horizontal bars at the top and bottom of the Fedora desktop that contain various tools and menus. At least, that's how they start out. But after a little bit of tweaking, you will soon discover that gray, horizontal, top, and bottom are all just loose concepts: the panels can look like nearly anything and be located in different places. It all depends on you.

One quick change you can make is relocating any panel.

1. Right-click the panel you want to move. A context menu will appear.

2. Click Properties. The Panel Properties dialog box will open.

3. Select a new Orientation setting.

4. Click Close. The panel will be fixed in its new position (see Figure 4.14).

Like menus, items can be added or removed from panels. Three categories of items can be added to a panel: a tool, such as an accessory or monitoring tool, an Application Launcher from the Applications menu, or a custom Application Launcher. We can walk through all of these in just a few steps, starting with a GNOME tool.

1. Right-click the panel to which you want to add an item. A context menu will appear.

2. Click Add to Panel. The Add to Panel dialog box will open (see Figure 4.15).

3. Click the item you would like to add. The item will be selected.

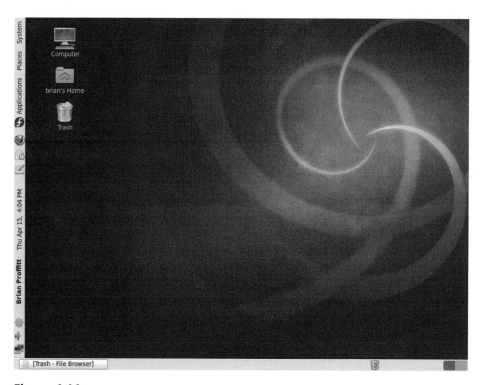

Figure 4.14
Moving a panel.

Figure 4.15
Adding items to a panel.

4. Click Add. The item will appear in the panel (see Figure 4.16).

5. To move the item, right-click its icon. A context menu will appear.

6. Click Move. The mouse cursor will change to a gripping hand.

7. Move the mouse cursor left or right across the screen. The panel item will move in a corresponding fashion.

8. When the item is positioned in the correct place, click the item. The item will be in the desired position.

9. Click Close. The Add to Panel dialog box will close.

Adding an application is just as simple. You can choose from any app on the Applications menu or run your own.

1. Right-click the panel to which you want to add an item. A context menu will appear.

2. Click Add to Panel. The Add to Panel dialog box will open.

The New Item: Weather Report

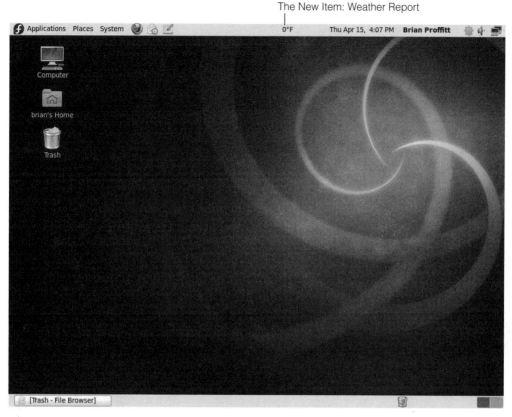

Figure 4.16
A new item, almost ready.

3. Click Application Launcher and then click the Forward button. The contents of the Applications menu will appear in the central window (see Figure 4.17).

4. Click the expansion arrow (triangle) to expand a group of applications.

5. Click the application you would like to add. The application will be selected.

6. Click Add. The application item will appear in the panel.

7. To move the item, right-click its icon. A context menu will appear.

8. Click Move. The mouse cursor will change to a gripping hand.

Figure 4.17
Any item on the Applications menu can be added.

9. Move the mouse cursor left or right across the screen. The panel item will move in a corresponding fashion.

10. When the item is positioned in the correct place, click the item. The item will be in the desired position.

11. Click Close. The Add to Panel dialog box will close.

You don't have to be limited to just the apps in the Applications menu; just use the Custom Application Launcher tool.

1. Right-click the panel to which you want to add an item. A context menu will appear.

2. Click Add to Panel. The Add to Panel dialog box will open.

3. Click Custom Application Launcher and then Add. The Create Launcher dialog box will appear.

4. Type the name of the application you want to add in the Name field.

5. Type the command used to start the program in the Command field or click the Browse button to locate the application in any of the places on your PC.

6. To add an icon, click the Launcher button. The Choose an Icon dialog box will open.

7. Click a desired icon and then click OK. The selected icon will appear in the Create Launcher dialog box.

8. Click OK. The Create Launcher dialog box will close, and the new menu item will appear in the panel.

9. To move the item, right-click its icon. A context menu will appear.

10. Click Move. The mouse cursor will change to a gripping hand.

11. Move the mouse cursor left or right across the screen. The panel item will move in a corresponding fashion.

12. When the item is positioned in the correct place, click the item. The item will be in the desired position.

13. Click Close. The Add to Panel dialog box will close.

To remove an item from a panel is a much faster process.

1. Right-click the item you want to delete. A context menu will appear.

2. Click Remove From Panel. The item will be deleted from the panel.

If the look of the panels is not something you can aesthetically appreciate, there's good news: you can change the panel look very quickly.

1. Right-click the panel that you want to configure. A context menu will appear.

2. Click Properties. The Panel Properties dialog box will open (see Figure 4.18).

3. Click the Background tab.

4. Click the Solid Color radio button. The color options will become active, as shown in Figure 4.19.

Figure 4.18
The Panel Properties dialog box.

Figure 4.19
Choose your panel's color.

5. Click and drag the Style slider toward the Transparent setting. The panel will become more transparent.

6. Click Close. The Panel Properties dialog box will close, and the panel will have become rather . . . clear (see Figure 4.20).

Figure 4.20
A more transparent panel.

Panel Design

Making a panel transparent is only one change you can make in the Panel Properties dialog box. Try experimenting with different colors, shading, and background images in the Background tab. In the General tab, you can adjust the panel's size, set it to Autohide, or even reduce its width.

Mouse and Keyboard

During the installation process, you were able to define the type of keyboard you were using. While it is unlikely that Anaconda got it wrong, there may come a time when you will swap keyboards or add a new user who prefers to plug in his own unique input device. And you were never given any options to set your mouse settings.

As you play with the Fedora desktop, let's take the time to see where such settings can be configured.

First, let's see how the mouse can be configured. You might think that there's not much to change with a mouse, but you might be surprised.

Click the System | Preferences | Mouse menu command. The Mouse Preferences dialog box will open (see Figure 4.21).

■ On the General page, you can set your mouse to be left-handed (which switches the button operations) and set the time between double-clicks—something very useful for those users with slower reflexes. Acceleration and sensitivity of the mouse can also be set, as well as the range a mouse can have when it is dragging and dropping desktop objects. You can also activate a control that will highlight the mouse on the screen when you press the Ctrl button on your keyboard.

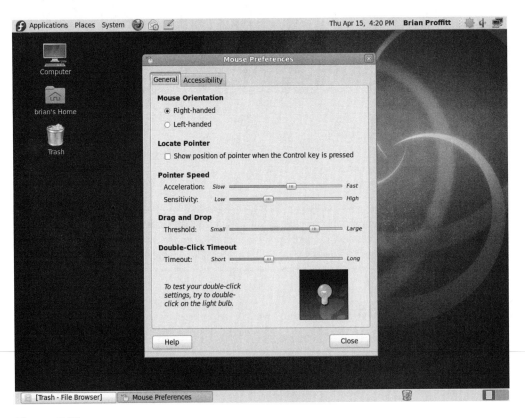

Figure 4.21
Everything a mouse needs but the cheese.

- On the Accessibility page, shown in Figure 4.22, you can set features that will make the mouse easier to use if you have more physical challenges. This includes setting a click action when you stop the mouse on the screen and creating custom mouse gestures.

The keyboard for your Fedora can also get a lot of attention, with features you may not have even heard of before, but that make perfect sense once you use them. To access the keyboard configurations, click the System | Preferences | Keyboard menu command. The Keyboard Preferences dialog box will open (see Figure 4.23).

- On the General page, the response time of repeating keys and cursor blinks can be set.

- On the Layouts page, you can select your keyboard type as you did in the installation of Fedora, and you can add additional keyboard configurations (see Figure 4.24).

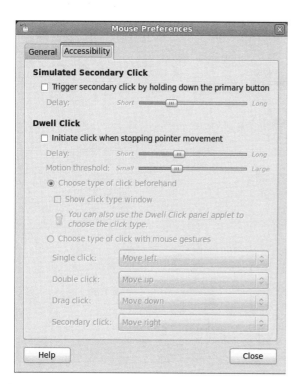

Figure 4.22
Setting mouse accessibility options.

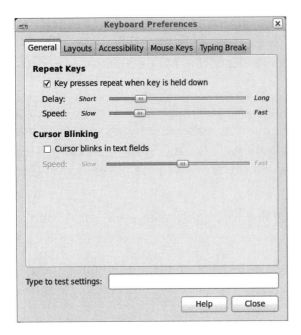

Figure 4.23
General keyboard settings.

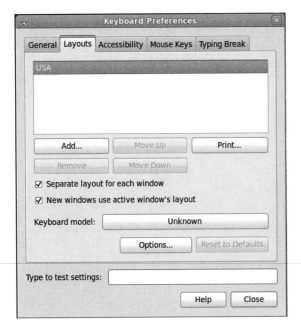

Figure 4.24
Choosing a keyboard layout.

- On the Accessibility page, you can configure features such as Sticky or Slow Keys to assist you if needed (see Figure 4.25).

- On the Mouse Keys page, you can set the keypad up to control the mouse pointer (see Figure 4.26).

- On the Typing Break page, you can force the keyboard to lock itself and make you take a break at any given interval (see Figure 4.27). This may seem like a time-waster, but regular breaks help prevent repetitive stress injuries that often come with excessive typing.

Time and Date

The Clock accessory that runs in your panel is pretty straightforward: it shows the date and the time. But it also can show your location on a world daylight map, as well as deliver weather forecasts.

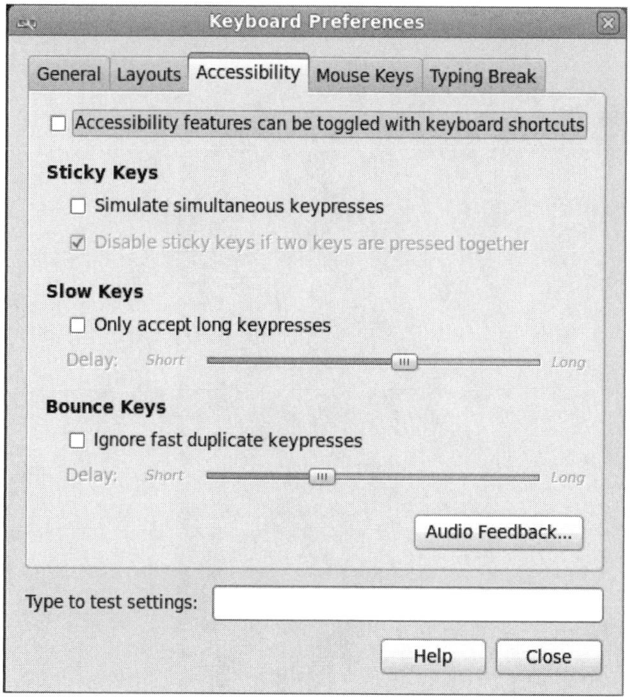

Figure 4.25
Setting keyboard accessibility options.

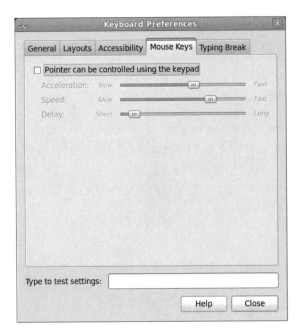

Figure 4.26
You can use the keypad to drive the pointer.

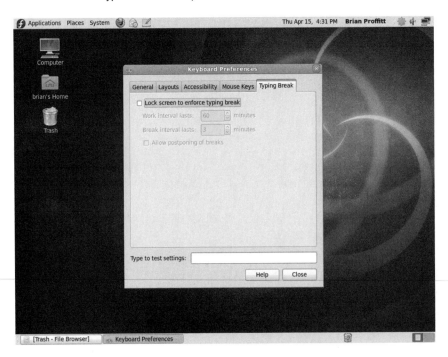

Figure 4.27
A feature for your health.

You can, if you want, set your time manually. But the really punctual people among you might be interested to know that you can synchronize the Clock to match the atomic clocks maintained by the world's governments.

1. Right-click the Clock. A context menu will appear.

2. Click Preferences. The Clock Preferences dialog box will open (see Figure 4.28).

3. To set the time on the desktop, click Time Settings. The Time & Date dialog box will open (see Figure 4.29).

4. Settings on the Clock can be done manually with the controls in this dialog box. Set the time and click the Set System Time button. An Authenticate dialog will open, as shown in Figure 4.30.

5. Type in the administrative password and click Authenticate.

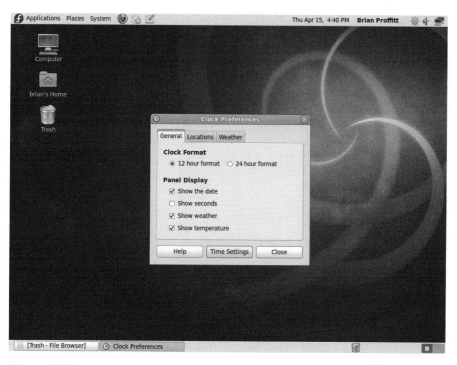

Figure 4.28
Setting Clock Preferences.

Figure 4.29
Setting your clock.

Figure 4.30
System settings need administrator permissions.

You can also set multiple locations within the Clock so you see what the time is at home or in a location anywhere in the world.

1. Right-click the Clock. A context menu will appear.

2. Click Preferences. The Clock Preferences dialog box will open.

3. Click the Locations tab. The Locations page will appear (see Figure 4.31).

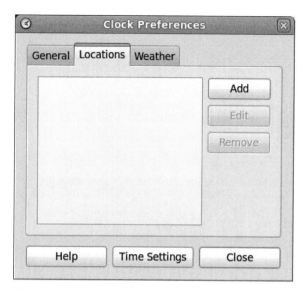

Figure 4.31
Setting your location.

4. Click Add. The Choose Location dialog box will open.

5. Type the name of the city or town you want. As you type, the names of various municipalities will begin to appear.

Where Are You?

If your town does not appear in the list, try a larger city near that location instead. Unfortunately, a complete gazette is not within the Clock. Alternatively, enter the latitude and longitude of the location in the appropriate fields of the Choose Location dialog.

6. Once the right name appears, press Enter. The geographic information for the city will appear in the appropriate fields (see Figure 4.32).

7. Click OK. The new city will appear in the Locations page.

Fedora's Clock will also provide the weather information for the first city listed in the Locations page. The Weather tab of the Clock Preferences dialog box will enable you to set the units of temperature and wind speed for your weather report, as shown in Figure 4.33.

Workspaces

Something that most Windows users haven't seen yet are the workspaces on the GNOME desktop. Workspaces are virtual desktops, in that each workspace can

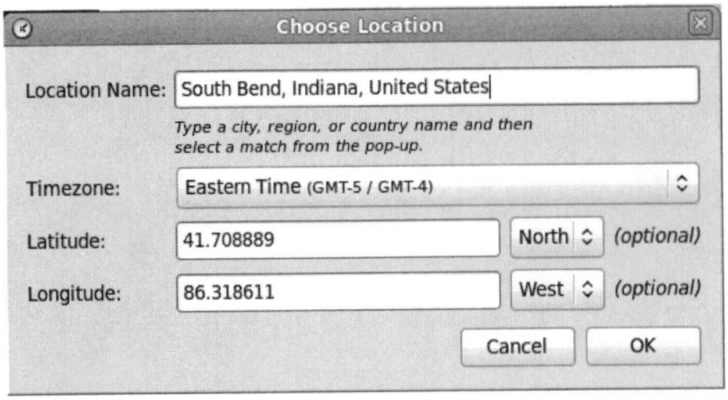

Figure 4.32
Home is where the coordinates are.

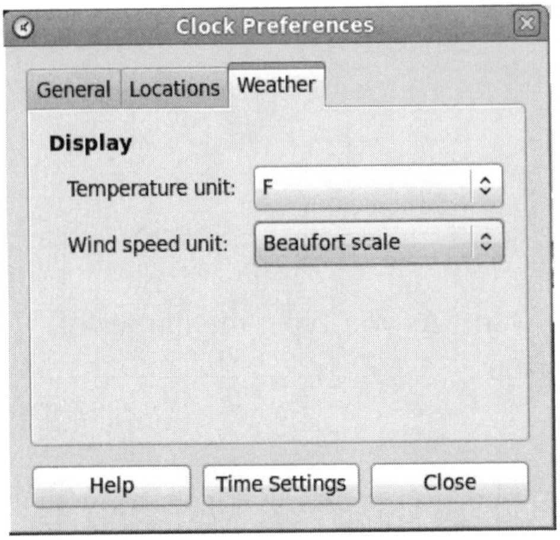

Figure 4.33
Beaufort scale buffs, rejoice.

contain its own windows, icons, and running applications. By default, Fedora give you two workspaces to start working with, but you can add a lot more if need be.

Workspaces are ideal for those users who need to separate one set of tasks from another. For instance, a certain author will keep all of the applications involved with writing his book in one workspace and the applications used for his day job in another workspace.

To switch between workspaces, simply click the workspace you want to view in the Workspace Switcher. You can control the number of workspaces by following these steps.

1. Right-click the Workspace Switcher. A context menu will appear.

2. Click Preferences. The Workspace Switcher Preferences dialog box will appear, as shown in Figure 4.34.

3. To change the number of workspaces, type the number you want in the Number of Workspaces field. A new workspace will be added to the switcher.

4. To give each workspace a unique name, slowly click the default name twice and then type a new name. The name will be changed.

5. Click the Show Workspace Names in Switcher check box. The Switcher will display the new names, as shown in Figure 4.35.

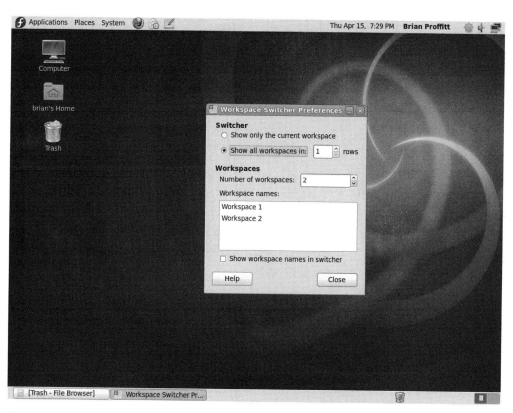

Figure 4.34
Control the number of workspaces.

Figure 4.35
Workspaces can have proper names.

To open windows in workspaces, either you can navigate to a workspace and open the application there or you can move any window to a workspace in just one step. Simply click the Window Menu icon in the upper-left corner of any open window and select the Move to Another Workspace menu. Then click the destination workspace for this window.

Window Dressing

Like custom cars, people seem to love to customize their PCs with the flashiest themes and colors. And for the best eye candy bang-for-your-buck, very few desktop environments compare with the GNOME desktop. So, for the sheer enjoyment of it, let's touch on how to start tricking out your Fedora ride.

Backgrounds

Backgrounds are the easiest thing to change in Fedora, though unfortunately, to save space on the installation CD, there are only a few backgrounds included. It would therefore be a good idea to get a background first from another source, such as the Internet or a personal graphic file.

Making Things Pretty

One of the best places to find beautiful wallpaper art for your Fedora PC is in the Wallpapers section at GNOME-Look, which is found at http://www.gnome-look.org. Be sure to visit the section that matches your desktop's resolution.

1. Right-click anywhere on the desktop. A context menu will appear.

2. Click Change Desktop Background. The Background page of the Appearance Preferences dialog box will appear (see Figure 4.36).

3. If you see a desired wallpaper, click it. The Fedora background will immediately update.

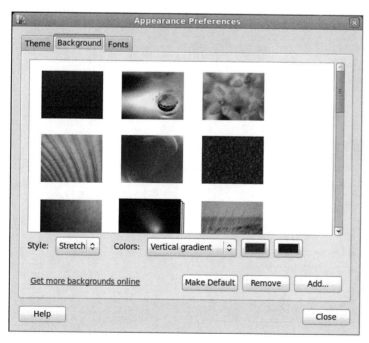

Figure 4.36
Changing wallpapers is easy.

4. To use another file for wallpaper, click Add. The Add Wallpaper dialog box will open.

5. Navigate to and select the file you want to use for wallpaper.

6. Click Open. The Add Wallpaper dialog box will close, and the new wallpaper will appear, already selected in the Appearance Preferences dialog box.

7. Click Finish. The dialog box will close, and your new wallpaper will be displayed (see Figure 4.37).

Themes

Themes are used in Fedora to change whole color and window schemes at one time. They are very fun to play with, and even if you download a theme from the Internet, you can customize any part of it to make it truly unique.

Figure 4.37
The only limit is your imagination.

To load a new theme, follow these steps.

1. Click the System | Preferences | Appearance menu command. The Appearance Preferences dialog box will open to the Theme page (see Figure 4.38).

2. Click a desired theme. The theme's settings will be immediately reflected on the Fedora desktop (see Figure 4.39).

3. To change part of a theme, click the Customize button. The Customize Theme dialog box will open (see Figure 4.40).

4. Explore the various controls and see what happens. When finished, click Close. If you made any changes, the theme will be displayed as a Custom theme.

5. Click Save As. The Save Theme As dialog box will appear.

6. Enter a Name and Description for the theme and click Save. The new theme will be saved in the list of themes.

7. Click Close. The theme will now be set.

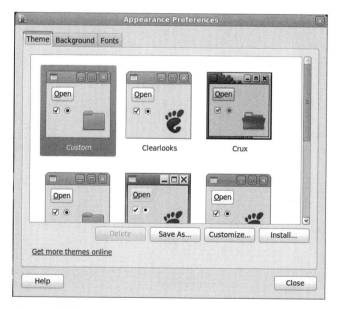

Figure 4.38
Fedora has varying themes to choose from.

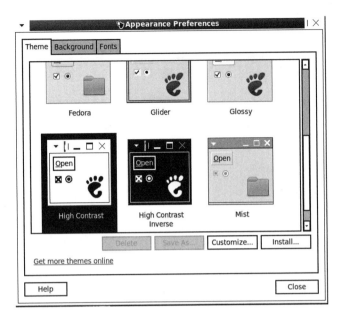

Figure 4.39
Themes are applied instantly.

Figure 4.40
You can change any part of a theme.

Sensing a Theme

Like wallpapers, many excellent themes can be found at the GNOME-Look Web site.

Conclusion

In this chapter, we took a tour of the Fedora interface itself, the GNOME desktop. You have seen that it is very similar to Windows and OS X desktops, although there are some important differences.

There is a lot to see and play with in the GNOME desktop, and before you continue on to the next chapter, you are invited to take a moment and do just that—play. Then we'll get to the important business of any PC, which is connecting to the Internet.

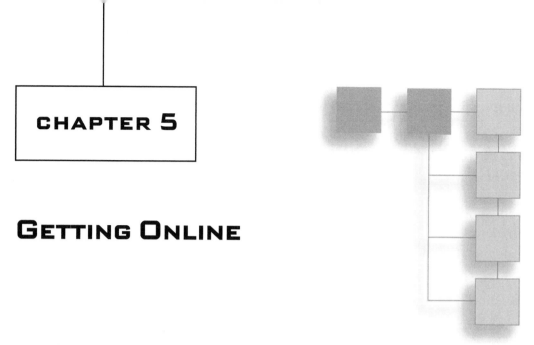

CHAPTER 5

GETTING ONLINE

Now that you have run through some of the basic configuration steps for your Fedora PC, it's time to take a look at how you can get Fedora talking to other computers, namely through that ubiquitous medium of the twenty-first century, the Internet.

In this chapter, you will learn how to configure Fedora to connect to the Internet through:

- A home or office network
- Broadband cable/DSL modems
- Dial-up connections
- Wirelessly via WiFi

How to Get on the Internet

Much has been said about the Internet this past couple of decades. Although much hoopla and hype has been associated with this phenomenon—the largest of all public computer networks—it should be noted that the Internet is not even close to being finished, even in developed nations.

The growth of the Internet (thus far) is in many ways similar to the growth of the telephone in the United States in the late nineteenth century. For the first five years of its commercial existence, the telephone was in about 10 percent of U.S.

households. In five more years, it was in 50 percent of American homes. And in another five years, it was in 90 percent of all U.S. homes.

The Internet matches this growth pattern fairly closely. By 1994, five years after the Internet broke out of its pure academic setting, connections to the Internet could be found in about 10 percent of U.S. homes. Now, 16 years later, the pervasiveness of Internet access in the United States has reached almost 80 percent. Incredible as it may seem, the United States is still just over the three-quarter mark toward full Internet usage. (The Internet's presence in other nations is now catching up and has even surpassed the U.S. in terms of percentages, even though the U.S. had a head start.)

Whether you are one of the new kids on the Internet block or have been surfing since the days of Mozilla, you will find the Internet is becoming less of a place to play and more of a place to work. Every day people are turning to the Internet to handle banking needs, shop for holiday gifts, and talk to friends and family through Web-based phone services.

The history of Linux and the Internet is an intertwined one. Linux's predecessor, UNIX, was *the* operating system upon which the Internet was built. In fact, much of the syntax of the Internet ("http://," FTP commands, forward slashes for directory separators) is directly derived from UNIX line commands, which in turn can be found in Fedora today.

So it should come as no surprise that Fedora provides a rich set of Internet tools for access. All you have to do is get yourself connected.

Getting to the Internet is fairly simple these days. Broadband access is provided by a variety of carriers, which boils down to cable from the cable companies or digital subscriber line (DSL) access from the phone companies. Within some cities, wireless access to the Internet is freely or cheaply available in some neighborhoods. Offices and retail buildings are almost always wired for network access for tenants. And there's always narrowband access: when your computer's modem dials up the Internet on a regular phone line.

Fedora can handle them all. Often seamlessly.

Configuring Connections

For the most part, Fedora comes Internet-ready. This means if you plug in some kind of cord to your computer that's connected on its other end to the Internet, chances are pretty good that Fedora will recognize what's going on and go ahead and make that connection for you.

Still, there are some parts of the process that might need your help. Dial-up, for instance. Dialing up to the Internet is not a complicated business for Fedora, but figuring out how to use the modem that came with your computer could present a hurdle, since many modem manufacturers don't have Linux drivers to operate them. Wireless connections can be tricky sometimes as well, for the same lack of drivers for WiFi cards.

Most of these situations have been discovered, however, and solutions have found their way into Fedora. In the next sections, we'll step through the processes of connecting to the Internet, no matter what method you prefer. In Chapter 7, "Making Things Work," we'll review the troubleshooting techniques needed in case something doesn't work as planned.

Dial-Up

The "language" of the Internet is called TCP/IP (Transmission Control Protocol/Internet Protocol). This language is how data is sent from your computer to a Web server computer anywhere in the world.

Even though TCP/IP is a UNIX-based product, Fedora needs additional protocol help connecting to the Internet through a dial-up connection. TCP/IP, after all, does not transmit the IP (Internet Protocol) data packets through serial lines very well—serial lines like those for phones, for example.

To get all of the data packets through a modem, an additional protocol, PPP, is used. The irony of this is that PPP is not a UNIX invention—it and its predecessor, SLIP, were developed to connect Windows computers to the Internet. Despite the Windows origins of PPP, Fedora has absolutely no problems handling this protocol.

While dial-up, or narrowband, connections comprise just under 20 percent of all Internet connections—a number that falls every year—it is still prevalent enough that you should know how to use it. Many broadband Internet accounts, DSL especially, will provide you with dial-up access to use in case the main DSL connection is under repair, or you are traveling and need to access the Internet from another location.

Here's how to start the dial-up process. Before you begin, you should have your Internet service provider (ISP) information in hand, specifically your username, password, and the phone number to dial.

1. Click on System | Administration | Network. You will be asked to provide your administrative password.

2. Enter your password. The Network Configuration dialog box (see Figure 5.1) will appear.

3. Click New. The Add New Device Type dialog box will open.

4. Click Modem Connection, then the Forward button. The Select Modem page will open, as shown in Figure 5.2.

5. Fedora is usually accurate on detecting your modem's capabilities. Check the speed (baud) settings and determine the volume of the modem you want. Click Forward. The Select Provider page will appear (see Figure 5.3).

6. Type the dial-in number in the Phone Number fields.

Figure 5.1
The Network Configuration dialog box.

7. Type your ISP username and password in the appropriate fields. Your information should be similar to that shown in Figure 5.4.

8. Click Forward. The IP Settings page will appear (see Figure 5.5).

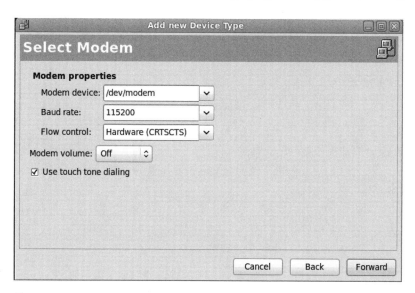

Figure 5.2
Configuring your modem settings.

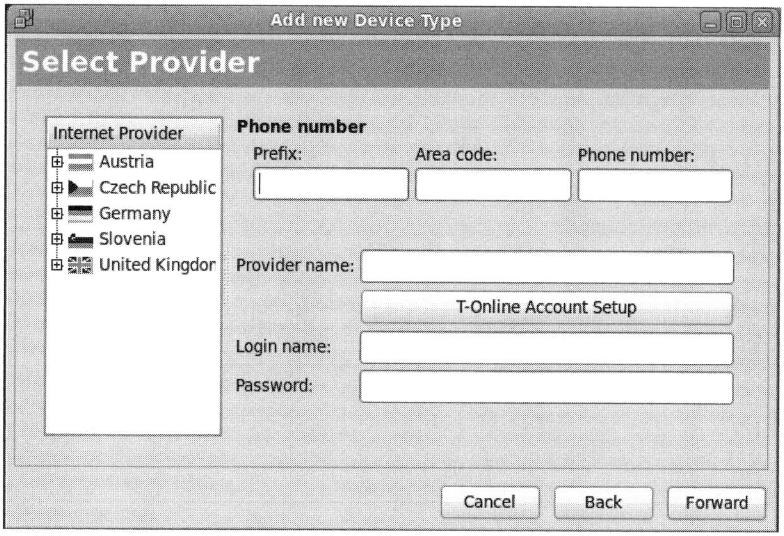

Figure 5.3
Configuring your dial-up settings.

9. Most dial-in providers assign your computer an Internet address automatically, so you can leave these settings alone and click Forward again. The Create Dialup Connection page will appear.

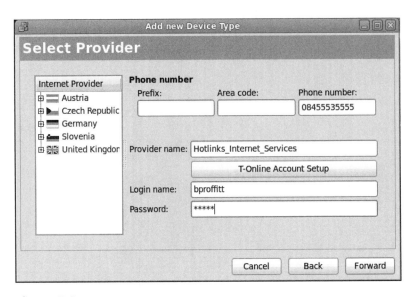

Figure 5.4
Example dial-up settings.

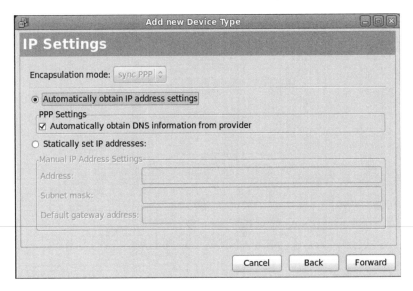

Figure 5.5
The IP settings for your dial-in provider.

10. Click Apply. The Add New Device Type dialog box will close.

11. Select the File | Quit menu command. A confirmation dialog will appear.

12. Click Yes to save the new profile. The Network Configuration dialog box will close.

Now all that you need to do is start the dial-up connection.

1. Make sure that your phone cord is plugged into your modem (and your modem is connected to your computer).

2. Click on the NetworkManager applet in the upper panel. A context menu will appear.

3. Click on Dial Up Connections | Connect to ppp0 via Modem. The modem will automatically dial up and connect to the Internet.

Disconnecting a dial-up connection is just as simple.

1. Make sure that your phone cord is plugged into your modem (and your modem is connected to your computer).

2. Click on the Network Manager applet in the upper panel. A context menu will appear.

3. Click on Dial Up Connections | Disconnect to ppp0 via Modem. The modem will disconnect from the Internet.

Where's My Modem?

Presumably your modem was correctly recognized by Fedora, and all of these steps went smoothly. Unfortunately, if your modem is inside your computer, then it is likely that things did not go as well. Internal modems, and software-only modems called *winmodems*, are notorious for not working for Fedora and other Linux distributions, because of the lack of Linux support by the modem manufacturers. This is not to say, however, that using an internal modem is not possible. See the "Modems" section in Chapter 7 for the steps needed to get internal modems up and running.

DSL

DSL is one of the two main forms of broadband used in the U.S. today, the other being cable. There are, of course, other ways of getting broadband into your home, such as broadband cellular, satellite, fiber optic, or municipal WiFi. But in many cases, these methods are not common or are far too expensive to justify using them.

DSL uses the same copper phone lines that run into your home or business; in fact, you can make a voice phone call and still maintain Internet access on the same line at the same time. This is because a DSL line sends the digital "Internet" signal at frequencies that are far above the range of human hearing. Once the signal gets back to the phone company, the voice and the network signals are split by a switcher, with the voice signal routed to the person on the other end of your conversation and the network signal sent out to the Internet.

There is, though, a catch to all of this techno-brilliance: because of the very high frequencies involved, a digital signal in a DSL line can only travel a short distance in the wires before degrading, about one and a quarter miles. So, people who live or work in rural settings are unable to enjoy DSL—at least, until their phone company gets a switcher near their location.

There are two types of DSL modems that a phone company will provide for you. One is the older type, which acts like a traditional modem that you have to connect and disconnect to the Internet as the need arises. The newer models of DSL modem essentially behave as routers: they are always connected to the Internet and manage that connection with onboard software.

Connecting with this latter type of modem, known as an *Ethernet DSL modem,* is very straightforward: computers are connected to the DSL modem/router via network cable or by WiFi, and the Ethernet DSL modem/router handles all the rest. In fact, you can visit the next section, "LAN/Cable," to proceed with connecting to the Internet.

The older types of DSL modems are known as USB modems, because they connect to your PC through the USB port. These, unfortunately, are not ideal for any broadband connection on any computer, Fedora, Windows, or otherwise. That's because PCs are designed with hardware (network interface cards or NICs) made specifically to go out and talk to other computers. Using a USB port to accomplish this is like asking your nose to start speaking instead of your mouth.

This is the one place in the book where you are strongly encouraged not to use a piece of hardware. This is because of the limitations of the hardware itself, not Fedora. If your computer doesn't have a NIC, they can be purchased and installed relatively cheaply. If your telephone carrier didn't give you an Ethernet modem, ask for one.

LAN/Cable

Most broadband connections in the home or office these days will connect to your PC's NIC port through what's known as a Local Area Network (LAN). The cable itself (known in the IT biz as "Cat 5" or "Cat 6" wire) looks like a phone cord, with a rectangular head that plugs into a matching port on your network router and your PC. Another term you have heard bandied about is "Ethernet," which describes the specific kind of network you are plugged into, namely many PCs connected to one central router.

The router is the heart of your network, and it is important to keep it running nice and smoothly. Make sure it's got plenty of ventilation, a steady stream of power, and updated software. A happy router is a functioning router.

Routers and PCs speak to each other via the TCP/IP protocol described earlier in this chapter. And, because no phones are involved, there's no need to apply additional software to translate anything to PPP or anything else a phone line needs.

What's nice about using a LAN or Ethernet connection is that nine times out of ten, it just works. Plugging in the Cat 5 cable into your PC tells Fedora to start the network connection software.

A router has two main functions. First, it acts as a switchboard, sending and receiving signals from the PCs on the network with great speed. Second, to keep these signals straight, the router is often responsible for assigning each PC or device that's connected to the network a unique IP address.

An IP address is a unique combination of four numbers (1.2.3.4) that belongs to only one device on a network at a time. Users can specify their own IP addresses if they want, but often the router does it for them using a tool known as DHCP, which automatically assigns IP addresses to a device whenever it is physically connected to the network.

Most home and small office networks have a combination router/modem at their hub, which not only connects the network devices together, but also handles communication with the outside world. Most ISPs will assign modems coming in to their network a unique IP address via DHCP. Any computer connected to that router/modem will in turn be assigned a different set of IP addresses by the router's DHCP system.

This is a good thing, too, because there is a physical limit to how many IP addresses there can be on the Internet. If every computer in the world were to have its own IP, we would quickly run out of addresses. The solution is, every router connecting to the Internet gets its own IP address, while computers and other devices using that router get similar sets of numbers.

For instance, your modem's IP address might be 64.123.45.1, and your neighbor's modem might be 64.123.45.2. But on your network, your computer may be 198.162.2.1, and on his network, his computer might have the same exact IP address. But there's no conflict, because as far as the Internet is concerned, it only cares about the routers' addresses.

Anything on the individual router's network is said to be "behind the firewall." A firewall is the metaphorical representation for the very real function a router/modem often has: to keep bad traffic out of its network.

Understanding this is important, because sometimes things don't always work the first time with network connections, and this basic knowledge of networking will help you apply quick fixes to your connection setup if the need arises.

Let's start with a look at how things work normally. These steps will apply to any Ethernet connection, and the steps assume that DHCP is enabled on your network.

1. Click on System | Administration | Network. You will be asked to provide your administrative password.

2. Enter your password. The Network Configuration dialog box will open.

3. Click on the Ethernet Connection (usually eth0) and then on the Edit button. The Ethernet Device dialog box will open, as shown in Figure 5.6.

4. Confirm that the Configuration field's value is set to Automatically Obtain IP Address Settings with dhcp.

Dynamic Versus Static IP

If your network, for some reason, is set up so that individual devices use specific IP addresses, set your configuration to static IP address. See your network administrator to get the necessary values for the Address, Subnet Mask, and Default Gateway Address fields.

5. Click OK. The Ethernet Device dialog box will close.

6. Select the File | Quit menu command. A confirmation dialog will appear.

7. Click Yes to save the new profile. The Network Configuration dialog box will close.

Now all you need to do is plug in your Cat 5 cable to your PC's NIC port. The Network Manager icon in the upper panel will display a swirling animation and then notify you of a successful connection.

Now you can access the Internet or other computers and printers on your network.

WiFi

WiFi is one of the real success stories of Fedora. There used to be a time not too long ago when wireless network connectivity on Fedora, or indeed any Linux

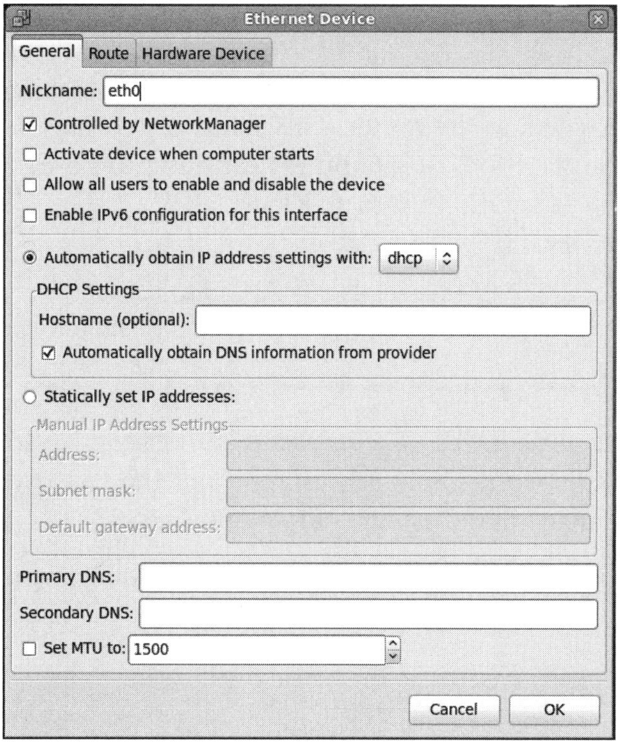

Figure 5.6
Configuring an Ethernet connection.

distribution, was a sketchy thing at best. Those times are past, and most wireless solutions work very well with Fedora.

Almost all new laptops have wireless built in, which is why most mobile users are interested in this section. But even in a home or office PC, wireless can be a good option because it saves you the time, materials, and hassle in setting up a wired network.

Configuring wireless is, on one level, exactly like configuring wired network access. You still need to connect to a router, and you still need a unique IP address for that router to recognize your machine. And, like an Ethernet connection, DHCP is the best way to have that IP address automatically assigned to your PC.

Wireless requires an additional level of configuration. Think of your wireless card as a radio (which it is) that needs to tune into a specific radio station (on your router). You have to tell your WiFi card exactly which radio station to look for. Or, if you move around with a laptop, it needs to be able to seek out all the wireless routers within its range and give you the choice of which router to connect.

Once the whole radio/radio station connection is worked out, you will have to tell your WiFi card how to actually talk to the router. This is because most routers' signals are encrypted so no unauthorized computers can jump on a network. This is usually done with an encryption protocol known as WEP.

Get Secure

If WEP is not enabled on your wireless router, it should be. See your router's documentation on how to set this up.

Wireless connections, then, have three levels of complexity to deal with: the network addressing, the wireless network signal acquisition, and the security. Fortunately, Fedora's NetworkManager handles them all in one place.

1. Click System | Administration | Network. You will be asked to provide your administrative password.

2. Enter your password. The Network Settings dialog box will open.

3. Click the Wireless connection and then Edit. The Wireless Device Configuration dialog box will open, as shown in Figure 5.7.

4. Confirm the Activate Device when Computer Starts check box is selected.

5. Click on OK. The Wireless Device Configuration dialog box will close.

6. Click on Close. The Network Settings dialog box will close.

That should be it. Your WiFi card will now automatically look for a WiFi network whenever you turn your computer on. It may slow down your start-up time a bit, but if you are on the go, this will save you from having to turn the WiFi card on later. It makes using the wireless feature almost ridiculously easy.

Conclusion

In this chapter, you discovered how easy it is to connect to a network and the Internet with Fedora's NetworkManager tool. There's not a great deal of mystery to this process, which is how it should be.

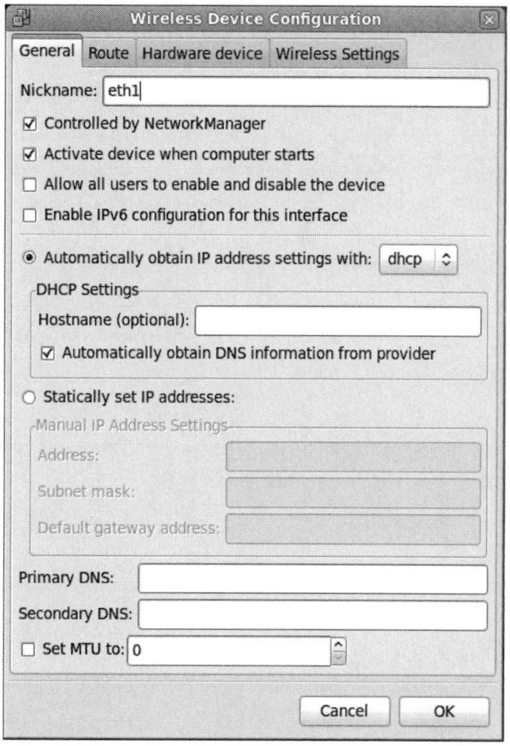

Figure 5.7
Configuring a wireless connection.

Every once in a while, however, things don't always go the way you plan. Because of a lack of hardware manufacturers' support for Linux, some networking devices don't always function. But there are a great many fixes out there, and in Chapter 7 you will learn how to use them.

Before that, however, you need to learn how to find, update, and install software on your Fedora PC. Chapter 6, "Installing and Updating Software," will show you all you need to know.

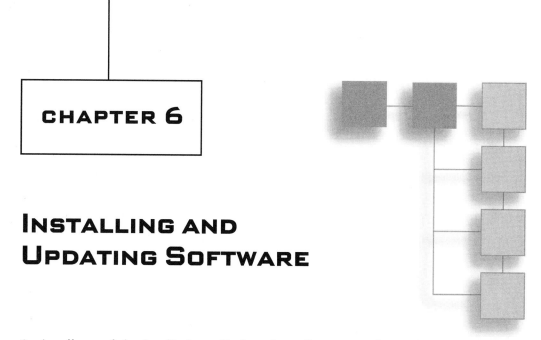

CHAPTER 6

INSTALLING AND UPDATING SOFTWARE

Saying "out of the box" about Fedora is really a metaphorical statement. After all, there's no real box from which you unpacked your software. Still, it's a phrase that gets used a lot in the software business to refer to features and applications that come with a given piece of software or operating system when you first install it on your computer.

One of the really interesting things about Fedora, and Linux in general, is that it comes with a lot of software out of the box. If you recall from Chapter 1, "What is Fedora?", by its very modular nature, Fedora essentially *is* a collection of separate software applications all coordinated to work together so that the operating system behaves like a single, functioning tool.

Philosophy aside, however, Fedora still has a lot of applications packaged for users, enough to get started right out of the box. That doesn't mean there aren't more applications out there ready for you to use.

In this chapter, you will learn:

- How Fedora handles software installation

- About software repositories and how to manage them

- How to use Software Update, PackageKit, and yum

- How to use the command line to install software

How Fedora Installs Software

In the Windows world, there is usually one way to install software: clicking on an installation application that starts up and runs the whole setup for you from start to finish.

In Fedora, like most Linux distributions, there are three methods of software installation. Admittedly, one way to install sure sounds attractive and less confusing, but the one-size-fits-all installation service comes with a potentially bad price: Windows installation routines can often overwrite important underpinnings in the operating system for the sake of the application that's currently being installed. This is good for your installed application, but potentially very bad for any pre-existing application on your system that was using that same section of Windows' code.

In Fedora, all of the three installation methods take great pains to install applications using only what's already in Fedora. If what the application needs is not installed in Fedora already, it has what is known as a dependency. The installing user (that would be you) will be told about any dependencies and asked how to proceed.

A description of the three installation methods is easy to provide:

- **Self-Contained Installation Program.** This methodology is very much like the method used by Windows. A special installation application is run that *automagically* handles the application's setup on your PC. This type of installation is not common on Fedora machines, though some of the larger consumer applications (OpenOffice.org or Firefox) can be installed in this manner. There is one important difference from Windows: no existing software is changed by the installation application. Dependencies are usually handled well, but it's not foolproof.

- **Compiled from Source.** Remember how any user can get to the source code of any free software application? Well, once you have that code, you can perform what's known as a compilation to turn that code (which only humans, at least the smart ones, can read) into something the PC can read and work with. Software compilation isn't hard, but it is time-consuming at times, and dependencies are not automatically handled.

- **Package Management.** This method is unique to UNIX-based systems. All of the files and settings needed to install and run an application are included in one package. Fedora uses RPM-based, or .rpm, packages. (Other Linux distributions, such as Debian or Ubuntu, use Debian-based, or .deb, packages.)

As you may have guessed, package management is the preferred method of software installation in Fedora. Package installation is actually performed by an application known as a package manager. It helps keep track of all of the applications that are already installed on your PC and also helps keep track of those dependencies we mentioned. If you install a package that needs some additional software tools to properly operate on your Fedora system, it's the package manager that will figure out what other packages you need.

In Fedora, there are actually three package managers that will assist you in your installation needs:

- **PackageKit.** This robust graphical package manager lists every package available for Fedora, which lets you search for software applications from a very big list. Applications are categorized by type, status on your system (installed or not), or origin.

- **Software Update.** Another graphical tool, this package manager has one job to do: keep your system as up to date as possible. If there's a new version of any of your installed applications out there, Software Update will know about it and flag it for you to download and install.

- **yum.** The core package manager for Fedora, this command line application makes getting new packages as easy as typing one line of text and pressing the Enter key.

Each of these three package managers is configured to find all of the packages from Fedora's package repositories. In the next section, we'll walk through repositories and how they work.

Understanding Software Repositories

One of the brilliant features of Fedora is that it only comes on one CD disc. Not every operating system can brag about that. Indeed, many Linux distributions are delivered to users through multiple disks.

Formerly, the strategy in delivering a Linux distribution to your home or office was not very complex: all of the applications a user needed or would ever need in the future would be delivered on one complete set of CDs (or, later, one or two DVDs). The advantage here was that once you downloaded and burned all of those CDs, you would be all set to run that distribution without having to download additional software later. But the average CD image download, discussed in Chapter 2, "Before You Install Fedora," is nearly 700MB. That's a lot of data, even for today's broadband connections. Having to do this for three, five, or even seven CDs is a very time-consuming undertaking for most users, unless they are willing to pay to have those same CDs delivered by mail.

Fedora flips the model around a bit. Working with the knowledge that a majority of Internet users now have broadband access, the Fedora Project has decided to send out just the absolutely necessary Fedora applications on one CD and leave the rest online on servers scattered around the world for users to download as needed.

This may seem inefficient, since you must have Internet access of some kind to make this work. But consider that most operating systems update themselves via Internet anyway, so in order to keep Fedora up to date, online access was needed anyway. And only downloading and burning one CD is a lot faster than downloading and burning CDs plural. Delivering a "core" distribution also gives users much greater flexibility in picking and choosing what software applications they want on their system. It also means their hard drives won't be loaded with stuff they don't need.

To give you an idea of just how much more software is available, consider these numbers: a standard installation of Fedora has around 1,100 packages. Currently, there are over 12,000 total application packages available.

Fedora, like its sibling Red Hat Enterprise Linux, organizes its software in repositories. There are three primary repositories for Fedora, each holding a specific class of software. Let's walk through them now.

Touring the Repositories

The three official Fedora repositories are pretty clearly named, but let's examine them anyway.

- **Fedora.** This repository holds all of Fedora's officially supported software. Everything that Fedora must have to actually run is in here, and all of the software is under a free software license. Additional applications in this repository include AbiWord, Evolution, Firefox, Gaim, OpenOffice.org, and Thunderbird.

- **Updates.** This repository contains any software that has been updated because of a bug or security fix.

- **Source.** All of the source code packages for Fedora software are found in this repository.

Adding Repositories

These are not the only repositories that Fedora can use. There are many community-run repositories on the Internet for Fedora, each holding specialized software that the Fedora Project does not want to host.

There are many software applications out there that can run on Linux, but because their licenses are completely proprietary, some Linux distributions won't touch them with a 10-foot pole. By virtue of its Linux origins, Fedora's makers feel obligated to abide by this philosophy, keeping totally commercial packages away from Fedora.

But there is an important distinction here. While the Fedora Project does not release commercial software with Fedora, that does not preclude letting users have access to a commercial repository after they have downloaded and installed Fedora. A fine distinction, to be sure, but it gives users the advantage of making their own choices about what software they want to use.

All of the package managers in Fedora work off a master list of repositories stored on your PC. From this file, known as sources.list, the package managers know which repositories to check for new software and if there are any updates available for software installed on your system. If you want these managers to peruse another repository, you will need to modify sources.list with the new information.

Fedora users in the know are aware of three such third-party repositories that will get you access to the latest in cutting-edge software for Fedora. These are the Dribble, Freshrpms, and rpm.livna.org repositories. Fortunately, you won't have to add these repositories one at a time. Instead, you can use one command to add RPM Fusion to your sources.list, which will accomplish the same thing.

This operation will be done using a command-line application. Command-line applications are always run in a Terminal window, one of the plainest and most versatile tools found in Fedora. To start Terminal, click on the Applications | System Tools | Terminal menu command (see Figure 6.1).

User Name   Computer (Host) Name   Command Prompt

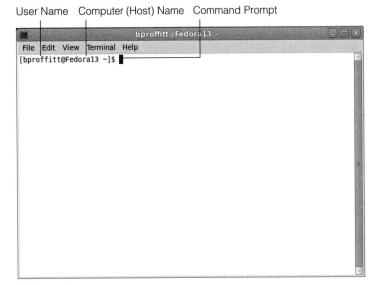

Figure 6.1
The Fedora Terminal.

Entering commands in Terminal is just a matter of typing the command and pressing the Enter key. To see a list of all of the files in the current directory, type ls and then press Enter.

There are lots of very cool command-line tools to use, but for now, let's stay with adding repositories and examine other tools later in the book. The following task will add a very important set of repositories, so even though it involves a very long command, it will be worth it.

1. Type the following command in the terminal:

   su

   You will be asked for your administration password.

2. Type your administration password and press Enter. The prompt will change to the root prompt.

3. Type the following command:

   ```
   rpm -Uvh http://download1.rpmfusion.org/free/fedora/rpmfusion-free-
   release-stable.noarch.rpm http://download1.rpmfusion.org/nonfree/
   fedora/rpmfusion-nonfree-release-stable.noarch.rpm
   ```

   This will add three new RPM repositories to your computer's sources.list.

Now, the next time you run any of Fedora's package managers, it will be aware of the new repositories and will let you view and install software from them.

What's a package manager? Good question! Let's take a look.

Using Software Update

Of all of the Fedora package managers, you will likely use the Software Update the most because it's the one that constantly runs in the background to see what, if any, updates are available for software you have installed on your PC. This is nice, because it has a set-it-and-forget-it quality that means you don't have to worry about whether you might have an older, buggy version of your software.

Updating Current Software

By default, the Software Update is configured to notify you when software updates are available—something it checks on a daily basis when your PC is connected to the Internet. When updates for your installed software are found, an orange starburst icon will appear in the upper panel, as shown in Figure 6.2.

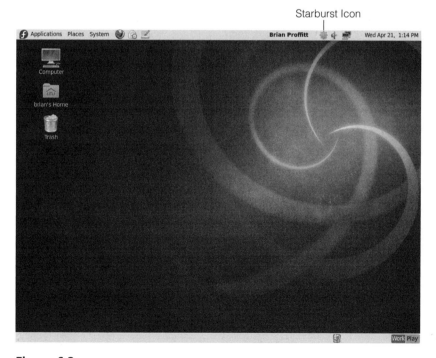

Figure 6.2
A heads-up about new updates.

The notification icon will remain in the panel until Software Update is actually run.

1. Start Software Update by clicking the notification icon. The Software Update window will open, and the start process will immediately begin, as shown in Figure 6.3.

2. When the process is complete, you will see a list of updates Fedora suggests you install (see Figure 6.4). Click any application to update. A list of changes for the selected application will appear in the description field.

3. If you choose not to update an application, click on its check box to deselect it.

4. When your choices are complete, click on Install Updates. Software Update will begin the update process by first resolving any dependencies for the selected packages.

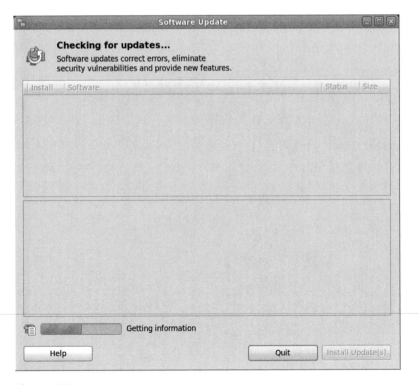

Figure 6.3
Starting Software Update.

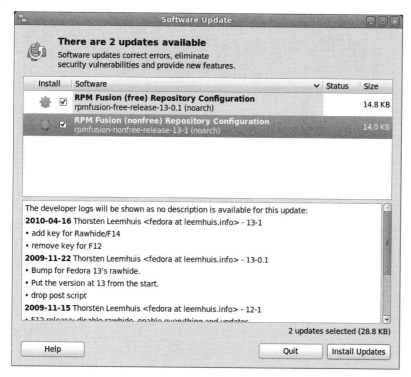

Figure 6.4
The update list.

5. If there are any additional packages that need to be added or removed to accommodate the current update, a confirmation dialog similar to the one in Figure 6.5 will appear.

6. Confirm the changes and click Continue. The download and installation process will begin, as shown in Figure 6.6.

   When finished, an up-to-date message box will appear (see Figure 6.7).

7. Click OK to shut down the message box. Software Update will close.

Occasionally, you may be required to restart your Fedora system after an update. This is not very common, because the modular nature of Fedora means that typically changes to one application won't affect others. But some updates, such as a newer version of the Linux kernel, do require a system restart for the changes to kick in. If that is the case, a light switch will appear in the top panel, and you will be asked to restart your computer when Software Update is finished.

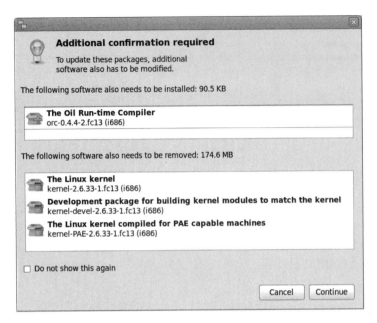

Figure 6.5
Confirm any additional packages.

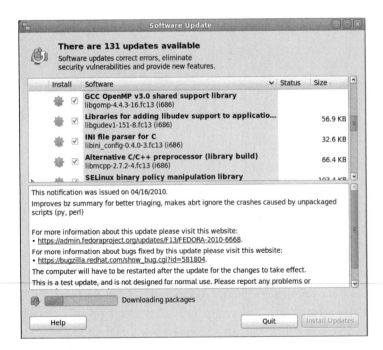

Figure 6.6
Updating is automatic.

Figure 6.7
A completed update.

Choose the option you want. It is recommended that you restart as soon as you can, but if you have other work to do, you can wait and restart later. (A system shutdown at the end of the day will count as a restart.)

Scheduling Updates

Because of the small possibility of a restart after updating, try to update your Fedora system at the start of your workday or near the end, so you won't interrupt any ongoing work.

Using PackageKit

As useful as the Software Update is, it doesn't compare to the robust nature of the PackageKit, Fedora's secret weapon. This package manager is very popular among Linux users, and the Fedora team has enhanced it to make it even easier to use.

Unlike Software Update, which just updates existing packages, PackageKit can update, install, and uninstall applications with just a few clicks.

Navigating PackageKit is easy. You can start the application by clicking on the System | Administration | Add/Remove Software menu command, which brings up the PackageKit window, as shown in Figure 6.8.

Installing New Software

Repository-based package installation is a powerful way of installing software. Not only is it easy, but once PackageKit installs it, you can be assured that any future updates of the application will be tracked and applied when they come up.

Search　　　　　　　　Package List

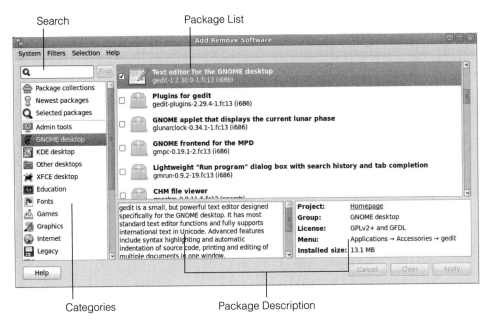

Categories　　　　　　Package Description

Figure 6.8
The PackageKit interface.

Looking for Packages

For any package installation or uninstallation, you can use the Search function in PackageKit to find any given package in PackageKit's list.

1. Explore PackageKit until you locate a package you want to install and select it. The description of the package will appear in the Description pane.

2. Click on a package's Selection check box. The package will be selected.

Important Dependencies

When you install new software, PackageKit may request to install other software (as shown in Figure 6.9). These are dependencies for the application you wanted to install in the first place. You must install them if you want your desired package to install.

3. Click Apply. The Authenticate dialog box will appear.

4. Enter your administrator password and click Authenticate. The software installation will begin.

5. When the Run New Application dialog box appears, click the Run or Close button, as desired.

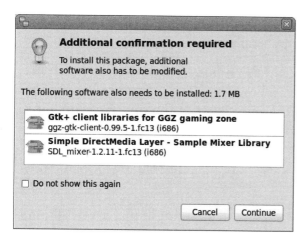

Figure 6.9
Be sure to install dependencies for your application.

Uninstalling Software

Sometimes—not often—you will run into a situation where you need to remove an application from your Fedora system. "Not often," because Fedora only installs what you really need, and anything else is software you likely added in the first place.

Still, just in case the need arises, here is how to uninstall any application with PackageKit.

1. Explore PackageKit until you locate a package you want to uninstall and select it. The description of the package will appear in the Description pane.

2. Click on a package's Selection check box. The package will be deselected.

3. Click Apply. The Authenticate dialog box will appear.

4. Enter your administrator password and click Authenticate. The software uninstall will conclude automatically.

Managing Software with yum

Unlike the other two package managers in Fedora, *yum* is what is known as a command-line application. Much of what users see in any Linux distribution is driven by these command-line programs. In fact, both PackageKit and Software

Update use yum at their cores to do much of their work. PackageKit and Software Update serve as easier-to-use graphical interfaces for yum.

"yum" is shorthand for Yellow Dog Update Manager, and is common to most Red Hat-based Linux distributions. "Yellow Dog" is a version of Red Hat that ran on Apple's Mac machines before Apple shifted its computers to Intel processors. Yellow Dog built such a good update tool that Red Hat and Fedora soon incorporated it into their own distributions. It is a very powerful manager and because it doesn't have to take up system resources creating neat-looking interfaces, it's pretty fast, too.

One thing that must be noted is that yum is an application that needs administrative permissions to run (just like Software Update and PackageKit). To do this on the command line, type the command su (which stands for super—or administrative—user) before you enter any yum commands. You will be asked for your administrative password. After that, you will have root access and can install and uninstall apps as needed. When you are finished running root commands, type exit in the terminal to leave su mode.

The first thing you should do, particularly if you have made any changes to your repositories list, is make sure yum knows about it. To do this, type:

```
yum update
```

A long list of package lists will appear. When the screen reads Done and the command prompt reappears, it's finished. Once you do this, you have complete access to the latest repository lists. You can also use the search parameter to search for applications in the repositories. To find a chess game, for example, type:

```
yum search chess
```

This will return information on eight packages:

```
gnuchess.i686 : The GNU chess program
pychess.noarch : Chess game for GNOME
chess.i686 : 3D chess game
eboard.i686 : Chess board interface for ICS
xboard.i686 : An X Window System graphical chessboard
gamazons.i686 : GNOME Amazons
maxr.i686 : A classic turn-based strategy game
xarchon.i686 : Arcade board game
```

If a package is listed, then installing it is as simple as running:

```
yum install gnuchess
```

This will get you this result:

```
Loaded plugins: langpacks, presto, refresh-packagekit
Adding en_US to language list
Setting up Install Process
Resolving Dependencies
- -> Running transaction check
- - -> Package gnuchess.i686 0:5.07-14.fc12 set to be updated
- -> Finished Dependency Resolution
Dependencies Resolved
==============================================================
 Package      Arch      Version         Repository    Size
==============================================================
Installing:
 gnuchess     i686     5.07-14.fc12      fedora       2.3 M
Transaction Summary
==============================================================
Install    1 Package(s)
Upgrade    0 Package(s)
Total download size: 2.3 M
Installed size: 3.8 M
Is this ok [y/N]:
```

Type y. The installation process will quickly finish.

Extra Packages

Whenever you install a new package, you may notice that yum adds additional packages you didn't ask for. That's because if there are any packages to be updated, yum will automatically include those packages whenever any installation activity occurs.

Removing a package is just as easy. Type:

```
yum remove gnuchess
```

Which will display this output:

```
Loaded plugins: langpacks, presto, refresh-packagekit
Adding en_US to language list
Setting up Remove Process
```

```
Resolving Dependencies
- -> Running transaction check
- - -> Package gnuchess.i686 0:5.07-14.fc12 set to be erased
- -> Finished Dependency Resolution
Dependencies Resolved
===============================================================
 Package      Arch      Version          Repository    Size
===============================================================
Removing:
 gnuchess     i686      5.07-14.fc12     @fedora       3.8 M
Transaction Summary
===============================================================
Remove     1 Package(s)
Reinstall  0 Package(s)
Downgrade  0 Package(s)
Is this ok [y/N]:
```

Type y. The uninstall process will quickly finish.

If you want to have yum download the latest versions of your installed applications, type:

```
yum upgrade
```

This will perform the same function as the Software Update.

Conclusion

By now you know the three ways you can use package management to update, install, or uninstall software in Fedora. Now you have much more ability to play and work in Fedora.

These functions will also help get things to work in Fedora. As mentioned in earlier chapters, sometimes things in Fedora don't work as smoothly as they should. Fixes abound in the Fedora community, and now that you know how to install software, you can quickly apply any needed fixes to your Fedora PC. You'll learn how in the Chapter 7, "Making Things Work."

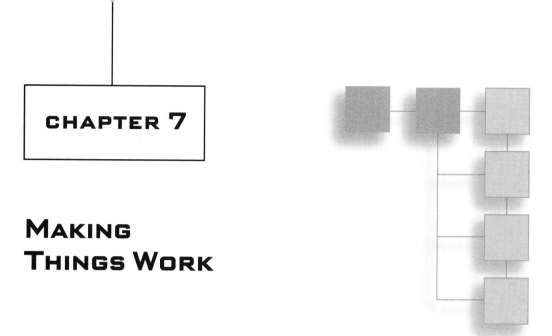

CHAPTER 7

MAKING THINGS WORK

Fedora is not perfect.

It will come as a surprise to some reading a Fedora book when this passage is found, but the truth must be told. Installing any operating system on an untried computer is a bit of a risk to begin with, because unforeseen hardware conflicts can trip up any operating system installation. (Just ask recent Windows 7 users who are finding hardware and software compatibility problems with their new purchase.)

If you installed Fedora on a desktop PC, then you may not have had any problems or concerns show up thus far. And that's great because eventually almost all of the trouble spots mentioned here won't be affecting users in the near future.

Even if you are not having difficulties making something work, this chapter will still be useful to you. There's still some unfinished business for most users to contend with:

- Creating and managing additional user accounts

- Setting up a printer

- Using USB storage

- Working with digital cameras

- Troubleshooting some hardware concerns

Setting Up User Accounts

When you first installed Fedora, two user accounts were created: the administrator (root) and your own. *Root* is the name of Fedora's "super" account. Like all Linux distributions, the root user account is the most powerful—and the most dangerous. That's because root can literally do anything possible on a Fedora machine. This is very, very helpful if you are trying to accomplish a lot of administrative tasks quickly and don't want to keep typing in the administrative password. But it's very, very bad if you make a mistake and accidentally end up deleting a critical file on your system.

Not to mention what could happen if you walked away from a machine logged in as root and someone happened to walk by and decided to play with your computer. Or hack into it from the outside, no matter where you are.

Another Warning About Root

Don't log in to your PC as root. Ever.

The account you created when you installed Fedora has some administrative capabilities by virtue of the fact that the original, installing user of a system is going to be the one administering it. There are times, however, when the user who installed Fedora is not the administrator, or you may simply want multiple user accounts, each with its own workspace. If that's the case, you need to know how to set up a new account. To do so, follow these steps:

1. Click on the System | Administration | User and Groups menu command. After entering your administrative password, the User Manager window will open, as shown in Figure 7.1.

2. Click on the Add User button. The Add New User dialog box will open (see Figure 7.2).

3. Using the user's information, fill in the information in the top section of the Add New User dialog box.

4. Confirm that the Create Home Directory and Create a Private Group for the User options are selected.

5. Click OK. The new user will be added to the User Manager (see Figure 7.3).

6. Click the File | Quit menu command. The User Manager window will close.

After any user is created, you can modify the account if need be.

1. Click on the System | Administration | User and Groups menu command. The User Manager window will open.

2. Click on a user to select the account.

3. Click the Properties button. The User Properties dialog box will open (see Figure 7.4).

4. Make the changes you need in any of the four pages.

5. Click OK. The User Properties dialog box will close.

6. Click the File | Quit menu command. The User Manager window will close.

If a user will no longer be using this computer, such as when an employee leaves a company, it's a good idea to remove the user's account.

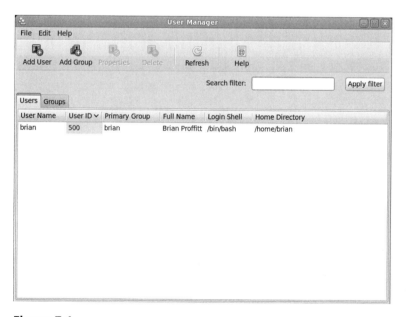

Figure 7.1
The User Manager.

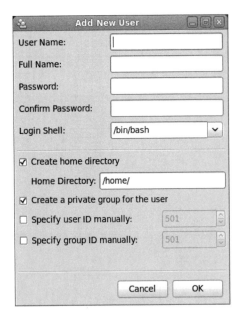

Figure 7.2
Basic user account information.

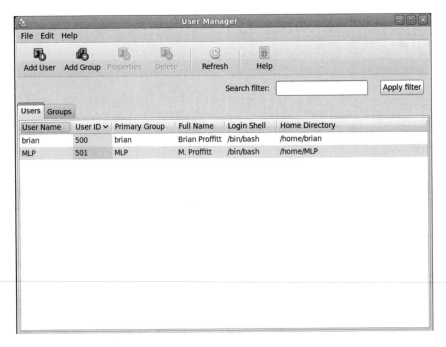

Figure 7.3
Adding new users is easy.

1. Click on the System | Administration | User and Groups menu command. The User Manager window will open.

2. Click a user to select the account.

3. Click the Delete button. A warning dialog box will appear (see Figure 7.5).

4. Click Yes. The user account will be removed from the list of accounts.

5. Click the File | Quit menu command. The User Manager window will close.

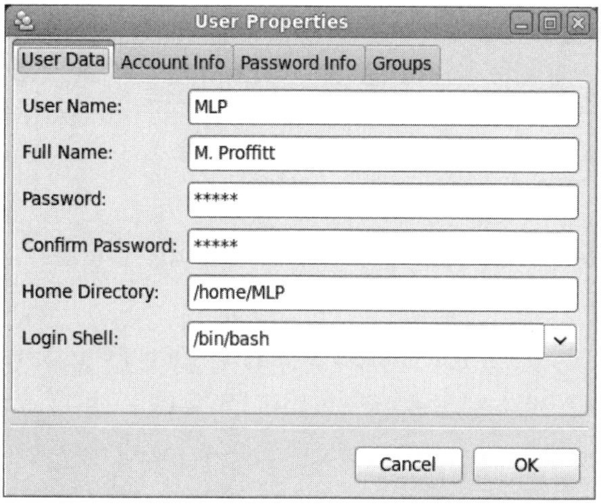

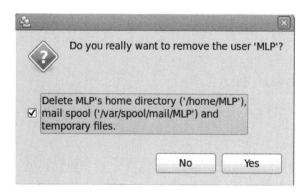

Figure 7.4
Editing user information.

Figure 7.5
Make sure that you want to delete a user account.

Using Printers

Early computers did not communicate well. The first digital calculating device that could safely be called a computer was the Harvard Mark I, a five-ton, 750,000-component device that read its programming code from paper tape and its data from punch cards. Data was output on a similar medium.

Multimedia was a bit of a wash as well. The only sound the Mark I generated was the internal clicking of its components, which sounded a bit like a "roomful of ladies knitting." Hardly multimedia.

For those of you old enough to remember the Apple I and II microcomputers released in 1973, you'll recall that they weren't big on multimedia, either. Little beeps and clicks were about all the sound they emitted. Printing was coming along, though, as dot-matrix printers wound out reams of perforated paper.

Today, the number of communication devices that can be connected to PCs is phenomenal. Printers, speakers, television tuners, cameras, alarm systems... even cars.

In the meantime, you can focus on more immediate concerns, such as getting your own peripheral communication devices hooked up to your Fedora PC—namely, a printer.

Setting Up a Local Printer

There are two ways of connecting a printer to your Fedora PC. The first is locally, by plugging your printer in via your computer's parallel port or, more frequently these days, one of its USB ports.

Once your printer is physically connected to your system and is powered on, it should automatically begin to configure itself, as shown in Figure 7.6. If not, follow these steps to get your printer working.

1. Click the System | Administration | Printing menu command. The Printing window will open (see Figure 7.6).

2. Click Add. After entering your administrative password twice, the New Printer window will open, and your system will begin to search for a connected printer. When found, the printer will appear in the Devices list (see Figure 7.7).

3. Select the printer you want to add and click Forward. The application will search for available drivers and install them. If additional options are available, the Installable Options page will appear (see Figure 7.8).

4. Select the desired option(s) and click Forward. The Describe Printer page will appear (see Figure 7.9).

Printers with Multiple Personalities?

Sometimes a single printer will show up as a multiple listing. This is because some printers (particularly newer ones) have a separate on-board memory card that the CUPS database reads as a separate device. Pick the listing with the most information and proceed. If this does not work, you can always come back and connect to the other option.

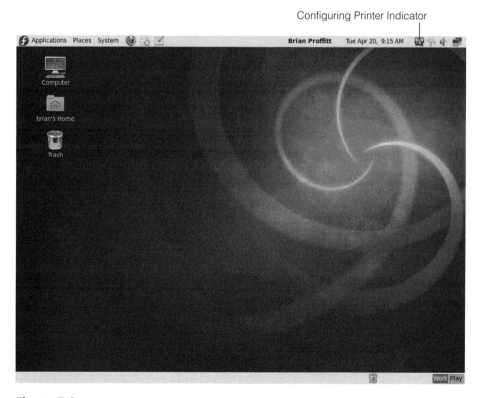

Figure 7.6
The Printing window.

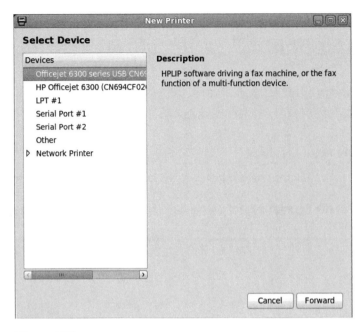

Figure 7.7
Printers are usually located with ease.

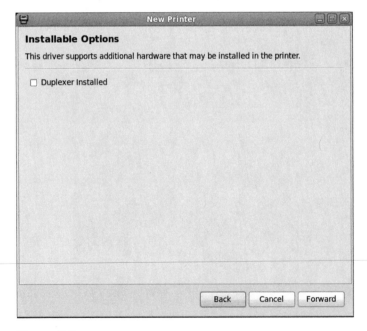

Figure 7.8
Sometimes, printers can have some add-on options.

Good News for HP Printer Users

HP has done some excellent work making their printer drivers available for Linux users. If you have an HP printer and an HPLIP option is available, definitely choose that one. HPLIP is an HP-developed control application for HP devices.

5. Click Apply. An Authenticate message box will appear.

6. Enter your administrative password and click Authenticate. The CUPS Root dialog may appear.

7. If asked, enter your root password (same as your administrative password) and click OK. The printer will be added, and a message window will appear asking if you would like to print a test page.

8. Click Yes. If properly configured, a test page will print on your printer and a notification dialog box will open.

9. Click OK. The notification dialog box will close.

10. Click Cancel. The Printer Properties dialog box will close, and the Printer will now appear in the Printing window (see Figure 7.10).

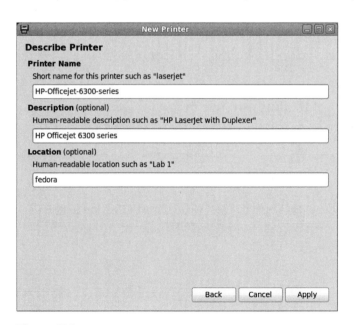

Figure 7.9
Describe your printer in user-friendly terms.

Figure 7.10
The newly added local printer.

Setting Up a Network Printer

The steps involved in connecting to a remote printer somewhere out on a network are very similar to getting a local printer connected. You just have to identify where on the network that printer is.

Most of the time, Fedora will do the work for you and detect networked printers. If that's the case, then follow the steps outlined in the previous section to connect to a detected network printer. If for some reason the printer wasn't found, follow these steps:

1. Click the System | Administration | Printing menu command. The Printing window will open.

2. Click Add. After entering your administrative password twice, the New Printer window will open.

3. Expand the Network Printer list and click Find New Printer. The Network Printer page will appear (see Figure 7.11).

4. Enter the IP address on your computer. Click Find, and your system will begin to search for a network connected printer. When found, the printer will appear in the Devices list.

Finding Your Printer's Address

To find the IP address of your printer, contact your system administrator. If this is on a home or small business network, refer to your printer's documentation to find out how it can report its IP address. Most network-connected printers have utilities to report where on the network they reside.

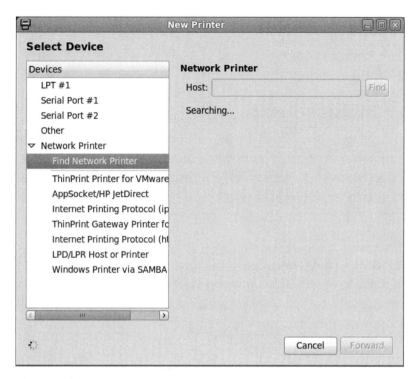

Figure 7.11
Find a network printer.

5. Select the printer you want to add and click Forward. The application will search for available drivers and install them. If additional options are available, the Installable Options page will appear.

6. Select the desired option(s) and click Forward. The Describe Printer page will appear.

7. Click Apply. An Authenticate message box will appear.

8. Enter your administrative password and click Authenticate. The CUPS Root dialog may appear.

9. If asked, enter your root password (same as your administrative password) and click OK. The printer will be added, and a message window will appear asking if you would like to print a test page.

10. Click Yes. If properly configured, a test page will print on your printer, and a notification dialog box will open.

11. Click OK. The notification dialog box will close.

12. Click Cancel. The Printer Properties dialog box will close, and the Printer will now appear in the Printing window.

Using USB Mass Storage Devices

One of the latest and greatest inventions in digital technology is the portable mass storage device that can hold anywhere from 1 to 1,000GB worth of data. These portable devices come in a variety of configurations, from the small memory sticks or thumb drives that you carry in your pocket or on a lanyard, to the portable external hard drives that can hold, at the time of this writing, anywhere up to 2TB (2,000GB) of data.

The common feature to these devices is that they all connect to your computer via a USB port. Fedora is very good at recognizing USB storage devices; literally, all you have to do is plug the storage hardware into your PC. A drive icon will appear on the desktop, and the Nautilus file manager will open to show the contents of the device, as displayed in Figure 7.12.

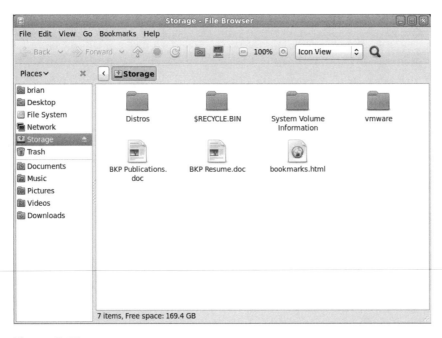

Figure 7.12
Transparent USB drive support.

Removing the drive just has one extra step. You could just pull the physical connection, and likely that would be okay. To allow Fedora to make sure all data is flushed from any buffers and written to the drive before it is removed, you can have Fedora to remove its own awareness of the device. Then you can physically remove it.

In Nautilus, click on the Eject icon next to the USB drive's icon in the Places pane. The device icon will disappear from the desktop, and the device can be physically removed.

Setting Up a Digital Camera

Digital cameras are very commonplace these days, and being able to move your photos to your computer is a necessity, since that's where any editing and long-term storage of your snapshots is going to take place.

Fedora handles digital cameras in one of two ways. If it does not recognize the specific camera model, it will treat a connected digital camera like a USB storage device. When this happens, you can simply use the file manager to transfer photos from your camera's drive to your hard drive.

If Fedora does recognize your camera, then you will have access to some nifty tools that will speed your digital camera work right along.

1. Connect your camera to your computer and turn on the camera's power. If properly detected, the Digital Camera dialog box (shown in Figure 7.13) will open.

2. Confirm the Open Shotwell Photo Manager option is selected and click OK. The Shotwell window will open (see Figure 7.14).

Figure 7.13
The camera was detected.

Figure 7.14
The Shotwell Photo Manager.

3. Select the camera in the Camera list. An Unmount confirmation dialog box will appear.

4. Click Unmount. The photos on your camera will be scanned and displayed in Shotwell (see Figure 7.15).

5. Click Import All or click on individual photos and click Import Selected. The photos will be imported, and the Import Complete dialog will appear (see Figure 7.16).

Selecting Multiple Photos

To select the photos you want to import, hold the Ctrl key on your keyboard while clicking on the desired photos.

6. Click the option you want. The imported photos will appear in the Shotwell photo library (see Figure 7.17).

Figure 7.15
Previewing photos.

Figure 7.16
Choose to keep or delete your pictures on the camera.

Figure 7.17
Starting a photo collection in Shotwell.

Shotwell enables users to sort, categorize, tag, and search images within a photo collection. You can even display a set of images in a full-screen slideshow to share with family and friends.

Special Hardware Concerns

After the normal hardware needs are set, you should be completely ready to go. Alas, not every installation goes smoothly, and some known hardware bugaboos can creep in and make things more . . . interesting. In this section, you will learn about the most prevalent issues that occur with Fedora and hardware and get on track to fix them.

This is by no means a comprehensive group of solutions; there are too many different kinds of hardware out there to try such a thing in this book. But the most common problems should be addressed.

Modems

Unfortunately, nearly every internal modem in a PC is going to have problems running in Linux. That's because these devices, as well as software-only modems referred to *winmodems,* have drivers written only for the Windows environment.

There are two ways around this problem, should you need a modem for your Fedora PC. One is to acquire an external modem. These modems, as a rule, do tend to work in Fedora, because the way they plug into a PC (through the serial or PCMCIA port), allows Fedora to communicate more freely with them.

If you don't want to spend the money, you can try the solutions presented by the Linmodem Project (http://linmodems.technion.ac.il/Linmodem-howto.html), a community service designed to get those winmodems running on Linux PCs.

Basically, there are two big steps to getting a winmodem to run on Fedora. First, you need to run an application called *scanModem* to determine exactly what kind of internal modem your system has (unless the modem is an ISA-type device, in which case no solution will help). Second, you need to apply specific solutions based on the modem's manufacturer.

To download and run scanModem, open the Terminal and follow these steps:

1. Type

   ```
   wget -c http://linmodems.technion.ac.il/packages/scanModem.gz
   ```

   The package will be downloaded to your home directory.

2. To decompress the compressed .gz file, enter

   ```
   gunzip scanModem.gz
   ```

3. Now type

   ```
   chmod +x scanModem
   ```

4. Become the administrative user by entering su and then your administrative password.

5. To run scanModem, enter

   ```
   ./scanModem
   ```

   Several new folders will be created in the home directory.

6. Click on the Applications | Accessories | Gedit Text Editor menu command. The Gedit application will open (see Figure 7.18).

7. Click the Open button. The Open dialog box will open.

8. Navigate to the Modem folder in your home directory.

9. Select 1stRead.txt and ModemData.txt and click Open. The files will be opened in Gedit.

10. Read the files to determine what type of modem you have.

After you have the modem type discovered, you will need to do a specific search for the modem's compatibility with Fedora. You may find that the modem simply will not work, because if Fedora hasn't detected it at this point, it is very likely incompatible. Hopefully, however, a specific solution will exist.

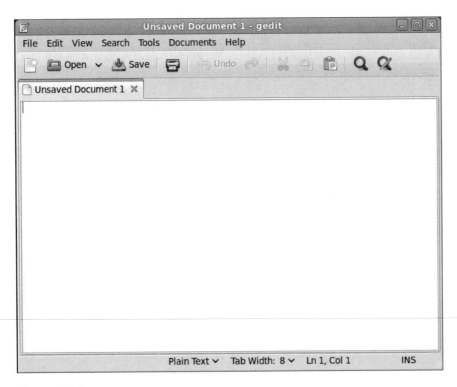

Figure 7.18
The Gedit application.

Sound Cards and Microphones

Sound is another concern that shows up in some Fedora installations. Curiously, though, Fedora (and Linux) pretty much has sound card compatibility licked. Yet, there is this one strange problem that may crop up: the sound card is properly detected, and yet the microphone may not work. This happens quite a bit on laptops, which often have a tiny internal microphone (that really should be avoided) as well as whatever external microphone you've plugged in.

If your sound is working but your microphone isn't, try these steps.

1. Right-click the Volume icon in the upper panel and select Sound Preferences from the context menu. The Sound Preferences dialog box will open (see Figure 7.19).

2. Click the Input tab. The Input page will appear.

Figure 7.19
The Sound Preferences dialog box.

3. Click the Connector combo list and look for an additional microphone input connector. Select that new connector option.

4. Speak into your microphone. If successful, you will see the Input Level bars light up (see Figure 7.20).

5. Click Close. The Sound Preferences dialog box will close.

6. Click on the External Amplifier check box.

7. Click on the File | Quit menu command. The Volume Control window will close.

There are other sound concerns that do appear, and there are many resources on the Web that deal with manufacturer-specific problems. This one, however, seems to come up quite a bit, and it would be remiss not to mention the easy solution.

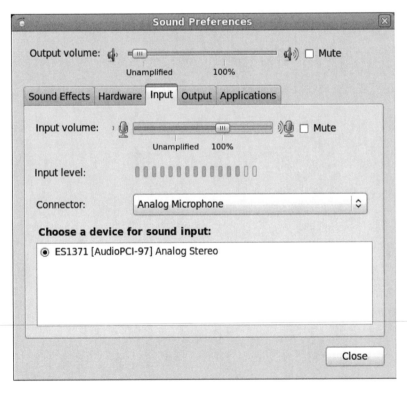

Figure 7.20
Testing, one, two, three, four...

Conclusion

In this chapter, you learned how to complete hardware installation on your Fedora PC. You also learned to navigate some of the trickier spots in Fedora/hardware compatibility.

In Chapter 8, we'll begin to explore the Fedora operating system and see what kinds of tools it has to make your home or office experience a great one.

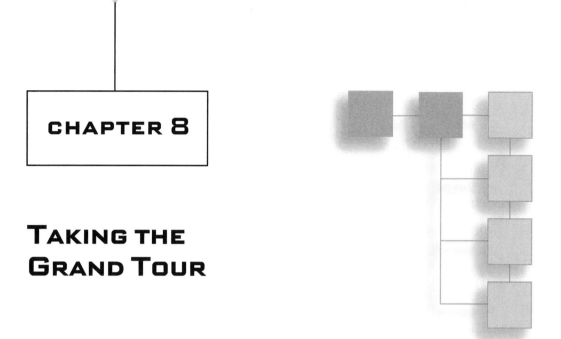

CHAPTER 8

TAKING THE GRAND TOUR

It's installed, it's running smoothly, and now you have a whole Fedora operating system to play with. After all of this configuring and customizing, you're probably wondering: does Fedora actually *do* anything?

Indeed it does. For instance, when you hear people comparing Linux to Windows, one of the big gripes you will hear is about the perceived lack of available Linux applications. At the moment, Windows has some 100,000-plus applications available. While there are not quite that many Linux applications, the number of available applications is greater than many people realize.

Because Fedora applications typically are not commercially advertised, they are far less known than their Windows counterparts. Word, PowerPoint, and Excel—most people have heard of these applications. But how many have heard of Writer, Impress, and Calc? Not many, although that's changing rapidly. Those who have heard of them know that these are part of a very robust office suite, fully comparable to *and* compatible with Microsoft Office.

The GIMP is another prime example of an application that is just as feature-rich as its Windows counterpart, Adobe Photoshop. But, since GIMP, like most of its Linux brethren, is not on the public radar, it is often treated as nonexistent—for the time being.

In this chapter, you will visit some of the essential tools packaged with Fedora, including:

- Firefox, a popular browser on any platform

- Evolution, a powerful Outlook-like email application

- OpenOffice.org, the fastest growing office suite in the world

- Additional Fedora applications that you will find many uses for

Introducing Firefox

In the olden days of the Internet (all of 17 years ago), life was uncomplicated. The simple concept of hyperlinks on a text page was just emerging. Some links went to other pages; others went to files to be downloaded—perhaps a picture or two. Browsers such as Lynx only had to contend with text—life was good.

In 1993, everything changed forever. The National Center for Supercomputing Applications (NCSA) at the University of Illinois created Mosaic—a browser capable of displaying text and pictures. Suddenly, users could see illustrated Web pages, which facilitated the flow of information. A year later, one of the Mosaic developers left NCSA and launched his own browser—Netscape Navigator 1.1.

Since then, the capability of browsers has grown even more in response to more complex content. Need to hear a sound file? The browser will take care of it. Need to view a Flash animation? Not only will a browser display it for you, but the browser can also automatically go get the required viewer if you don't already have it.

These sophisticated features are a long way from the early Internet days, that's for sure.

One of the direct descendants of that early Netscape browser is Firefox, a cross-platform open-source browser that has taken the desktop world by storm, no matter what the platform. Even on Windows, traditionally the bailiwick of Internet Explorer, Firefox has a 10+ percent browser share, which may not seem like a lot, except when you consider it's only been around for a couple of years.

What makes Firefox special is its speed, stability, and security. Unlike Internet Explorer, which is tied closely to the Windows operating system on a code level,

Firefox is a separate application. So, even if someone can figure out how to maliciously hack Firefox, it won't damage anything beyond the browser. When Internet Explorer is hacked, all of Windows can become vulnerable.

Another unique feature of Firefox is the available extensions. Because Firefox is open, developers can create small add-on programs that can handle a variety of tasks, like displaying newsfeeds, synchronizing a user's settings with any Firefox browser they use, blocking advertising . . . it's a long list.

Finally, something that Firefox has had for quite some time, before Internet Explorer picked it up, is a tabbed interface (see Figure 8.1). Tabs let you display multiple pages in a single window, a very useful feature for power surfers.

In Chapter 10, "Surfing the Web," you will take a closer look at Firefox, as well as some of the other browsers available in Fedora. For now, let's take a quick look at Fedora's flagship email client, Evolution.

Figure 8.1
The tabbed Firefox interface.

Introducing Evolution

In 1999, GNOME founder Miguel de Icaza made mention of the Camel mail code-set, which was the very beginning of the Evolution email client. Originally called Helix Code, de Icaza's company would start working on what would become one of the most popular mail clients on Fedora or any other Linux flavor, for that matter.

Though the GNOME interface already had plenty of mail clients, calendars, and address books, a certain level of integration was missing. Few of the mail clients, for instance, took advantage of the address book. None of the programs available offered the sort of all-in-one convenience of a Groupwise or Outlook application. Evolution was designed to change this (see Figure 8.2).

The application has seen a lot in its day: a name change of its originating company to Ximian and then Ximian's subsequent purchase by the large IT company

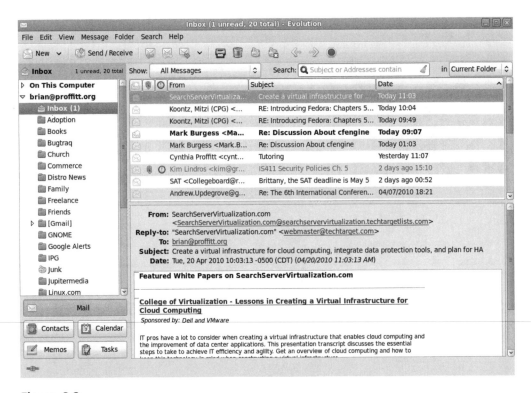

Figure 8.2
The Evolution application.

Novell. But through it all, Evolution has remained closely tied to its GNOME origins, and since Fedora Desktop is primarily a GNOME distribution of Linux, it makes sense that it would be featured so prominently here.

Chapter 11, "Mail Call," will demonstrate how to use Evolution and other Linux email clients. Now, let's turn our attention to OpenOffice.org.

Introducing OpenOffice.org

OpenOffice.org is a product that definitely deserves some attention. Is OpenOffice.org the *Greatest Office Suite Ever Made*? No. Everything can be improved upon, and not everyone will like using OpenOffice.org. But Open-Office.org does offer something other office suites do not: a unique, totally integrated interface that seamlessly blends its different components.

It's time to start it up (using the Applications | Office menu command) and see for yourself how this powerful office suite is put together.

Writer

The written word is still a major component of our daily lives. Newspapers, Web pages, and books—the written word comprises them all. Even our audio and visual media stem from written scripts and news copy.

Writer was the first product developed by the original Star Division for the old StarOffice suite and is therefore the most complete. You can see its robust nature in Figure 8.3, which shows a typical Writer window. You can see that Writer offers a number of familiar tools.

The uses for Writer, which are as boundless as your imagination, will be examined in Chapter 15, "Documenting with Writer." You can create any form of written document and use elements from any other part of OpenOffice.org to suit your needs.

Calc

Spreadsheets get their name from the old-fashioned ledger sheets used by desk-bound accountants. In their work, they would lay out numbers on what were at times huge sheets of grid-lined paper. Sometimes, these sheets would be yards long, and if a mistake were made in just one cell . . . well, let's just say the mistake would be rather tedious to find and fix.

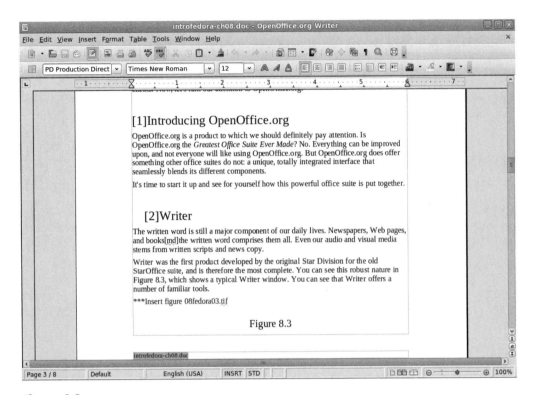

Figure 8.3
The key elements of Writer.

The concept of these paper sheets has been carried over to electronic form. It made sense to keep data in this familiar tabular format. Thus, the first spreadsheet program, VisiCalc, was born. Although no relation to Calc, a lot of the concepts introduced in VisiCalc provide the basis for Calc's design.

Cells are the heart of a spreadsheet. They contain the data. The data values can be numbers, letters, words—whatever you want to keep track of. Cells can also contain formulas. Formulas are mathematical equations that take the value of one cell and relate it to the value of another cell to come up with a unique answer. If needed, formulas can equate whole ranges of cells.

Figure 8.4 shows that the basic elements common to all spreadsheets are in Calc: cells, rows, and columns. You can't have a spreadsheet without these elements. Spreadsheet programs differ in the way they present and utilize these elements, but Calc uses a very intuitive interface, as you will learn in Chapter 16, "Analyzing with Calc."

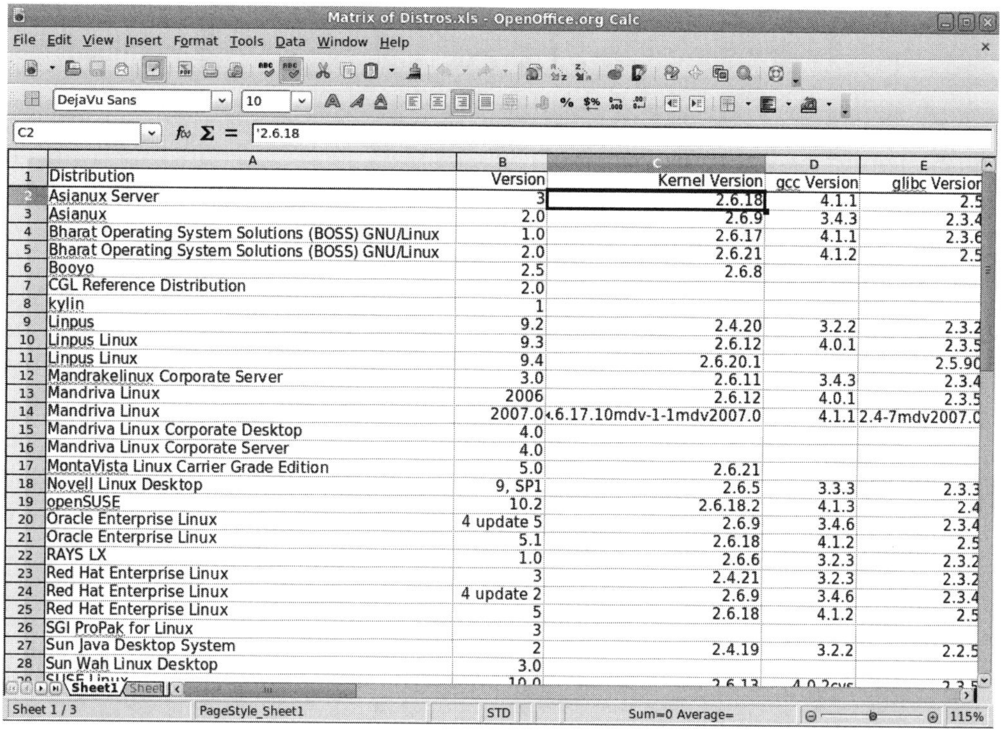

Figure 8.4
The Calc interface.

Calc does not just display data in neat little columns and rows. Nor does it just perform mathematic functions, although it does so rather well. You can create multiple scenarios with your data. What would happen to my overall revenues if the price of asparagus rocketed to a new high this season? How much profit could I make if asparagus stayed at its current level? Calc is a great way to plan ahead for mortgages, loans, and other business concerns (such as asparagus).

Impress

There was a time in the business world when average workers were not expected to share their knowledge with the rest of the workplace all at once. But in these days of open communication, there are more and more opportunities to do what most people hate to do: public speaking.

OpenOffice.org has a component that helps relieve some of that anxiety. Impress is a robust presentation tool designed to show your ideas to the world. Figure 8.5 shows a sample Impress presentation.

Impress can let you create a presentation from scratch or build one from an existing outline. You can use the Presentation Wizard to add templates, backgrounds, and even additional slides all in one easy process, as will be demonstrated in Chapter 17, "Presenting with Impress."

Perhaps best of all is that any presentation created in Impress not only can be used in a standard slide show, but also can be converted for use on the Internet, giving you a chance to create flashy Web pages in a snap.

Base: Track Your Data

Databases are scary. There, it's said, out in the open.

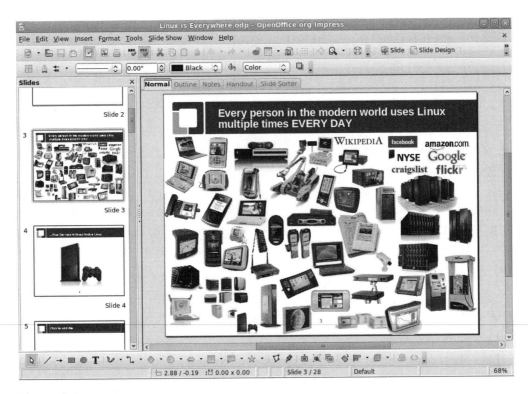

Figure 8.5
An Impress presentation.

Many people often think of databases as dark, shadowy beasts that lurk in their PCs, chewing up and spitting out data and reports only if coaxed out with strange and cryptic queries.

Not necessarily. In recent years, personal databases have become more friendly and intuitive. Base is no exception.

Of all the OpenOffice.org components, Base needs the most input from the user before creating a database. As simplified as databases have become, you still can't snap one together with a single command. You need to know what tables will hold what data, what the data entry form will look like, and what reports the database will need to generate.

Sounds scary again, doesn't it? It's really not, and to demonstrate this, take a look at Figure 8.6, which displays the Base application.

In Chapter 18, "Organizing with Base," you will learn more about this so-called shadowy beast and learn to tame it.

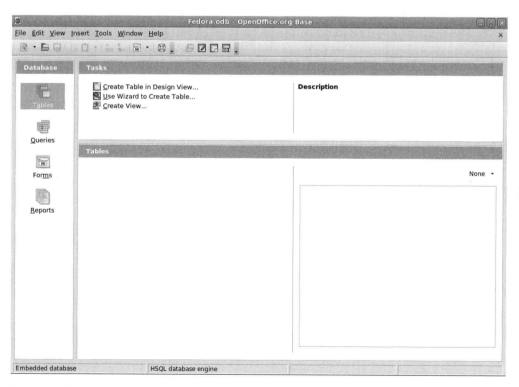

Figure 8.6
The Base interface.

Other Nifty Fedora Tools

There are many applications that will run in a Fedora installation, far too many to review in any single work. But there are some amongst the many good applications that stand out as great and worthy of note.

Empathy

Empathy is the primary instant messaging client for Fedora. Empathy is now compatible with a whole host of messaging systems, including AIM, MSN, Yahoo!, Jabber, ICQ, IRC, SILC, SIP/SIMPLE, Novell GroupWise, Lotus Sametime, Zephyr, Gadu-Gadu, and QQ.

All at the same time.

If you have a messaging account on any of these services, and your friends and colleagues do, you can use a single Empathy client to talk to any of them when you need to.

Figure 8.7 shows the Buddy List for Empathy, where all of the online contacts are stored. In Chapter 12, "Messaging Tools," you'll delve more into Empathy.

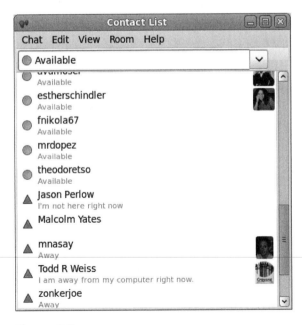

Figure 8.7
The Empathy application.

GIMP

GIMP (short for *GNU Image Manipulation Program*) is a free-of-charge app often compared to Adobe Photoshop because it has many of the same capabilities.

GIMP has some special features that make it necessary for you to perform a secondary installation when you first start the application. When the GIMP Installation dialog box appears, click Install. When the installation is successfully completed, a message box will appear informing you of the completed installation. Click Continue to open the GIMP interface, shown in Figure 8.8.

The GIMP interface is sort of odd, in that there is no "canvas" screen immediately visible—just a Toolbar and (if your options are set for it) a Tip of the Day message box. But once you begin working with the program, you will find its capabilities amazing.

Figure 8.8
The unusual GIMP interface.

Skype

Imagine having the capability to make a call to anyone on the planet—for free. That's what Skype will allow you to do, using a networking system known as *Voice over IP* (VoIP). Instead of data packets carrying data, VoIP clients break down auditory signals into digital data packages and then into IP data packets, which are sent on their way out into the Internet. That's the very simple explanation of VoIP. We'll cover it in more detail in Chapter 12, as well as go over the interface shown in Figure 8.9.

VLC Movie Player

Movies in Linux have been another long-standing sore spot for users. Not that Linux was technically incapable of displaying movies, but rather that the software makers who created movie formats like AVI, WMA, or DVD

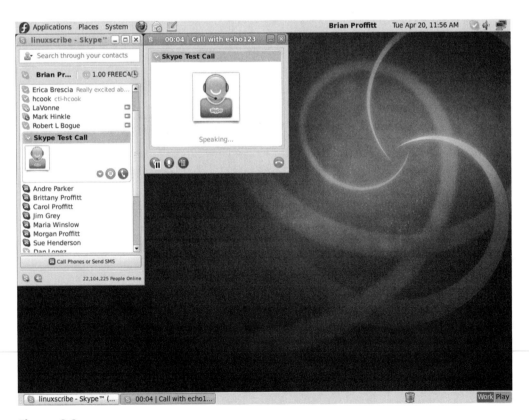

Figure 8.9
Skype on Fedora.

were unwilling to let Linux players use their formats without paying very large fees.

Some Linux players have eventually reverse-engineered these formats to the point that they can be displayed. One of the best of these is the VLC Player (see Figure 8.10).

In Chapter 13, "Multimedia Tools," you will learn how to use the VLC Player, as well as other audio/visual applications.

Rhythmbox

A very important expectation for any computer these days is the capability to play music. Whether it is MP3 files or CDs from your collection, you will expect Fedora to have something to handle this important task.

As a matter of fact, the application for this task is Rhythmbox, a sophisticated audio player that can handle standard audio files, CDs, podcasts, and streaming Internet radio (see Figure 8.11). Rhythmbox will be examined more closely in Chapter 13.

Figure 8.10
The VLC Player.

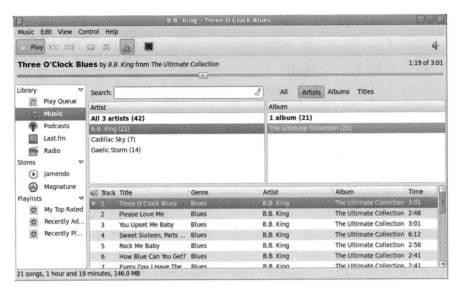

Figure 8.11
The Rhythmbox interface.

Conclusion

This chapter hasn't been very big on detail, but it gives you an important preview of the rest of the book. Chapters 9–14 will tour the most important Fedora applications. Chapters 15–18 will explore the powerful home and office tools included free of charge in Fedora.

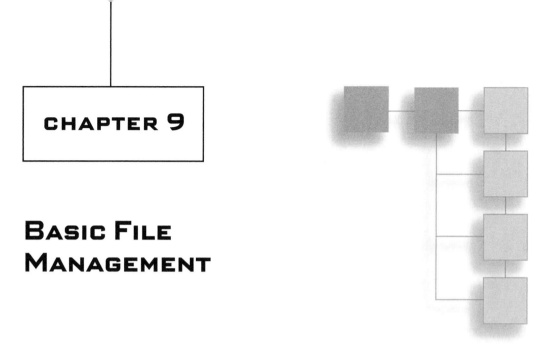

CHAPTER 9

BASIC FILE MANAGEMENT

Before you start exploring the Fedora applications, it is important for you to take a look at where and how Fedora stores your personal data files.

"Personal data files" refer to any file that you can access within Fedora, such as an OpenOffice.org document, or a music file, or an application file you've downloaded. The reason why the "personal" definition is applied is because unlike the Windows operating system, there are many, many files that you don't have permission to access.

In fact, if you recall the directory structure of Fedora from the "Partitions Fedora Will Need" section of Chapter 3, "Installing Fedora," the only Fedora directory you will have ready access to is the /home directory—and even then, just the one that belongs to your user account.

Still, there's going to be times where you will need to perform some file management duties. In Fedora, there are two good ways to accomplish this. In this chapter, you will learn:

- How to use the Nautilus file manager to manage files

- How to use the command line to perform the same functions and more

Using Nautilus

Nautilus is the name given to the default file manager in GNOME, the Fedora desktop environment. When you look at Nautilus for the first time (see Figure 9.1),

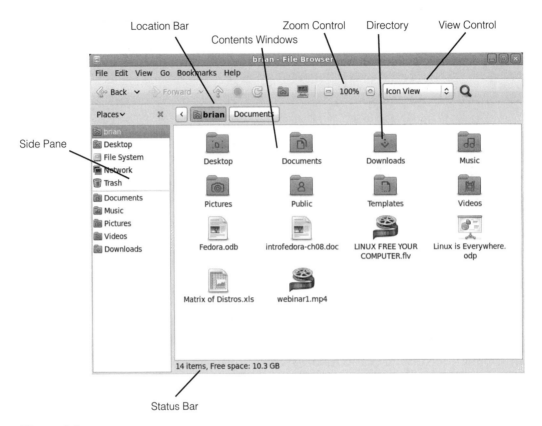

Figure 9.1
The Nautilus interface (Browser mode).

you will see a lot of things that will look rather familiar to a Windows user. To open Nautilus, select any option in the Places menu, such as Home.

There are actually two modes to view Nautilus: the Browser mode, which you have seen in Figure 9.1 already, and the Spatial mode, which has fewer navigation tools and instead displays the contents of each directory as a separate window (see Figure 9.2). Spatial mode, which we will examine in more detail later in this chapter, may seem awkward, but anyone coming to Fedora from OS X will recognize the same functionality in the OS X Finder application.

We will examine how to switch modes in the "Configuring Nautilus" section later in this chapter. For now, we will stay in the Browser mode to demonstrate basic file management tasks.

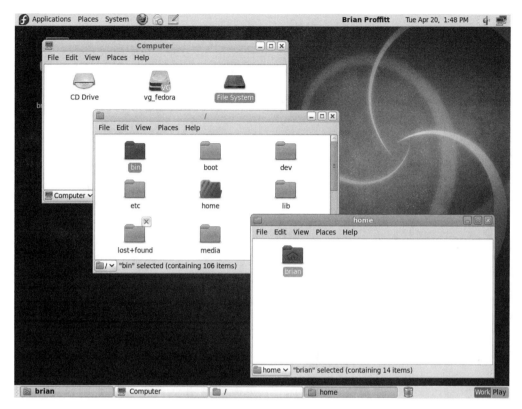

Figure 9.2
The Nautilus interface (Spatial mode).

Moving and Copying Files

Moving and copying files with a graphical file browser is a simple process: you pick up the file or directory you want to move or copy and drag and drop it into its new location. But there are some details that will help.

1. Click the Places | Home Folder menu command (or double-click the Home folder on the desktop). The Nautilus file manager will open.

2. Double-click the Documents directory. The contents will be displayed.

3. Click and drag a file to your home directory in the side pane.

4. Release the mouse button. The file will be moved to the home directory.

5. Click your home directory in the Location bar. The window will display the contents of your home directory.

6. Locate the file you moved to this directory.

7. Holding the Ctrl key, click and drag the file over the Documents directory icon. The folder icon will open to receive the file.

8.   Release the mouse button. The file will be copied to the Documents directory.

Deleting Files

Like other operating systems, deleting a file or a directory in Fedora doesn't really delete it. Instead, the file is moved to the Trash directory, where it will sit until you decide to delete the contents of the Trash directory permanently.

This eliminates most worries about accidentally erasing something that you don't want to disappear.

There are three ways to send a file or directory to the Trash directory.

- Click the file and press the Delete key.

- Drag and drop a file onto the Trash icon.

- Right-click the file and select the Move to Trash command on the context menu.

If you decide to remove the files from the Trash directory permanently, follow these quick steps:

1. Click the Trash icon in the lower panel. Nautilus will open, displaying the contents of the Trash directory (see Figure 9.3).

2. Review the contents of the directory. Be sure that everything is safe to delete.

3. Right-click on a file and click Restore to move it automatically back to the location from which it was deleted.

4. When ready, click Empty Trash. A warning dialog box will appear (see Figure 9.4).

5. Click Empty Trash. The files will be permanently deleted and the Trash directory emptied.

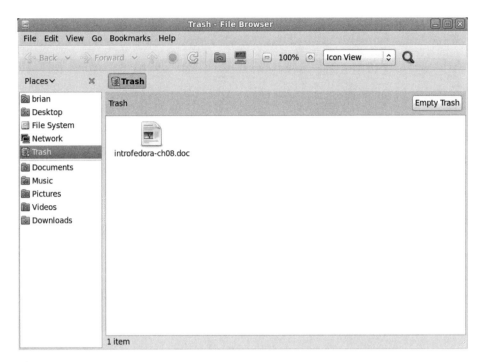

Figure 9.3
The Trash directory.

Figure 9.4
Confirming final deletion.

Finding Files

When you get a lot of files and directories, it will become increasingly difficult to remember where everything is. And why should you? Storing and remembering things is what we have built computers for!

Nautilus has an easy-to-use tool to locate files. Nautilus searches only your current location, so if you are in your Home folder, it will search all your personal files. If you want to only search your Music folder for a song, for example, first select the Music folder on the left in Nautilus and then click the Search icon.

1. Click the Search button. The Location bar will change to a Search tool (see Figure 9.5).

2. Type in a search term and press the Enter key. The results will be displayed, as shown in Figure 9.6.

3. You can add additional search parameters. Click the Plus icon. A new filter will be added to the Search Results section of the screen (see Figure 9.7).

4. Click the criterion lists to add additional parameters.

5. Click Reload. The new results will be displayed.

6. To leave the Search screen, click the Back button.

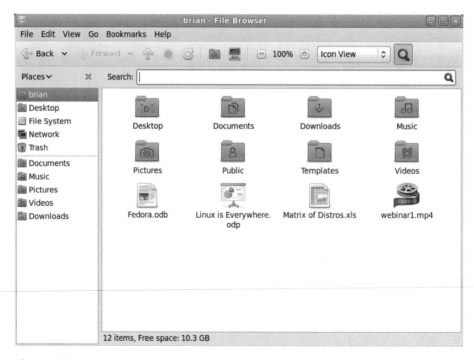

Figure 9.5
Searching for answers.

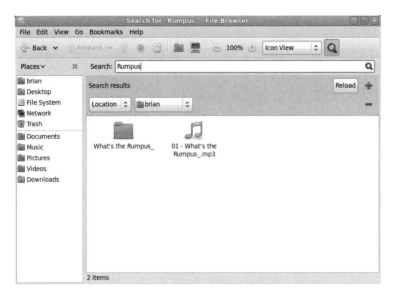

Figure 9.6
Where's the rumpus?

Figure 9.7
Narrowing the search.

Configuring Nautilus

As mentioned earlier, Nautilus has two distinct modes: Browser and Spatial. Thus far, we have been working in the Browser mode, but if you want to use Nautilus in Spatial mode, here's how to do it.

1. In Nautilus, click the Edit | Preferences menu command. The File Management Preferences dialog box will open (see Figure 9.8).

2. Click the Behavior tab. The Behavior page will open (see Figure 9.9).

3. Click the Open Each Folder in Its Own Window check box. The option will be deselected.

4. Click Close. The File Management Preferences dialog box will close.

5. Restart Nautilus. It will now be in Spatial mode.

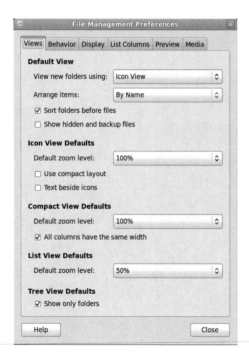

Figure 9.8
Defining your preferences.

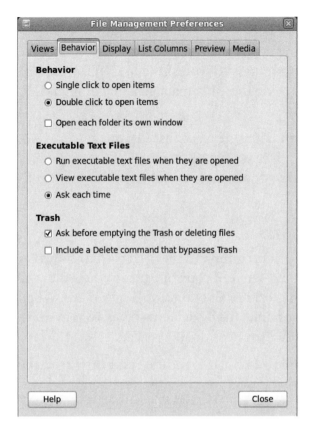

Figure 9.9
Changing modes.

In the Browser mode, you can tweak your settings quite a bit. Try these actions to experiment on the presentation of Nautilus.

- Click the drop-down list on top of the Side Pane and select one of the options.

- Test the Zoom control settings.

- Change the View control value from View as Icons to View as List.

After playing around with the settings, you may find a configuration of Nautilus that you prefer, which Nautilus will remember moving forward. This can only help your efficiency and satisfaction with Fedora.

Command-Line File Management

One of the best benefits of Linux is the power and simplicity to be found in the command line. Even if you plan to spend most of your time in GNOME or one of Fedora's other GUIs, you will find using these file management commands in Terminal very useful.

Are the solutions in this section easier than using Nautilus? In some respects, no, especially if you are used to using GUI-based file managers. But the command line offers a lot of flexibility and power: try out these examples and see if they fit your work style.

Copying Files: The cp Command

The cp command is similar to the MS-DOS command copy; it's used to copy files or directories from one place to another. You can copy one file to a new file, one file to another place, or a large number of files all at once to a new place. When you copy a file, you do not delete the original file by default. If you want to move a file rather than make a copy of it, use the mv command instead.

To use the cp command, type **cp**, followed by any options, and then type the directory or filename(s) you want to copy, followed by the destination. If you want to copy multiple files, you can use a wildcard character (which can stand for any character), or you can list multiple files separated by spaces.

Table 9.1 lists some of the available options for the cp command.

Let's say that you download a .zip file called program.zip into your home directory, and you want to unzip it, but you don't want to do it in your home directory. You can cp the file into the /tmp directory and work with it there. To do this, type in the following:

```
cp program.zip /tmp
```

Note that you do not get an error message if the file already exists, unless you use the interactive option. If the file exists, you are asked whether you want to overwrite the file or not, like this:

```
cp -i program.zip /tmp
cp: overwrite /tmp/program.zip'?
```

If you answer y, the file is overwritten; if n, the file is not overwritten.

Table 9.1 cp Command Options

Option	Name	Description
-f	Force	Removes any existing files of the same name.
-i	Interactive	Prompts the user if there is an existing file of the same name in the destination directory.
-p	Preserve	Tells the cp command to preserve the original file's permission, ownership, and timestamp data, if possible.
-R, -r	Recursive	Copies directories located under the starting directory. The default is not to copy subdirectories.

If you have a group of files you want to move into another directory without having to type each filename individually, you can use wildcards. If you want to copy all files in the current directory to another directory, type:

```
cp * /tmp
```

This copies all files in the directory to the /tmp directory; however, it does not copy directories unless specifically told to. To copy files and directories, use the recursive option.

```
cp -R * /tmp
```

If you'd like to copy all files with a specific extension to another directory, you can use wildcards to selectively copy groups of files like this:

```
cp *.jpg *.gif images
```

This copies all JPEG and GIF files to the images directory without copying any other files with them. You can also use the question mark character (?) to match a single character rather than a group of characters.

Moving Files: The mv Command

The mv command can be used to move a file or files to another directory, or to rename a file or files. The mv command is similar to the move command under

MS-DOS, but the `mv` command is much more powerful than its MS-DOS equivalent. The `mv` command does delete the original file that is being moved, so be sure to use the command carefully. The `mv` command is also used to rename files in Fedora, so it also takes the place of the `REN` command under MS-DOS.

To move a file, type `mv`, followed by any options, then the name of the file(s) or directories to be moved, and then the destination to which you want the file(s) moved. As with the `cp` command, you can use wildcards to move multiple files rather than typing individual filenames.

Table 9.2 lists some of the available options for the `mv` command.

To move the file `index.html` to another directory without making a backup or being prompted in the event of an overwrite, use the `mv` command, followed by the name of the file and its destination (where *username* is your login name):

```
mv index.html /home/username/backup/
```

Table 9.2   mv Command Options

Option	Name	Description
-b	Backup	Creates a backup file of any files that would be overwritten by moving a file. By default, backup files have a tilde character (~) extension.
-f	Force	When trying to move a file, removes any files of the same name without prompting the user.
-i	Interactive	Prompts the user if moving the current file will overwrite another file. If there are no conflicting files, mv simply moves the file with no complaint.
-S	Suffix	Appends a suffix to any backup files. By default, the tilde suffix is applied, but you can specify any type of suffix, such as .bak or .tmp.

If you're not certain whether a file of the same name already exists, use the interactive mode of mv. If the file already exists, your output looks like this:

```
mv -i index.html /home/username/backup/
mv: replace /home/username/backup/index.html'?
```

You can use wildcards to move more than one file to another directory. Be careful! The mv command can move directories as well as regular files. Be sure you actually want to move everything under a directory before using the wildcard (*).

If you want to move all of the .html files in the current directory to the /home/ httpd/ directory, you can use this command:

```
mv *.html /home/httpd/
```

The *.html specifies that you want to move all files that end in .html to another directory. If you want to move all files in the current directory to the /home/ httpd/ directory, you type:

```
mv * /home/httpd/
```

Fedora does not have a separate rename command, so the mv command is used to rename files. If you want to rename index.html to index.html.old, for instance, you use the mv command like this:

```
mv index.html index.html.old
```

As far as Fedora is concerned, moving a file and renaming it are the same thing.

Creating Directories: The mkdir Command

The mkdir command is pretty straightforward. It behaves the same way that the MS-DOS command MKDIR works. The Fedora command does have some additional functionality—you can set the permissions of the directory when it is created.

To create a new directory, simply type mkdir and any options and then the name of the directory you want to create.

Table 9.3 lists some of the options for the mkdir command.

To create a new directory called html under the current directory, use the mkdir command followed by the name of the new directory:

```
mkdir html
```

Table 9.3 `mkdir` Command Options

Option	Name	Description
-m	Mode	Creates a directory with specified permissions.
-p	Parents	Creates parent directories as needed.
-v	Verbose	Gives a written report for each directory created.

If you want to create a new directory called download under the /tmp directory:

```
mkdir /tmp/download
```

You do not need to be in the /tmp directory to create a subdirectory for it. If a file or directory named /download already exists in the /tmp directory, you'll receive the following error message:

```
mkdir /tmp/download
mkdir: cannot make directory download': File exists
```

Listing and Finding Files: The ls Command

The ls command lists the contents of a directory. This command is similar to the MS-DOS command DIR. In fact, typing dir in Fedora is the same as typing ls -c. The ls command is one of the commands you use the most in the Fedora Terminal. You can also use the ls command to get information about a specific file in a directory.

To use the ls command, you simply type the command, followed by any options you want to invoke and any filenames (including wildcards) that you want to specify.

Table 9.4 lists some of the available options for the ls command.

You probably want to know what files are in your home directory from time to time, so it's a good idea to know how to check. To list the files in your home directory, type the following command:

```
ls ~
```

That's all you need to type. The ~ character is a shortcut that refers to your home directory.

Table 9.4 ls Command Options

Option	Name	Description
-a	All	Using the -a option lists all files in a directory, including hidden files.
-A	Almost all	Lists all files in a directory, except for . and ...
-l	Long	In addition to the filenames, lists the file type, permissions, owner name, size of the file, and the last time the file was modified. Also known as the *verbose mode*.
-r	Reverse	Lists the directory contents in reverse order.
-sk	Kilobytes	Lists file sizes in kilobytes. The s specifies that, yes, you want to see the sizes.
-X	Extension	Sorts files by their extension; files with no extension will be sorted first.

If you decide you want to edit configuration files, you probably have to look for hidden files—files that do not show up in a standard listing. To list all files in a directory, type in the following:

ls -a

When listing all of the files in your home directory, you find that there are quite a few more files than you might have thought.

If you want to see all of the files in a directory and their attributes, combine the -a and -l options, as follows:

ls -al

You'll see a listing of all files in the directory, as well as their permissions, modification dates, to whom they belong, and the size of the files. The first letter indicates whether it is a file, directory, link, or other. A file is a dash (-), a directory is d, a symbolic link is an l, and a hard link is represented as a regular file. Other characters indicate it is a special type of file. After that letter, the permissions come. There are three groups of three letters.

Although detailed information on permissions is beyond the scope of this book, "r" stands for "*read*," which means—depending on in which group the "r" appears—that the owner, group, or anyone can read or view that file. A "w" stands for "*write*" and means—depending on in which group the "w" appears—that the owner, group, or anyone can write or change that file. And lastly, an "x" stands for "*execute*" and means—depending on in which group the "w" appears—that the owner, group, or anyone can write or change that file.

The first set is the permissions given to the owner of the file. The next set of three is for the group of the file, and then finally the permissions for everyone else. Then you'll see the owner of the file, followed by the group to which the file belongs. By default, the size of each file is displayed in bytes. Next in the listing, you'll see the last time the file was modified, or touched, and then the name of the file itself, as shown in this excerpt:

```
total 15244
drwxr-xr-x 43 username users   4096 2007-05-03 19:03 .
drwxr-xr-x 4 root    root    4096 2007-01-20 22:15 ..
-rw-r--r-- 1 username users  656308 2007-02-21 18:09 13969-crystal-1.0.2.
tar.bz2
-rw-r--r-- 1 username users  526684 2007-02-21 10:11 42804-domino-0.4.tar.bz2
-rw-r--r-- 1 username users  603993 2007-02-21 18:20 51302-Dark Plastic 2.
tar.gz
-rw------- 1 username users   1358 2007-04-19 21:43 .bash_history
-rw-r--r-- 1 username users   1177 2007-01-20 22:15 .bashrc
drwx------ 7 username users   4096 2007-05-03 19:04 .beagle
drwxr-xr-x 2 username users   4096 2007-01-20 22:15 bin
-rw-r--r-- 1 username users  132063 2007-01-20 23:40 bookmarks.html
drwxr-xr-x 6 username users   4096 2007-04-27 09:42 Books
-rw-r--r-- 1 username users   62048 2007-02-26 07:12 example.pdf
```

Touchy Files

The expression *touch* is not one I coined. In UNIX-style operating systems, like Fedora, a file is said to be touched when it is modified or viewed by a user in some way. A file is not touched when you just list the contents of a directory the file is in or view the contents of the file.

Moving Around the Filesystem: The cd Command

The cd command changes your working directory to another directory that you specify. This command is used to navigate the directory structure in Linux. Typing only cd returns you to your home directory. The cd command works similarly to the CD command under DOS. However, the cd command is a little more flexible in that it allows for shortcuts to change between your home directory and the previous working directory.

Use the cd command to change directories. Specifying no directory returns you to your home directory.

The parent directory is denoted by .. (two periods). To go up one level in the directory structure, simply type the following:

cd ..

Careful Typing

You must have a space between the .. and cd. If you type cd.. with no space, you'll get an error message telling you that the command cd.. is not found.

If you want to go up a couple levels in the directory structure, you can do so by typing this:

cd ../../

This moves you up two levels from your current directory.

To change to a specific directory, issue the cd command and then type the name of the desired directory. If you're working in your home directory and decide to switch to the /tmp directory, you use this command:

cd /tmp

Know Where You Are

It is important to note that /tmp and tmp are not the same in this instance. The /tmp command means you want to go to the tmp under the / (root) directory and not a tmp directory under the present working directory.

To get to your home directory quickly, simply use the cd command with no arguments, like this:

cd

If you do not specify a directory, the command line interface assumes you want to go back to your home directory. You can also use the tilde (~) symbol to specify your home directory, as in the following example:

cd ~

If you want to jump quickly back to the directory you were last in, without typing the full pathname of that directory, type this shortcut:

cd -

After you get the hang of the cd command and Fedora's directory structure, you may find that using the command-line interface is not as unfriendly as you might have thought when you first started.

Where the Heck Am I?: The pwd Command

The command pwd is simple: it's a one-trick pony. If you have lost track of where you are in the directory structure, you simply use pwd to get the shell to print out the present working directory.

At the command shell, type in:

pwd

The output is the current working directory. The pwd command does not take any options or arguments.

Conclusion

In this chapter, you learned how to manage files and directories both in the Nautilus file manager and on the command line. As you have seen, it is very similar to any operating system you've used in the past, so the transition to Fedora should be that much easier.

In Chapter 10, "Surfing the Web," you'll start looking beyond your Fedora desktop and find out about one of the best ways to browse the Internet: Firefox.

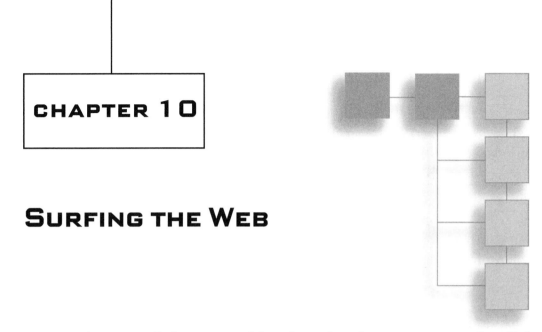

CHAPTER 10

SURFING THE WEB

Browsers have actually been around for a long time, but were never really called browsers. Instead, they were called *text readers* or *read-only applications,* because what these programs did was open simple files of text and let someone read them—like a book. These programs were on computers called *dumb terminals.*

It seems odd to call a computer *dumb,* but compared to the computers used today, these computers weren't very smart. All they did was display information from big, monster servers called *mainframes* that were the size of an average living room. These servers weren't all that smart, either, but they were good enough to take a lot of information and help businesspeople and scientists make sense of it.

The problem was that all these dumb terminals could only talk to the servers they were connected to. There was an Internet back then, but there was no World Wide Web; Internet traffic was mainly limited to messaging and file transfers, using tools such as Usenet, Archie, or Gopher.

Then, in 1990, a scientist in Switzerland, Sir Tim Berners-Lee, got a brilliant idea. What if you could read files on any computer connected to the Internet any time you wanted? You could put those files on a special server that had one job—showing those files to anyone who asked for them. Sir Berners-Lee, who was knighted for his work at the CERN institute, knew this idea would only work if all of these files were made readable by any computer. File compatibility was (and still can be) a huge obstacle for users to overcome.

So, Sir Berners-Lee suggested that people use HyperText Markup Language (HTML) files. Because they are essentially ASCII text files, HTML files could be read by any computer, would let people create any content they wanted, and would have hyperlinks—something that would revolutionize the way people absorbed material.

Browsers came about as instruments to read all of these new HTML files. As with the dumb terminals, Sir Berners-Lee just wanted people to read information quickly in files—not to change their content. So he and his colleagues figured out a way to make a program that did nothing but read and display HTML. Other people got involved and made the application read more complicated HTML code.

People began reading the information on the Web page and calling the process of reading those pages *browsing*—and that's where the browser name comes from. Later, when the general public started using the Web, the verb *browsing* got morphed into *surfing*. The name *browser* stuck, though, because it still more accurately describes what this type of application does. You can call any program like this a browser, of course. A program that does nothing but show pictures could be a picture browser. But these days the name is more synonymous with Web browsers, such as the most famous open-source browser today: Firefox.

In this chapter, you will learn about:

- The origins of Firefox

- Basic browsing tools

- Using tabs and live bookmarks

- Adding extensions and themes

Using Firefox

If you missed the infamous Browser Wars or have blocked it out of your mind along with the rest of the '90s, here's a quick summary.

In 1994, a young programmer named Marc Andreessen left the National Center for Supercomputing Applications (NCSA), the academic home for the first graphical browser for the Web, called *NCSA Mosaic*.

Andreessen founded Netscape Communications, and the company's first browser, Netscape Navigator 1.1, surpassed Mosaic in many important ways—not the least of which were added HTML extensions that only Netscape would support, such as tables, colors, text size, and (Lord help us all) blinking text. None of these functions was included in the original HTML specifications; Netscape added them because they looked good. And they did look good (except for the blinking) and eventually led to the adoption of these extensions by early Web developers, who in turn encouraged visitors to their sites to download and install Netscape to see their cool new Web site. This viral marketing had its effect—soon, Navigator controlled more than 90 percent of the browser market.

Around this time, Microsoft realized that this Internet thing was a good idea, and they were clearly missing the boat. To lure people away from the Web itself, the company started the Microsoft Network. MSN 1.0 was a flop, however, which prompted Microsoft to go head-to-head against Netscape.

Meanwhile, fearful of a complete lack of standards for this rapidly growing facet of the Internet, the World Wide Web Consortium (W3C) was established to implement standards for HTML, the basis of all of the Web sites in that day. The W3C took too few innovative steps while working on the HTML 3.0 specifications in 1995, because right at the beginning of 1996, Navigator 2.0 was released, supporting just a few of the HTML 3.0 specs and quite a few of its own. In as pure a case of market-driven events as you will ever see, the W3C threw up its collective hands and released HTML 3.0 soon after, which many of the Netscape extensions included.

One of these new extensions was the support of the new programming language, JavaScript, which along with the related Java language, offered Netscape users a platform-independent way of accessing innovative tools on any Web page.

Soon after this, Microsoft released Internet Explorer (IE) 2.0, which was very similar to Navigator 1.1 and contained some of its own extensions, such as background music and scrolling text. As far as releases go, it would have been no big deal—save for the fact that IE 2.0 was released free of charge. Then, to make it worse for Netscape, Microsoft announced that it would only implement support for "true" standardized HTML from that point on. In the first half of 1996, Web designers started to make sites that were "optimized for Netscape" or "optimized for MSIE."

The Browser Wars had begun.

Critics of IE (and there were plenty) knew that the only way Microsoft would ever be on equal footing with Netscape would be if IE supported something similar to

JavaScript. In August 1996, the critics got what they wanted, when Navigator and IE 3.0 were each released within a single week, with IE 3.0 including a new technology called *ActiveX*. ActiveX went beyond the simple scripting model of JavaScript and the plug-in methodology of Navigator. Now, IE users could pick up the tools they needed to read any special Web media automatically—they didn't need to find and install any helper apps like Navigator did.

No one would be laughing at IE anymore.

The next targeted release of the Big Two browsers would be 4.0, and each company had its own plan for changing the face of the desktop itself. IE would become integrated directly into the Windows desktop (a decision that has since come back to bite them), while Navigator would become more powerful and versatile so it would essentially become the platform upon which every application a user needed would run. The desktop would become the Internet, it was announced at a Netscape conference in 1997. But it was too late—Netscape's market share was dropping like a rock. By the end of that same year, Navigator held anywhere from 10 to 20 percent of the overall browser market share.

By the turn of the century, IE's market share was consistently 95 percent or higher.

There was no clear end to the Browser War, though many believe it came to a halt in December 1997, when the U.S. government levied charges of unfair competitive practices against Microsoft because of its decision to integrate IE into the then-upcoming Windows 98.

But what may have seemed like the end for Netscape may have actually turned into the beginning of the end for IE. In 1998, Andreessen announced the release of the Netscape Communicator 5.0 application suite, which contained the Navigator browser and Messenger email client, as well as a calendaring function under the open source Mozilla Public License. "Mozilla," once the name of Netscape's lizard mascot, would now become the name of the project created to manage the now-free Netscape code.

The Netscape Communicator suite would eventually be known as the *Mozilla Application Suite*, and many spin-offs would be created from this rich repository of source code, including several browsers for Linux, such as Galeon, Epiphany, and K-Melon. The Mozilla Foundation, the organization charged with maintaining the Mozilla code, continued to work on the entire suite, but some application developers felt that the suite itself (code-named *SeaMonkey*) was just too big to be fast and effective. Even the Mozilla browser (or its commercial offspring Navigator, which was still being produced by Netscape's new parent company, America Online) was considered by many to be rather slow and cumbersome.

In 2002, two developers, Blake Ross and Dave Hyatt, started working on a new kind of browser, a stripped-down, lean and mean bit of code that was called *Phoenix*. And even though the name didn't stick, it would prove to be prophetic.

Two years and two name changes later (Phoenix was already taken, and so was the next chosen name, *Firebird*), Firefox 1.0 was released for Windows, Mac OS X, and Linux. It was very fast and minimalistic: early versions had just a Back button and a Location Bar. Everything else was just frills. What kept people flocking to this sleek little browser were two things: tabbed browsing, where one browser window could have many open Web pages; and the capability to add extensions to Firefox. These were not like the HTML extensions of the prior century: these extensions were actually small applets that worked in much the same way as the old Netscape plug-ins. Need to view a certain type of media on a Web page? Download and install an extension. But, unlike plug-ins, extensions were easily installed and managed in a uniform way, while Netscape plug-ins were sometimes inconsistent with regard to these features.

Slowly, but surely, it became apparent that Firefox was rising quickly to become a serious challenger to IE's dominance. IE's own nearly constant security failings didn't help: because of that fateful decision to integrate IE into Windows—a decision that started the whole trouble with the Justice Department—crackers could more easily use IE's vulnerabilities to break into Windows. Firefox, a completely separate application, had no such problems in Windows (and certainly not in Fedora).

The Browser Wars, it seems, are back. Only this time, the battle is being fought over features, not the shifting sands of HTML standardization.

Browsing

Browsing is more than just clicking through a collection of hyperlinked files. What really makes the whole thing work is the Uniform Resource Locater (URL). URLs are pseudo-English labels that make it possible to find and retrieve resources across the Internet in a consistent, predictable, and well-defined manner. Every Web server has an IP address, but URLs make it easy for regular folk to type an address into the Location Bar of Firefox and bring up a page.

Of course, when you look at URLs such as http://www.llanfairpwllgwyngyllgo-gerychwyrndrobwllllantysiliogogogoch.co.uk/, using the IP address might actu-ally be a blessing, but for the most part, URLs are easier.

We Can't Make This Stuff Up

Llanfairpwllgwyngyllgogerychwyrndrobwllllantysiliogogogoch is a village on the Isle of Anglesey in North Wales that currently holds the Guinness record for the longest English place name. The village's Web site holds the record for the longest valid URL.

You can begin browsing with Firefox as soon as you start the application. If you are not connected to the Internet yet, starting Firefox will prompt your computer to start making that connection, especially if you are on dial-up access.

1. Click Applications | Internet | Firefox. The Firefox application will start (as shown in Figure 10.1).

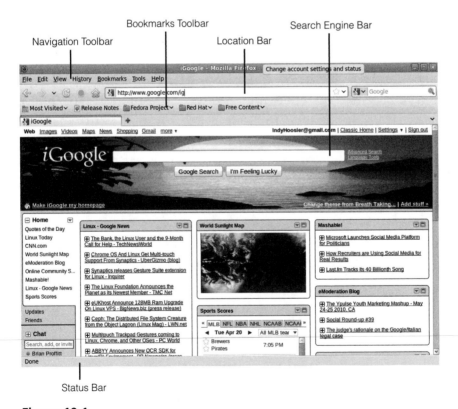

Figure 10.1
Firefox 3.6 in Fedora.

Starting Firefox

You can also start Firefox by clicking its launcher icon in the upper panel.

2. Double click the Location bar so the URL in the field is highlighted.

3. Type the URL for the Web site you want to visit in the Location bar.

A Helping URL Hand

You do not have to type the URL identifier http:// before the Web site address. Firefox will fill it in for you.

4. Press Enter to go to the new page.

5. Place the mouse cursor over a highlighted or underlined hyperlink. The link will change color, and the full URL for the link will appear in the Status bar at the bottom of the window.

6. Click the hyperlink to go to the new page.

You don't have to type in the full address every time you visit a Web site, thanks to the Autofill feature in the Location bar. Just start typing the URL, and Firefox will display a list of similar URLs for you to choose from.

After you have been browsing for a while, you may need to go back to a Web page you visited earlier in your current browser session. Two controls on the Navigation toolbar, the Back and Forward buttons, will enable you to navigate through the pages you have visited.

Note, however, that navigation through Web pages is not tracked for *every* Web page you visit during a session. Firefox uses a sequential navigation method that tracks only the pages along a particular path. For instance, assume you were browsing Page A, then Pages B, C, and D. On Page D, you found a hyperlink back to Page B and clicked it to visit that page. Now, from Page B again, assume you went off and visited Pages E and F. If you were to use the Back button in this session, the order of pages that would appear for each click of the Back button would be F to E to B to A. Pages C and D, because they were on another "track" of browsing, would no longer be a part of the browser's navigation—even if you were to cycle forward through the same pages again using the Forward button.

Of course, you can do more with the Back and Forward buttons than just cycle through Web pages one at a time.

1. After navigating to a few Web pages, click the drop-down list control to the right of the Forward button. A list of recently visited pages will appear (see Figure 10.2).

2. Click one of the options. That page will appear in the browser window.

One of the nicer features of Fedora is its capability to call up the default Web browser whenever any hyperlink or Web page shortcut is clicked—in any application. That capability is particularly handy in email clients, such as Thunderbird or Evolution, where you often receive URLs from friends or colleagues.

Tabs

Tabs are not unique to Firefox; they were a feature in other browsers before it came along. But Firefox can certainly get some credit for popularizing this feature.

Tabs allow you to visit many pages and give each one its own window within the Firefox browser. A visual example of this can be seen in Figure 10.3.

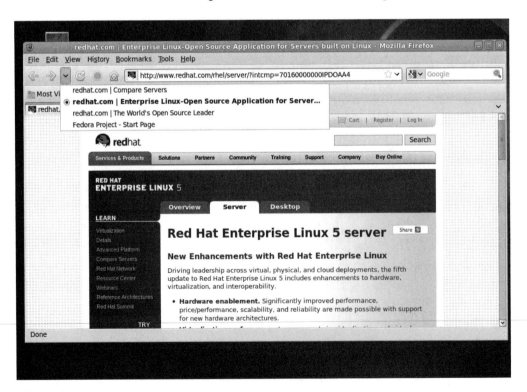

Figure 10.2
Stepping back through a browsing session.

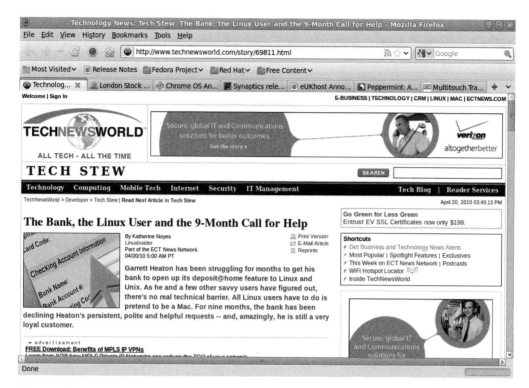

Figure 10.3
Tabs in action.

As you can see, each tab holds its own Web page. More than that, tabs are really independent browser sessions, all in one window. So, if you were to navigate through a series of pages, you could use the Back and Forward buttons just as described in the previous section. If you switch to another tab, however, the navigation rules will change to sites visited in the new tab.

To open a new tab, select the File | New Tab menu command. You can also press Ctrl+T on your keyboard. Once a new, blank tab is opened (see Figure 10.4), you can type in a URL in the Location bar or use a bookmark to navigate to a new page.

Another way to open a tab is to right-click a hyperlink. In the context menu that appears, click the Open Link in New Tab menu command. The linked page will open in a new tab. A shortcut to this action is to press the Ctrl key and click a hyperlink. The page will open in a new tab.

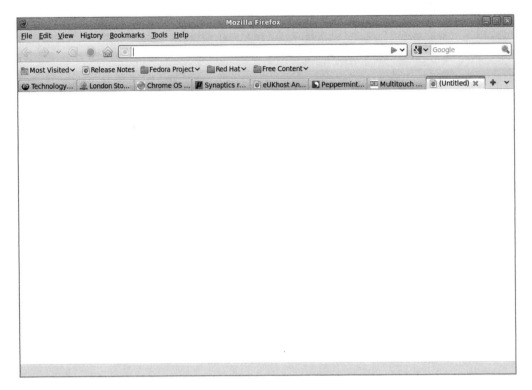

Figure 10.4
A blank tab.

Tabs can also be moved around and put in whatever order you prefer. Simply click a tab and drag and drop the tab in the new position, which will be indicated by a miniature preview of the screen and a small arrow in the Tab bar as you move the mouse pointer (see Figure 10.5).

More Tab Tricks

If you want to view another tab, just click it with the mouse pointer. If you want to cycle through the tabs in order, press Ctrl+Tab on the keyboard. This will take you to the right along the Tab bar. Pressing Shift+Ctrl+Tab will cycle through tabs to the left.

When you are finished with the contents of a tab, you might want to close it. This is not just for aesthetics; having a lot of tabs open can put a strain on any computer, even your Fedora machine. So once you are ready to close a tab, simply click the red Close icon on the tab you want to shut down. The tab and its contents will disappear.

Figure 10.5
The tab's new position is marked by an arrow.

If you made a mistake and closed the wrong tab, don't worry about it. You can get it back by right-clicking the Tab bar. In the context menu that appears, click the Undo Close Tab menu command. The last closed tab will reappear.

Undoing Closed Tabs

If you have closed the last tab in the browser, the Undo Close Tab command will not work, unless you have the Tab bar always enabled.

If you really want to clean up fast and reduce all of the tabs down to one, click the tab you want to keep. Then right-click that tab and select the Close Other Tabs menu command. Every tab but the one you selected will close.

Bookmarks

Human beings are creatures of habit, and often we find ourselves clinging to the familiar as we move through our busy lives. Firefox accommodates this trait with its Bookmarks feature. Bookmarks are markers that, when selected in a menu or clicked in the Bookmark toolbar, will take you directly to the Web page you want—without typing the URL address.

You can create a bookmark for one page or many, utilizing the tab feature in Firefox. Then, when you need to, you can open up one or multiple pages with just a click.

To open a bookmark, click the Bookmark menu and select the bookmark you want. If there is a bookmark in the Bookmark toolbar, all you need to do is click it. Finally, if the sidebar is open in Firefox, you can access bookmarks from there.

You can open the Bookmarks sidebar by selecting the View | Sidebar | Bookmarks menu command (see Figure 10.6).

Opening the Sidebar

Pressing Ctrl+B will also open the Bookmarks sidebar.

Figure 10.6
The Bookmarks sidebar.

When you find a page you want to save, you can bookmark it and add it to your bookmark collection.

1. From a page you want to save, select the Bookmarks | Bookmark This Page menu command. The Page Bookmarked message box will open (see Figure 10.7).

Bookmarking Tabs

Pressing Ctrl+D will also bookmark the current tab's contents. If you have multiple tabs open, right-click the desired tab and select the Bookmark This Tab menu command on the context menu.

2. Confirm or edit the name of the bookmark you want to use.

3. Click the Folder drop-down list if you want the bookmark to appear somewhere other than the main Bookmarks menu, and select a new location.

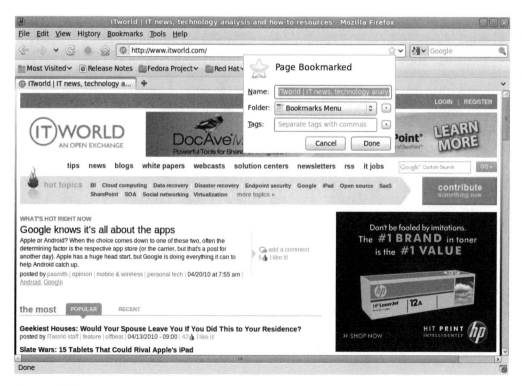

Figure 10.7
The Page Bookmarked message box.

4. Add any tags you might want in the Tags field.

5. Click Done. The bookmark will be added to the desired location, and the Page Bookmarked message box will close.

You can also bookmark multiple tabs at the same time. This is very useful, since opening a group of pages all at once is a huge time-saver.

1. From any page, select the Bookmarks | Bookmark All Tabs menu command. The New Bookmarks dialog box will open (see Figure 10.8).

Add New Bookmarks

Right-click the Tab bar and select the Bookmark All Tabs menu command on the context menu to open the New Bookmarks dialog box.

2. Enter the name of the bookmarks folder you want to use.

3. Click the Folder drop-down list if you want the bookmarks folder to appear somewhere other than the main Bookmarks menu, and select a new location.

4. Click Add Bookmarks. The bookmarks folder will be added to the desired location, and the New Bookmarks dialog box will close.

If you put a bookmarks folder in the Bookmarks toolbar, clicking the folder will open a menu that displays all of the contents of the folder (see Figure 10.9). You can click the pages one at a time to open them individually or select the Open All in Tabs option to open every page in a separate tab.

Too Many Tabs!

Opening many tabs at once can slow your system down, particularly if the pages have a lot of graphics or animated ads. If you notice this on your system, consider making smaller bookmark folders. Or don't open all your bookmarks at the same time.

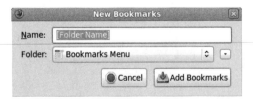

Figure 10.8
The New Bookmarks dialog box.

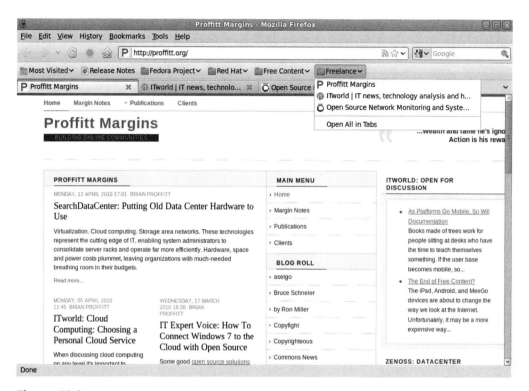

Figure 10.9
Listing a bookmarks folder.

As time goes on, you will find your collection of bookmarks has grown quite a bit. Firefox includes a solid tool to organize bookmarks in a way that makes the best sense for you.

1. From any page, select Bookmarks | Organize Bookmarks. The Library window will open (see Figure 10.10).

2. Click any folder's expansion icon. The contents of the folder will be displayed.

3. Click and drag any item up or down the list of bookmarks. A placeholder line will appear to mark the bookmark's position.

4. Release the mouse button. The bookmark will be moved to the new location.

5. Right-click any menu entry and select the New Folder option. The New Folder dialog box will open (see Figure 10.11).

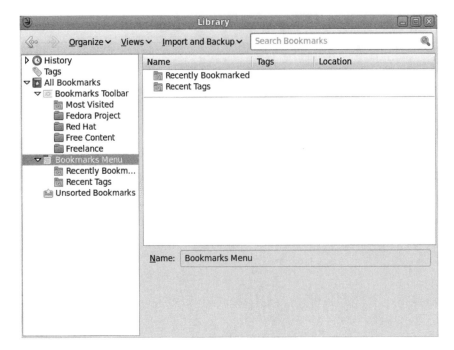

Figure 10.10
The Library manages bookmarks.

Figure 10.11
Manually creating a new bookmarks folder.

6. Enter the name of the bookmarks folder in the Name field.

7. Click Add. The folder will be added to the folder and the bookmark panes.

8. Click and drag a bookmark to a position over one of the folders in the folder pane.

9. Release the mouse button. The bookmark will be placed in the folder.

10. Click a bookmark or folder to remove it and click the Delete button. The bookmark will be removed.

Search Engines

Finding things on the Web used to be very easy; with only 500 or so Web sites in existence in the early '90s, you could almost index them by hand. Today, there are billions of Web pages, and finding useful things can be daunting sometimes. Firefox has a search tool that not only uses the most powerful search tools around, but also allows you to choose the search engines you prefer.

Using the Search bar is easy: just type in what you are looking for and press Enter. By default, the Search bar connects to the Google search engine, and it will display the results of your search in a new tab.

Suggested Searches

The latest version of Firefox will suggest search terms similar to what you type, in an effort to save you time. If you see the term you were looking for, select it and press Enter to start the actual search.

To change search engines, click the Search bar's drop-down list and select the engine you want to use instead, as shown in Figure 10.12.

Follow these steps to add or remove a search engine.

1. Click the Search bar drop-down list and select the Manage Search Engines option. The Manage Search Engine List dialog box will open (see Figure 10.13).

2. To remove a search engine, click the engine to select it.

3. Click Remove. The search engine will be removed from the installed list.

4. Click the Get More Search Engines hyperlink. The Manage Search Engine List dialog box will close, and a new Firefox window will open, displaying the Search Engines page on the Firefox Add-ons site (see Figure 10.14).

5. Click a search engine. The search engine's page will appear.

6. Click Add to Firefox. The Add Search Engine dialog box will open (see Figure 10.15).

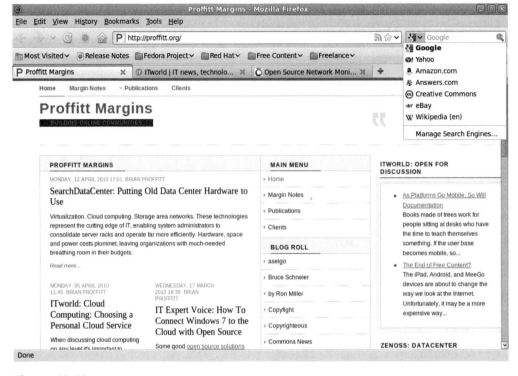

Figure 10.12
Initially available search engines.

Figure 10.13
Managing search engines.

Figure 10.14
Adding search engines.

Figure 10.15
You can use a new search engine right away.

7. Click the Start Using It Right Away check box.

8. Click Add. The new search engine will be added to the Search bar list.

Live Bookmarks

A relatively new phenomenon on the Web is the presence of Really Simple Syndication (RSS) feeds, or *feeds* for short. An RSS feed is typically a very brief synopsis of the contents of a Web site. Users can "subscribe" to a site's feed and be able to see just by looking at the brief synopsis if the site's content has been updated. Clicking a link in the RSS feed will take the user right to the content on the feed's site.

Many Web sites use RSS feeds to syndicate content from other sites. If you have a site about Fedora, for instance, you might want to display the headlines from various Linux sites, such as Linux Today, Linux Weekly News, or LXer.

Firefox has a feature that's very useful for those of us who don't have a Web site to add RSS feeds to—live bookmarks, which automatically update their content and display the source sites' content automatically.

Identifying sites that can have a live bookmark is easy. Any site that has an available RSS feed will be noted by an orange RSS icon in the far right of the Location bar. If you find such a site and want to subscribe to its feed, then just follow these steps.

1. From a site with an available feed, click the RSS icon in the Location bar. The site's feed page will appear, with a subscription prompt at the top of the page (see Figure 10.16).

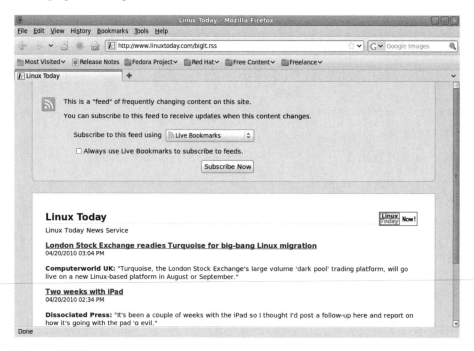

Figure 10.16
Subscribing to an RSS feed.

2. Click the Subscribe Now button. The Subscribe with Live Bookmark dialog box will open (see Figure 10.17).

3. Edit the name of the live bookmark you want to use.

4. Click the Folder drop-down list if you want the live bookmark to appear somewhere other than the Bookmarks Toolbar and select a new location.

5. Click Subscribe. The live bookmark will be added to the desired location, and the Subscribe with Live Bookmark dialog box will close.

Once a live bookmark is in place, it will periodically update itself and display the contents of the subscribed site just like a bookmarks folder.

Add-Ons

Another feature unique to Firefox over other browsers is the ability to add add-ons, such as extensions to enhance your browser experience or themes to dress up your browser. Getting these add-ons is very simple, since for the most part, they are all found in one place: the Firefox Add-ons Web site. But you don't need a URL to go there; Firefox's Add-ons tool will take care of everything.

1. Click Tools | Add-ons. The Add-ons window will appear (see Figure 10.18).

2. Click the Browse All Add-ons link. A new Firefox window will appear, displaying the Firefox Add-ons site (see Figure 10.19).

3. Navigate the site to find an extension you would like to install.

4. Click the Add to Firefox button. The Software Installation dialog box will appear (see Figure 10.20).

Confirm Compatibility

Please note the Works With column's information to be sure an extension will function with the version of Firefox you are currently using.

Figure 10.17
Live bookmarks are added like regular bookmarks.

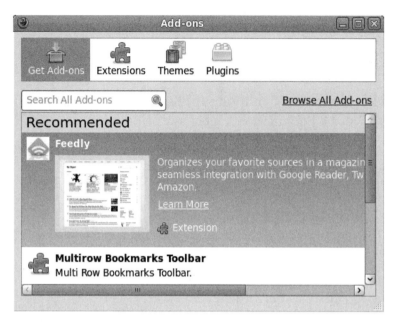

Figure 10.18
Managing add-ons.

Figure 10.19
The Firefox Add-ons site.

Figure 10.20
The Software Installation dialog box.

5. When ready, click the Install Now button. The installed extension will appear in the Add-ons window (see Figure 10.21).

Extension Tricks

You may need to restart Firefox to fully install an extension. If asked, click the Restart Firefox button. You may need to re-open the Add-ons window if this occurs.

The Add-ons tool does more than add extensions. It also handles access to each extension's preferences commands, as well as uninstalls them when the time comes. Clicking the Find Updates button will begin a search immediately for the latest versions of all of your extension software.

Beginning in Firefox 3.6, the browser has the ability to instantly load "skins" created by users around the world. These themes, or personas, can quickly give your browser a custom look. Finding personas and applying them is very easy.

1. Click Tools | Add-ons. The Add-ons window will appear.

2. Click Themes. The Themes page will open.

3. Click the Get Themes link. A new Firefox window will appear, displaying the Personas Gallery site (see Figure 10.22).

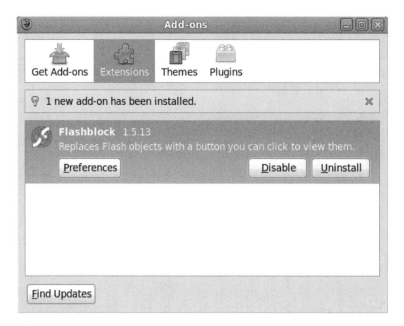

Figure 10.21
An installed extension.

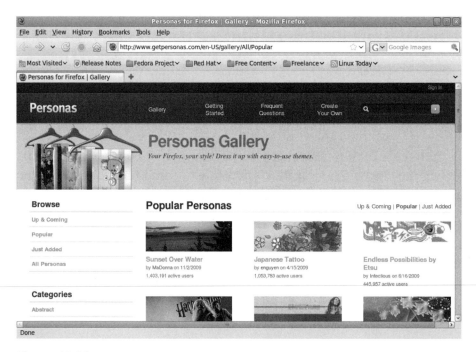

Figure 10.22
The Personas Gallery.

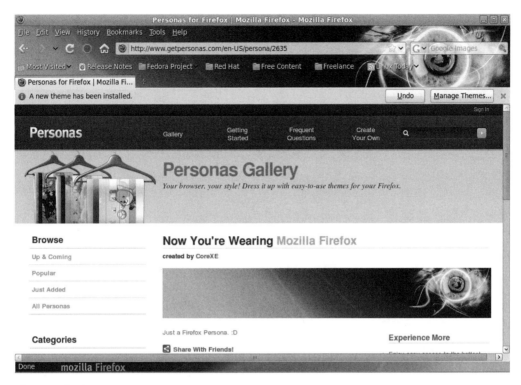

Figure 10.23
An installed Persona.

4. Navigate the site to find a persona you would like to install.

5. Click on any persona. In a few moments, the persona will be applied to your browser.

6. If you like the persona, click the Wear It button. The Persona will be applied to your browser (see Figure 10.23).

Conclusion

In this chapter, you learned some of the finer points of operating the Firefox browser. With the multitude of extensions, it is a very realistic statement to say that this tool will be the most powerful application in the Fedora toolset.

In Chapter 11, "Mail Call," we will examine how to use the other most-used aspect of the Internet—email—and how Fedora's email clients handle this important job.

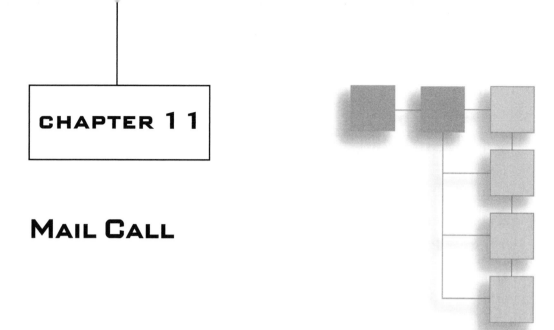

CHAPTER 11

MAIL CALL

In a new building in Austin, Minnesota sits the SPAM Museum, a shrine completely dedicated to a processed meat product that has earned itself a unique place in American culture. Here, at least, SPAM is a good thing.

Everywhere else and apart from culinary discussions, the term *spam* has decidedly less appeal. Unsolicited email messages comprise a very large majority of all email traffic in the world. Most of it, fortunately, we never see, as our Internet providers' and employers' mail servers clean most of it out. The part that does get through, though, is still unwanted. You need a good email client that will help you slog through spam, as well as organize all of the good emails that you want to receive.

Fedora, like most Linux distributions, is endowed with a very robust and capable email client: Evolution. But there is another application that's very popular among Fedora users that you might also want to try: Thunderbird. Rather than recommend which one to use, it is left to the reader to compare and choose based on personal preferences. After all, they both have similar features, are easy to use, and are noncommercial applications. In this chapter, for both applications, you will learn how to do the following:

- Create an email account
- Download your messages
- Organize your email
- Filter spam away forever

Using Evolution

Evolution is the GNOME environment's personal information manager and workgroup application. It hasn't been around long, since September 2004, when it was released as part of GNOME 2.8 (Fedora 13, to give perspective, ships with GNOME 3). Since Fedora is primarily a GNOME-using distribution, it makes sense that it would be included in Fedora as the default email application.

If you've used Microsoft Outlook, there's a lot about Evolution that you are going to recognize: email, calendar, address book, and task list functions are part of its feature set. If you are in an office that uses Microsoft Exchange Server, Evolution is one of the non-Microsoft clients that can fully connect to Exchange and utilize it. You can also sync your Palm Pilot and Windows Mobile device with your Evolution data.

This chapter will focus mostly on the email capabilities of Evolution.

Setting Up an Account

Getting an email account these days is a pretty simple thing. Most employers have them for their employees, universities have them for students and staff, and private Internet service providers often provide multiple email accounts per Internet connection: one for each member of the family, if you want.

Most emails (especially away from internal business accounts) are delivered over the Internet via the Post Office Protocol (POP) or Internet Mail Access Protocol (IMAP). A POP or IMAP account works something like this: someone sends you an email. The Internet's control servers route that message to your email server, which can be located anywhere in the world. There your message will sit, until you come along and download it (and any other messages) into your email client. Unless you have an email server in your home or cubicle, emails never come directly to you. This is actually good, because this two-step process gives both your mail server and your client (such as Evolution) a chance to clean out spam and junk mail.

Outbound mail is a little different. You type a message, address it, and hit Send. The message is immediately sent out to the destination server via Simple Mail Transfer Protocol (SMTP) server. It doesn't stay there long; the SMTP server has one job to do, and it does it very quickly. It checks the address in your message and makes sure there's actually a mail server ready to receive messages at the other end. If there is, boom! Off your message goes. If there isn't, the SMTP server will immediately bounce your message back to your client and tell you what went wrong.

Return to Sender

Note that the SMTP server on your end only checks for valid mail servers. If the username in the address is incorrect, or that user no longer has an account, it's the job of the receiving POP server to figure that out and send you the bounce message. It's a fine line, but if you get a bounce message, knowing from where it was sent will help you figure out what went wrong.

Whenever you set up a new email account, your Internet service provider will provide you with some important information that you need to memorize or store in a safe place somewhere. Specifically, you need:

- Your new e-mail address

- Your username for the POP server

- Your password for the POP server

- The Internet address of the POP server

- The Internet address of the SMTP server

When you first start Evolution, you will immediately be given the opportunity to set up an email account. You can set up as many accounts as you would like, but you should have the complete set of information for at least one of your accounts before working on these steps when you start Evolution for the first time.

1. Click the Applications | Office | Evolution Mail and Calendar menu command. The Evolution Setup Assistant dialog box will open (see Figure 11.1).

Opening Evolution

Clicking the Evolution launcher icon in the upper panel or any email link in a Web browser will also start Evolution.

2. Click Forward. The Restore from Backup page will open.

3. If you are restoring an Evolution file you backed up on another computer, you can click the Restore Evolution from the Backup File option and continue on. Otherwise, click Forward. The Identity page will open, as shown in Figure 11.2.

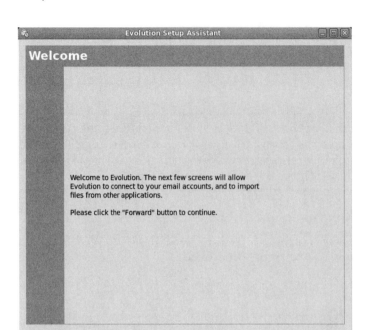

Figure 11.1
The Evolution Setup Assistant.

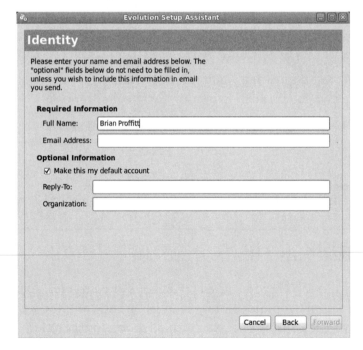

Figure 11.2
Declare your identity.

4. Type the appropriate information in the fields. It is important that you fill out the Required Information fields.

5. Click Forward. The Receiving Email page will open (see Figure 11.3).

6. Select POP from the Server Type drop-down list.

Non-POP Accounts

For this example, we are going to use POP accounts, although the setup for IMAP is essentially identical. Contact your system administrator and obtain the necessary information for whichever account type you need.

7. Type the address of your POP server in the Server field.

8. Confirm your username in the Username field.

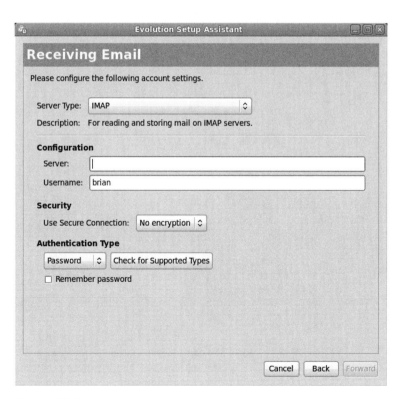

Figure 11.3
Specify the server type.

9. If your mail server uses encryption, select the appropriate value in the Use Secure Connection field.

10. Most POP servers use a password for authentication. If you are not sure, click the Check for Supported Types button. The POP server will be queried, and the correct authentication value should be inserted.

11. Click the Remember Password check box if you want Evolution to pick up mail without asking you for a password every time (though this could be a potential security risk).

12. Click Forward. The Receiving Options page will open (see Figure 11.4).

13. Check the appropriate check boxes to get the settings you want.

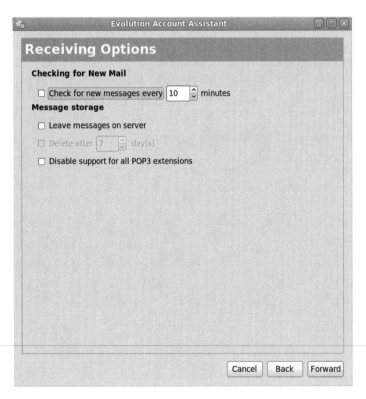

Figure 11.4
Detail your reception preferences.

Taking It Easy on the POP Server

You can set Evolution to download email automatically at a certain interval—no less than 10 minutes, so you don't overload your POP server. That's a good idea for those of you with an always-on Internet account. If you are using dial-up, consider leaving this option off. If you can control the timing of email downloads, you can manage the flow of traffic through your narrowband connection.

14. Click Forward. The Sending Email page will open (see Figure 11.5).

15. Set the Server Type as SMTP.

16. Type the address of your SMTP server in the Server field.

17. If your SMTP server uses encryption, select the appropriate value in the Use Secure Connection field.

Figure 11.5
Specify the SMTP settings.

18. Some SMTP servers use a password for authentication. If you are not sure, click the Check for Supported Types button. The SMTP server will be queried, and the correct authentication value will be inserted.

19. Confirm your username in the Username field.

20. Click the Remember Password check box if you want Evolution to send mail without asking you for a password every time.

21. Click Forward. The Account Management page will open (see Figure 11.6).

22. Name the account and click Forward. The Done page will appear (see Figure 11.7).

23. Click Apply. The Evolution Setup Assistant dialog box will close, and Evolution will open.

Figure 11.6
Name the account.

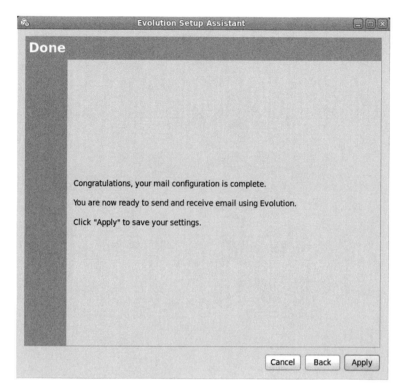

Figure 11.7
Finished and ready to go.

If you set your account to automatically check for mail, as soon as Evolution opens, the Enter Password for <Your Account Name> dialog box will open. Type in the password and click OK. The dialog box will close, and your mail will be downloaded.

If you want to add another email account to Evolution, you will need to use the Evolution Account Assistant, which is identical to the Setup Assistant. To access it, follow these few steps in Evolution.

1. Click the Edit | Preferences menu command. The Evolution Preferences window will open (see Figure 11.8).

2. Confirm the Mail Accounts option is selected and click the Add button. The Evolution Account Assistant dialog box will open, as shown in Figure 11.9.

3. Follow the steps you used for the Evolution Setup Assistant to complete the task.

Figure 11.8
Evolution Preferences.

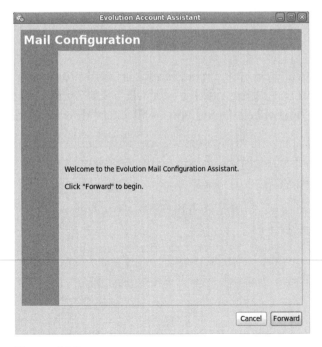

Figure 11.9
The Evolution Account Assistant.

Receiving and Sending Mail

Once you have one account set up in Evolution, you are free to send and receive email as long as you are connected to the Internet.

If you did not set Evolution to download messages automatically (or you just want to see what's out there before the next scheduled download occurs), click the Send/Receive button (or press F9 on the keyboard). Your messages will be downloaded.

As you can see in Figure 11.10, the Evolution window is very similar to Microsoft Outlook.

Reading a message is simple: just click a message in the Message list, and its contents will be displayed in the Preview window. Double-clicking a message will

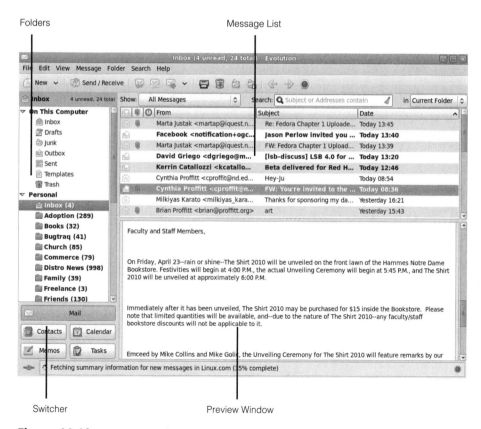

Figure 11.10
The Evolution window.

open the message in its own message window (see Figure 11.11), complete with a set of tools to use on the message.

After you have read an email, you will note that it is no longer bold in the Message list, and its envelope icon will be open.

You can do more with an email than just read it. In fact, more often than not, a message will warrant a reply. To reply to the *sender* of the message only:

1. Select a message to which to reply. The message will be displayed in the Preview window.

2. Click the Reply button. A preaddressed Re: message window will open.

3. Type your reply in the body of the message.

4. Click Send. The message window will close, and the message will appear in the Outbox until it is sent to the SMTP server.

If the message was sent to you and other people, you can send a reply to all the recipients and the sender.

1. Select a message to reply to all recipients. The message will be displayed in the Preview window.

2. Click the Reply to All button. A preaddressed Re: message window will open.

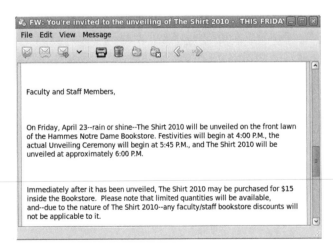

Figure 11.11
A Message window.

3. Type your reply in the body of the message.

4. Click Send. The message window will close, and the message will appear in the Outbox until it is sent to the SMTP server.

If you want to forward a message to someone else, it's just as easy.

1. Select a message to forward. The message will be displayed in the Preview window.

2. Click the Forward button. A preaddressed Fwd: message window will open.

3. Type an additional message in the body of the message.

4. Click Send. The message window will close, and the message will appear in the Outbox until it is sent to the SMTP server.

If you want to send a new message to a single or multiple recipients, here's how.

1. Click New. A Compose Message window will open (see Figure 11.12).

2. Type an email address in the To field.

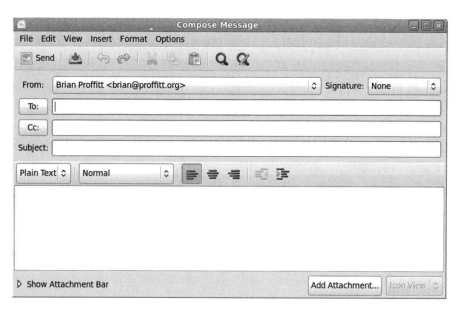

Figure 11.12
A new message window.

Contact Connection

If you use the Contacts tool in Evolution, you can create a database of names and email addresses. Then you can click the To button and open the Select Contacts from Address Book dialog box and quickly choose the addresses you need without typing a single ampersand.

3. If you need to blind carbon copy a recipient, select the View | Bcc Field menu command in the message window and type the address in.

4. Type a subject.

5. Type a message in the body.

6. Click Send. The message window will close, and the message will appear in the Outbox until it is sent to the SMTP server.

Organizing Mail

After you have read your messages and sent your replies, what next? You don't want to leave your Inbox cluttered, and unless it's junk mail, you don't want to delete everything, either.

Evolution is very good about handling lots of email at once. Let's take some steps to organize the Inbox first.

If you click the Show drop-down list, you will see a list of categories to filter the Message list. Click these, as desired, to see the results on your Inbox.

You can also sort messages based on the criteria of the columns in the Message list. If you want to sort by date, click the Date column header. A down arrow will appear in the header button, and the messages will be listed from earliest to most recent down the screen. Clicking the Date header again will change the sort order from most recent to earliest. You can do this for any column header.

The folder is a really useful tool in Evolution for organizing your information. Using folders, you can essentially treat messages as files (which, you should know, they are) that can be organized just like files in the Nautilus file manager, which you learned about in Chapter 9, "Basic File Management."

Creating a folder is very quick.

1. Right-click the Inbox folder. A context menu will appear.

2. Select the New Folder menu command. The Create Folder dialog box will open (see Figure 11.13).

3. Type a folder name.

4. Click Create. The Create Folder dialog box will close, and the new folder will be added to the Inbox.

5. To view the new folder, click the expansion icon next to the Inbox folder (see Figure 11.14).

After you have folders created, you can set up rules in Evolution that will examine incoming messages and automatically move certain messages into those folders. If you have a project you are working on, you can create a rule that will move any message containing a reference to that project into a folder you've created.

Evolution helps with this process by letting you choose a representative message and build the rule from that point.

1. Right-click the example message. A context menu will appear.

2. Select the Create Rule menu command; then select one of the Filter On options (Subject, Sender, or Recipients). The Add Filter Rule dialog box will appear (see Figure 11.15).

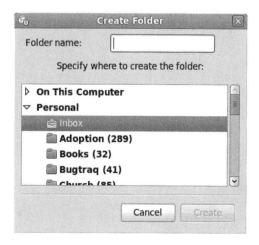

Figure 11.13
Making a new folder.

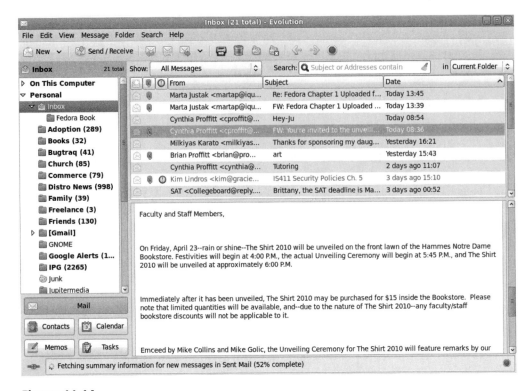

Figure 11.14
Viewing a new folder.

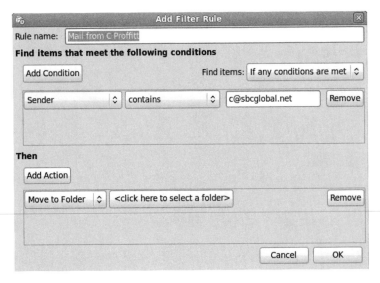

Figure 11.15
Creating a new rule.

3. Confirm or edit the rule name.

4. Confirm or edit the subject criteria. If one of the criteria isn't needed, click its Remove button.

5. Confirm that the Move to Folder option is selected.

6. Click the Click Here to Select a Folder button. The Select Folder dialog box will open.

7. Select the desired folder and click OK. The Select Folder dialog box will close.

8. Click OK. The Add Filter Rule dialog box will close.

To run the filter on your existing Inbox messages, select the Message | Apply Filters menu command.

Protecting Your Inbox

One of the sad truths about working on the Internet messaging is no one is ever immune to spam, or junk mail, as Evolution refers to it. There are ways to minimize it, the most important method being to keep your email address close to the vest. Sometimes that's not possible, especially with work accounts. But if you have a personal email address, just give it to family and friends and never post it on the Web.

When, not if, you start getting junk mail, Evolution initially will let it roll right into your Inbox, leaving you wondering where all this vaunted protection is. Don't worry, it's there.

Evolution uses a Bayesian filter to sort through junk mail. A Bayesian filter looks at messages and decides if they are spam or not based on criteria it has learned over the course of time. But in order to learn, it has to be trained, and that's where the user comes in.

When you select a junk message and mark it as *Junk*, two things will happen: first, the offending message will be removed from the Inbox and moved to the Junk folder. Second, the Bayesian filter will "learn" that messages with certain words and characteristics should be regarded in the future as junk mail. When more messages like that come in, the Junk filter should automatically dump the spam into the Junk filter, leaving your Inbox much cleaner.

1. Right-click the example message. A context menu will appear.

2. Select the Mark as Junk menu command. The message will be removed from the folder and input into the Junk filter.

There are a few things to remember when working with Evolution's Junk filter. To begin with, it takes a while to learn what's really junk or not, so for the first few sessions it may not seem like it's doing its job. Eventually, less spam will slip though as the learning process continues.

Another important point: the Junk filter is not infallible, especially early in its learning process. Not only will spam go unmarked, but genuine emails may get treated as spam by mistake. Therefore, it's very important that you periodically scan the contents of your Junk folder to look for real messages. If you do find any, be sure to click on the Not Junk button when the message is selected. This will help Evolution's Junk filter learn faster.

Using Thunderbird

As you learned in Chapter 10, "Surfing the Web," the Mozilla Application Suite is the source for the open source Firefox browser. The Mozilla Foundation, the organization charged with maintaining the Mozilla code, still works on the entire suite, but some application developers feel that the suite itself (codenamed *SeaMonkey*) was just too big to be fast and effective.

Just as a development team spun off a light and fast Web browser from Sea-Monkey, another team took the code for SeaMonkey's email and contact manager and created the Thunderbird application.

Compared to Evolution, Thunderbird is lighter on features. If you are looking for an all-in-one personal information manager application like Outlook, Thunderbird may not be the best choice. But if you don't need all of those tools, and you just want a fast email client, Thunderbird will definitely fit the bill.

Unlike Evolution, Thunderbird is not included in the default installation of Fedora. So, you will need to install it if you want to use it. Start PackageKit as demonstrated in Chapter 6, "Installing and Updating Software," and search for the Thunderbird package. Once found, mark it for installation and allow the dependent packages to be installed as well.

Setting Up an Account

When you first start Thunderbird, you will immediately be given the opportunity to set up an email account. Remember, you will need all of your account information to get things set up.

1. Click the Applications | Internet | Thunderbird menu command. The Mail Account Setup dialog box will open (see Figure 11.16).

2. Type the appropriate information in the fields and click Continue. Thunderbird will begin to poll the Internet for information (see Figure 11.17).

Figure 11.16
The Mail Account Setup dialog box.

Figure 11.17
Automatically connecting with your mail servers.

3. If the information is not correct when the automated search is finished, click Stop, fill in the appropriate information, and then click the Re-Test Configuration button. When the information is correct, green indicator icons will appear (see Figure 11.18).

4. Click Create Account. The Mail Account Setup dialog box will close, and Thunderbird will connect to your account.

If you want to add another email account to Thunderbird, you will need to use the Mail Account Setup again. To access it, click the File | New | Mail Account menu command. The Account Settings dialog box will open again.

Receiving and Sending Mail

When you have one account set up in Thunderbird, you are free to send and receive email as long as you are connected to the Internet.

To download messages, click the Get Mail button (or press Ctrl+Shift+T on the keyboard). Your new messages will be downloaded.

As you can see in Figure 11.19, Thunderbird is very streamlined.

To read a message, click a message in the Message list, and its contents will be displayed in the Message pane below. Double-clicking a message will open the

Figure 11.18
When the connection is good, Thunderbird will inform you.

Folders   Message List   Message Pane

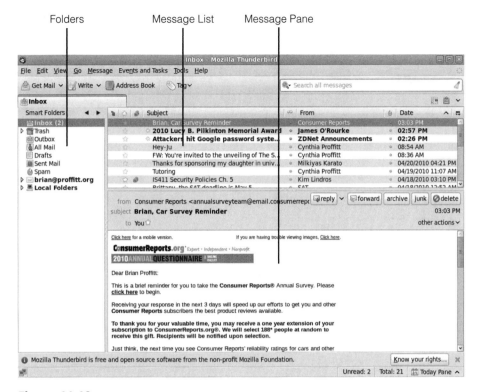

Figure 11.19
The Thunderbird window.

message in its own message tab (see Figure 11.20), complete with a set of tools to use on the message.

After you have read an email, you will note that it is no longer bold in the Message list.

To act on a message, you can reply, reply all, or forward it. To reply to the *sender* of the message only:

1. Select a message to which to reply. The message will be displayed in the Message pane.

2. Click Reply. A preaddressed Compose: Re: message window will open.

3. Type your reply in the body of the message.

4. Click Send. The message window will close, and the message will appear in the Unsent folder until it is sent to the SMTP server.

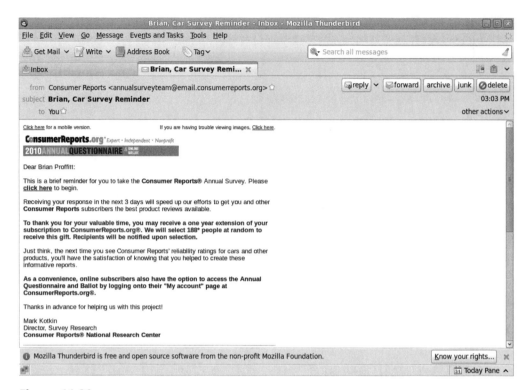

Figure 11.20
A message tab in Thunderbird.

If the message was sent to you and other people, you can send a reply to all the recipients and the sender.

1. Select a message to reply to all recipients. The message will be displayed in the Message pane.

2. Click Reply All. A preaddressed Compose: Re: message window will open.

3. Type your reply in the body of the message.

4. Click Send. The message window will close, and the message will appear in the Unsent folder until it is sent to the SMTP server.

If you want to forward a message to someone else, it's just as easy.

1. Select a message to forward. The message will be displayed in the Message pane.

2. Click Forward. A preaddressed Compose: Fwd: message window will open.

3. Type an additional message in the body of the message.

4. Click Send. The message window will close, and the message will appear in the Unsent folder until it is sent to the SMTP server.

If you want to send a new message to a single or multiple recipients, follow these steps.

1. Click Write. A Write window will open (see Figure 11.21).

2. Type an email address in the To field.

3. If you need to enter another recipient, click another address field and type the address in.

4. Select the Address type (To, Cc, Bcc, etc.) for the additional address.

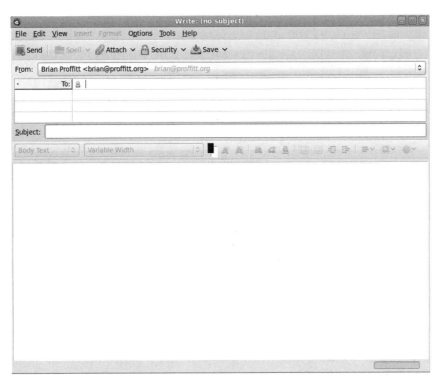

Figure 11.21
A new Write window.

5. Type a subject.

6. Type a message in the body.

7. Click Send. The message window will close, and the message will appear in the Unsent folder until it is sent to the SMTP server.

Organizing Mail

Like any email client, it is very easy to get your Inbox full of lots of stuff you may not want to keep around. Let's take a quick tour of some organizational methods.

If you click the View drop-down list, you will see a list of categories to filter the Message list. Click those as you desire to see the results in your Inbox.

You can also sort messages based on the criteria of the columns in the Message list. If you want to sort by date, click the Date column header. A down arrow will appear in the header button, and the messages will be listed from earliest to most recent down the screen. Clicking the Date header again will change the sort order from most recent to earliest. You can do this for any column header.

Folders are also a really useful tool in Thunderbird, just as with Evolution.

Creating a folder is easy.

1. Right-click the Inbox folder. A context menu will appear.

2. Select the New Folder menu command. The New Folder dialog box will open.

3. Type a folder name.

4. Click OK. The New Folder dialog box will close, and the new folder will be added to the Inbox.

Once you have folders created, you can set up filters in Thunderbird, too. And you can also choose a representative message and build the filter from that point.

1. Click the example message.

2. Select the Message | Create Filter from Message menu command. The Filter Rules dialog box will appear (see Figure 11.22).

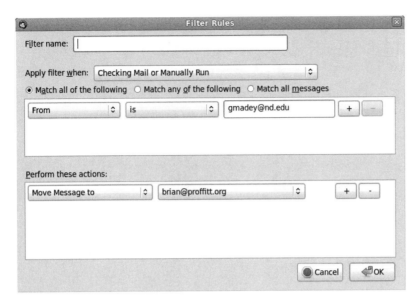

Figure 11.22
Creating a new filter rule.

3. Confirm or edit the filter name.

4. Confirm or edit the selection criteria.

5. Confirm that the Move Message To option is selected.

6. Click the Local Folders drop-down list and select the desired folder.

7. Click OK. The Filter Rules dialog box will close, and the Message Filters dialog box will appear (see Figure 11.23).

You can go ahead and close this dialog box. To run the filter on your existing Inbox messages, select the Tools | Run Filters on Folder menu command.

Protecting Your Inbox

Like Evolution, Thunderbird uses an adaptive Bayesian filter to sort through junk mail. But, unlike Evolution, you have more control over the junk mail controls.

If you select the Tools | Run Junk Mail Controls on Folder menu command, the Junk Mail Control will run.

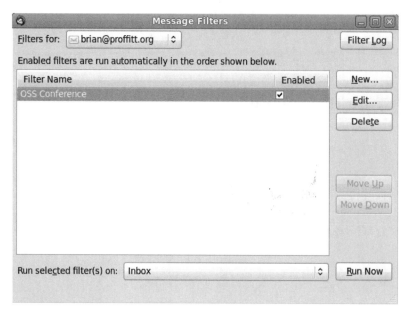

Figure 11.23
Message filters.

The only tab you need to worry about is the one selected: Settings. On this page, you can determine a little better what constitutes junk mail and also determine what to do with junk mail you've marked yourself.

Remember, no filter is foolproof, and you need to check the Junk folder periodically to make sure that nothing genuine has gotten tagged as spam.

Conclusion

There is a lot more to email these days than just reading and writing. With this medium becoming so integrated in our daily lives, it's good to see that there are excellent tools in Fedora that can make email use easy.

In Chapter 12, "Messaging Tools," you will learn about an even newer form of communication available in Fedora: instant messaging and Internet phone calls.

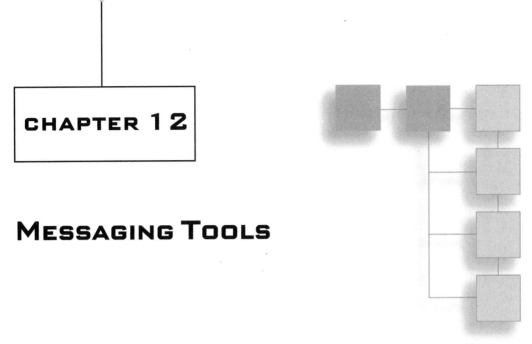

CHAPTER 12

MESSAGING TOOLS

When you come right down to it, the invention of the Internet was really meant as a way for scientists in academic and government environments to communicate vast amounts of data with each other in a very quick and reliable manner. The military saw uses for this kind of global network, too, which is why the U.S. Department of Defense sponsored the early DARPAnet infrastructure that would eventually become the Internet.

The kind of data they needed to transfer was voluminous and needed to be securely moved back in forth in a hurry; something that the phone system could not provide. So it comes with some irony that after all is said and done, companies are turning the Internet into another global voice network, just like the phone system.

Instantaneous communication is a really wonderful thing, which most of us take for granted. Imagine, you can pick up a cell phone, conduct an instant messaging (IM) session, or (more recently) use Voice over IP (VoIP) technology and communicate with someone thousands of miles away. To people living just 50 years ago, this would border on magic. Our children have all grown up with such advances, and we've adapted fairly well, so it's hard to step back and appreciate how cool this really is.

In this chapter, you will find out how Fedora provides the tools to conduct IM and VoIP conversations via the Internet, specifically learning how to:

- Obtain your own IM account
- Use Empathy to conduct an IM session
- Call anyone in the world with Skype

Using Empathy

Instant messaging, as we know it today, is actually a conglomeration of a variety of technologies. First, there was the Internet Relay Chat (IRC), the stream-of-consciousness chat sessions in which many users could participate at the same time. A little bit later, as private networking providers like America Online or Prodigy grew in popularity, they featured their own versions of chat sessions, although these chat sessions were between just two users at a time: a private chat session that was dubbed by these network providers as *instant messaging*.

Today, almost all of these types of instant text communications, whether in IRC, in an IM session, or through text messaging on cell phones, are given the moniker "instant messaging."

Empathy is a software client that allows you to connect to a huge variety of IM networks. These networks are simply different "channels" of IM that are available to users, much like the networks on your cable TV. The difference is, with Empathy, you can monitor and have conversations on many different networks at the same time.

The networks to which you can connect with Empathy include:

- AIM

- Facebook Chat

- Gadu-Gadu

- Google Talk

- GroupWise

- ICQ

- Jabber

- Internet Relay Chat (IRC)

- MSN

- MySpace

- QQ

- Yahoo!

- Zephyr

As you can see, that's a lot of flexibility, so there is a certain sense to the name *Empathy,* which means the ability to intuit and share another's emotions, regardless of language.

There are two steps that have to occur before you can conduct an IM or chat session on any of these networks. You need to get yourself an account on one of these networks (if you don't have one already), and you need to configure that account in Empathy.

The really great thing is that you can set up multiple accounts in Empathy and have them running all at once. If you are so inclined, you can hold many conversations with different friends and colleagues at the same time.

Getting an IM Account

With all of the protocols listed in the previous section, it's a good chance that you will already have an account on one of these private networks. If you do, gather your login information and skip ahead to the next section, "Signing On," to begin your Empathy session.

For those users who have not acquired an account on one of these networks, let's walk through setting up a Google Talk account. Google Talk is free to any Internet user who signs up, and a Google account will enable you to use many other features from the search engine company, such as Google Docs and Maps.

There are two ways to sign up for a Google account: you can use an existing email address or create a Gmail account first, which has the advantage of giving you the option to create a custom Google ID that can act as your personal "handle" on Google Talk and other Google services. In this example, you'll create a Gmail account and then a Talk account. If you already have a Gmail or Google account, skip ahead to the "Signing On" section.

First, connect to the Internet and open Firefox. Then follow these steps:

1. Type www.google.com/accounts/NewAccount?service=mail in the Location bar and press Enter. The Create a Google Account - Gmail page will appear (see Figure 12.1).

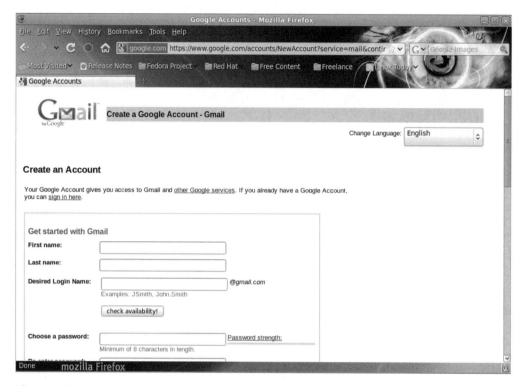

Figure 12.1
Create a Gmail account.

2. Fill in all of the fields on the page, making sure that you click the Check Availability button to confirm the login you want is available.

Name Flexibility

Try to be flexible with your desired login name choices. So many users have signed up for Google, it's sometimes hard to get your first choice of a login name.

3. After the fields are correctly filled in, click the I accept. Create My Account button on the bottom of the page. The Introduction to Gmail page will appear (see Figure 12.2).

4. Click the Show Me My Account link in the upper-right corner. You may see a promotional screen for Google Buzz.

5. Click the Just Go to My Inbox, I'll Try Buzz Later link at the bottom of the page. The initial Gmail page for the account will appear (see Figure 12.3).

Figure 12.2
The initial Gmail account screen.

Figure 12.3
The main Gmail page.

Now that the Gmail account is created, you will automatically have access to the Google Talk (or Chat) feature, so you can now sign on to Empathy.

Signing On

The first time you sign on to Empathy, you will be prompted to add information for at least one account before the application will start. Using the information from a pre-existing account or from the steps you took in the previous section, signing up is fast and painless.

1. Select the Applications | Internet | Empathy IM Client menu command. The Messaging and VoIP Accounts Assistant dialog box will open (see Figure 12.4).

2. Confirm the Yes, I'll Enter My Account Details Now option is selected and click Forward. The Enter Your Account Details page will appear (see Figure 12.5).

3. Select the Google Talk chat account option and fill in the Google ID and Password fields.

4. Confirm the No, That's All for Now option is selected and click Forward. The Please Enter Personal Details page will appear.

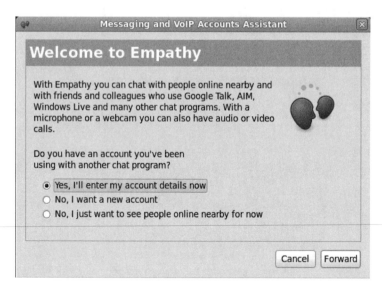

Figure 12.4
Entering accounts in Empathy.

Figure 12.5
Account configuration in Empathy.

5. Click Apply. The Messaging and VoIP Accounts Assistant dialog box will close, and the main Empathy Contact List window will open, as shown in Figure 12.6.

Figure 12.6
No contacts . . . yet.

Instant Messaging with Empathy

When you first create an account, you will be confronted with a temporary but unpleasant thought: you have no contacts.

Contacts are Empathy-speak for the online personas of your friends or associates. Empathy doesn't let you just IM anyone. You have to specify the person you want to IM first. Once you have people in your contact list, Empathy shows which are online and whether they are available, busy, or offline.

Adding a contact is the first step. Many people with Google Talk or other IM accounts send their contact information out via email or post it on their Web sites.

1. Select the Chat | Add Contact menu command. The New Contact dialog box will open (see Figure 12.7).

2. Type the identifier for the person you want to connect with. This will be their full Google Gmail address. You can add an alias (such as their given name) if you want.

3. Click Add. The New Contact dialog box will close, and after the requested contact verifies they know you, they will be added to your Contact List, as displayed in Figure 12.8.

The contact *Kent* displayed in Figure 12.8 is actually available, as the default icon is a bright green circle, and there is no "away notification" associated with the Kent icon. If Kent were online but not available to IM, a red triangle icon and an away message similar to the one shown in Figure 12.9 would be present.

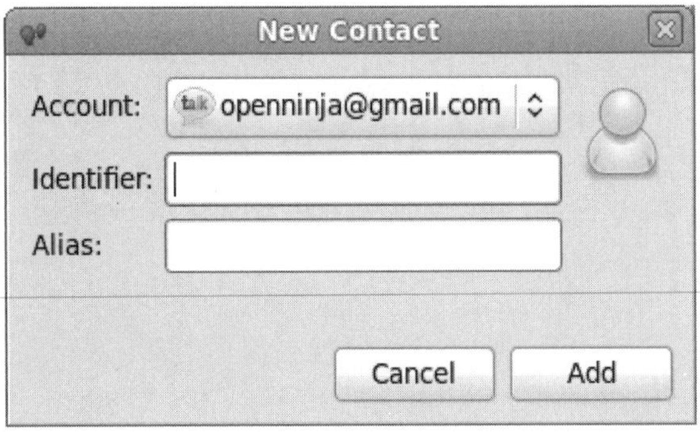

Figure 12.7
Add a contact.

Figure 12.8
A contact for your list.

Figure 12.9
Sometimes buddies are cranky.

If the contact were not connected to Google Talk (or another network), the icon would display an Offline status.

If you want chat with a contact, follow this set of steps.

1. Double-click a contact you want to IM. The conversation window for that contact will open (see Figure 12.10).

2. In the input line at the bottom of the conversation window, type a message to the contact and press Enter.

3. Depending on your contact, the reply could come back very quickly or in a few minutes and will be displayed in the IM window (see Figure 12.11).

4. If, in the course of a conversation, you would like to send a file to your contact, click the Contact | Send File menu command. The Select a File dialog box will open.

5. Navigate to the file you want to send and click Send. The File Transfers dialog box will open (see Figure 12.12).

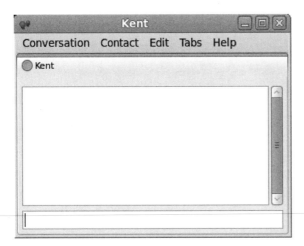

Figure 12.10
Starting an IM conversation.

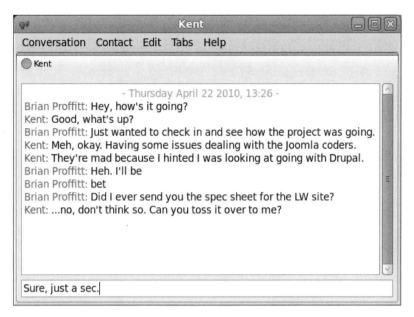

Figure 12.11
An IM conversation in progress.

Figure 12.12
Sending a file.

6. The recipient of the file will be directed to choose whether to accept this transfer. If they do accept, the transfer process will complete automatically (see Figure 12.13).

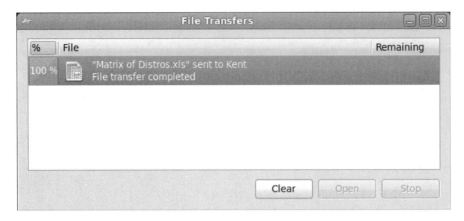

Figure 12.13
A successful transfer.

7. Click Clear to close the File Transfers dialog box.

8. If someone wants to send a file to you, a notification icon that looks like a paper airplane will appear in the upper panel (see Figure 12.14).

Security Concerns

Always make sure you know who you're talking to and what file they are supposed to be sending. Never accept files from anyone you don't know or that you were not expecting.

9. Click the icon if you were expecting this file. The Select a Destination dialog box will open, as shown in Figure 12.15.

10. Navigate to where you want to store the file and click Save. The file will be downloaded, and the File Transfers dialog box will open to mark the progress and completion.

11. Click Clear. The File Transfers dialog box will close.

12. To end the conversation, simply send your goodbyes and close the conversation window.

If you want to set yourself as away (unavailable), click the status drop-down list at the top of the Contact List window and select the Away option.

To create a custom away message, click the Custom Message option in the status drop-down list and fill in the status field on top of the Contact List.

Incoming File Notification

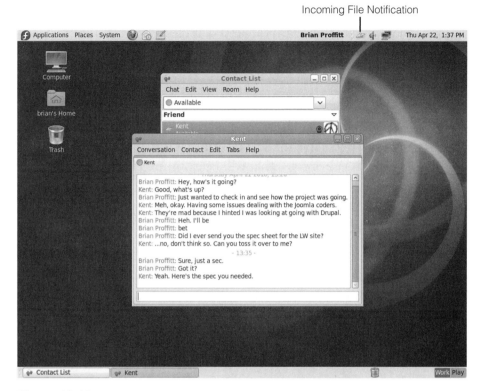

Figure 12.14
An incoming file notification.

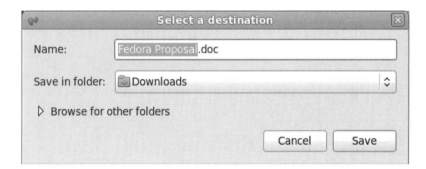

Figure 12.15
Saving the incoming file.

Using Skype

Skype is a popular application that enables VoIP communication, as well as video conferencing, if you have a webcam for your Fedora PC.

Using Fedora, you can talk or video conference to anyone in the world who is using a Skype client. For a pay-as-you-go fee, you can also dial up any regular phone.

At a minimum, to really get the benefit of this application, your Fedora PC will need a functioning sound card, with speakers, as well as a working microphone. This will get you voice communication capability, which will be very useful.

Because it is proprietary software, Skype is not available through PackageKit. However, the Skype developers have made a custom Fedora package that will let you install Skype very quickly, a process that will be examined in the next section.

Installing and Configuring Skype

Installing Skype is a very simple process: just download the RPM from the Skype Web site at www.skype.com and run it.

1. Click the Applications | Internet | Skype menu command. The Skype application will open, with a license agreement screen.

2. Click I Agree. The Skype window will open.

3. Click the Don't Have a Skype Name Yet? link. The Create a New Skype Account dialog box will appear (see Figure 12.16).

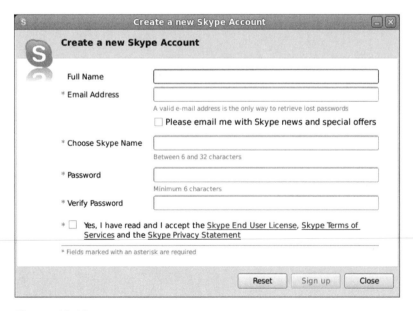

Figure 12.16
The initial Skype start-up screen for new users.

4. Complete the information on the screen and click Sign Up. The Create a New Skype Account welcome page will appear, and the Skype window will open (see Figure 12.17).

5. Click the Edit Your Profile So Friends Can Find You link. The Profile dialog box will open.

6. Fill in the appropriate fields and click Update. The Profile dialog box will close.

7. Click the Make a Test Call to Check Your Sound Configuration link. The Skype test call window will open (see Figure 12.18).

8. Follow the verbal instructions on the test call. If all goes well, you should hear your own voice from your microphone.

Can You Hear Me Now?

If you have any trouble with the sound configuration, check out Chapter 7, "Making Things Work," for more assistance.

Figure 12.17
The Skype welcome screen.

Figure 12.18
The test call will confirm that your sound and microphones are working.

Reaching Out and Touching Someone

Making Skype calls is very easy. Just find a contact and then click a button to connect.

1. Click the Add or Search for Skype Contacts icon at the bottom of the Skype window. The Add a Skype Contact dialog box will open (see Figure 12.19).

2. Type the name of the contact in the top field. You can use their full name, their Skype ID, or their email address.

3. Click Search. Skype will search for the person.

4. When the contact is found, click the contact and then Add Contact. The Say Hello dialog box will open (see Figure 12.20).

5. Click OK. The Say Hello dialog box will close, and the new contact will be added to your contact list.

Figure 12.19
Finding someone to talk to.

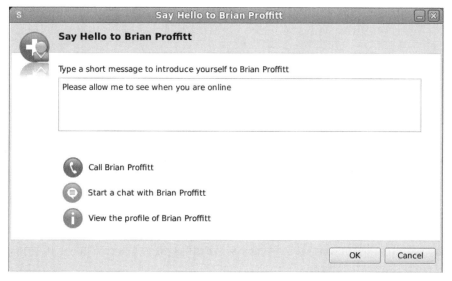

Figure 12.20
Introduce yourself to a contact.

Figure 12.21
Call a friend with Skype.

6. To start a call, click the green telephone icon next to the contact's name. The Call With window will open (see Figure 12.21).

7. To end the call, click the red hang-up icon. The Call With window will close, and you will be disconnected.

Conclusion

Now you are ready to communicate instantly with a whole new host of people using your Fedora PC. The advantages for business of such communications are enormous, and it is well worth your time to learn.

But the PC is not all about work, especially a Fedora PC with its advanced multimedia capabilities. In Chapter 13, "Multimedia Tools," you will learn how to enjoy your favorite multimedia presentations, whether they are music or movies. Get ready to rock the Fedora way.

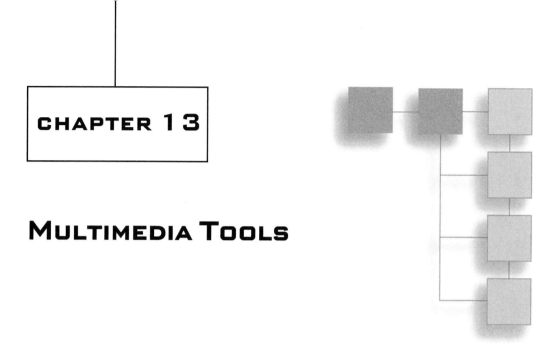

CHAPTER 13

MULTIMEDIA TOOLS

Computers were never really designed to handle audio and video. This capability was more of an afterthought that occurred when computer processors got really fast and video monitors came into existence. At this point, more users began noticing the similarities between computers and televisions.

If a computer has a screen and a television has a screen, folks wondered, why couldn't they both display pictures? Never mind the fact that computers and televisions were about as technologically alike as an elephant and a rhododendron. The new monitors represented a challenge to programmers: how to bring animation and video to these new devices.

Was all this multimedia? In the strictest sense, yes. Machines designed to create one form of media were being used to create another form. More than one medium on one device certainly qualifies as multimedia. Of course, what we think of multimedia is full-motion video with stereo sound blasting out of our speakers.

Sights and sounds on your computer are very necessary things, even though your boss might not always agree. The ability to play music and video files on a PC seems, at first, an indulgence. More and more, however, business workers are asked to put together multimedia presentations and interactive Web sites for their employers. It makes increasing sense to have that functionality built in to modern operating systems.

And it doesn't hurt to be able to play some tunes while typing that quarterly report for the boss, either.

In this chapter, you will review the following:

- Why some multimedia is not ready to play out of the box

- Playing CDs

- Playing MP3 files, including podcasts

- Getting tuned into Internet radio

- Burning CDs

- Playing video files

The Big Deal: Formats and Codecs

One of the biggest problems with running Linux in general is coming up against an incompatible file format. Many people who encounter this problem often blame the software developers for not being able to put together a decent program. In reality, it's not the developers' fault. It is actually not that hard to put together an application that will run MP3s or Windows Media files. The problem lies in the licenses that these formats often carry.

If you recall from Chapter 1, "What is Fedora?", there was a discussion on the nature of Fedora's free and open source software licenses and a comparison with how they worked versus proprietary licenses. When software companies use a proprietary license, they want to get paid when someone uses their software. There is nothing inherently bad about this—everyone's got to eat. But there is often conflict about this between the free and proprietary software worlds, and unfortunately it's the user who gets caught in the middle.

The conflict centers on the way developers in both camps want to get paid. (Because open source software developers have to eat, too.) Proprietary vendors have the revenue model that says: when people use our software, they need to pay us for using it because we invented it. The open source revenue model flips that around: when people use our software, we'll let them have it for free and make money providing support for our software.

The open source people would gladly pay the proprietary developers to use their software, but since they don't charge license fees for their open software, there's nothing to actually give to the proprietary vendors. There's the revenue generated from support, of course, but the profit margin is so tight for the pay-for-support-and-updates business model that there is still very little to send to the proprietary vendors.

The problem is exacerbated by what proprietary vendors have identified as theirs. It's not just the software application that's copyrighted; sometimes, it's the actual format of the file that's protected by an individual or company. The popular MP3 format is one example. Thomson Consumer Electronics has made several legal claims that it owns the patent for the code to play the MP3 file format (known as a *codec,* which stands for enCOder/DECoder) and has vigorously pursued software developers who make MP3 players and don't pay Thomson a fee for those applications.

Some software developers have just avoided the legal issues and moved to another format. Linux developers, for instance, prefer the open source Ogg Vorbis audio format. And some developers, like Apple, have gone ahead and settled in some manner with Thomson.

But there's still a lot of MP3 files out there, and as PC users, we want to be able to listen to them. Fedora 13 does not officially support any software that plays MP3s because of these ongoing legal pursuits, but there are ways to obtain software plug-ins to run MP3 files in some of the included audio software.

Some of you may be wondering at this point if this is illegal. While there is still ongoing patent litigation, and there are no injunctions for MP3 player inventors to stop what they are doing, then users are not going to be penalized for installing code on their systems.

Unfortunately, this is not the case with the codecs used to play DVDs on a PC. The Motion Picture Association of America has pushed through litigation in Congress that makes it illegal for anyone in the U.S. to use unlicensed software to play DVD movies. Note, that's *use* the software, not just *make.* So, if you are residing in the U.S., you cannot legally use software in Linux to watch DVDs, even though there's perfectly good software to do it. But since that DVD-on-Linux player software is given away, its makers are unable to afford a license to use the DVD codecs. Also, the very act of watching a DVD means you have to decrypt the content, which is illegal to do in the U.S.

It seems kind of strange, because all Fedora users want to do is watch a movie from a DVD they bought and paid for. But while the MPAA is hell-bent on battling movie piracy, which is a laudable goal, innocent users, like those who run Linux systems, could get caught in the crossfire.

For the record, it should be noted that libdvdcss has not been tested in any court decision, and thus far the movie industry has been reluctant to initiate any real legal fight—possibly because it knows most users just want to watch movies they own, not steal them.

Audio on Fedora

There's something nice about being able to stick a CD into your computer and listen to it, with no muss or fuss. But it's not just CDs that get music to your PC these days: there are plenty of Internet sites out there that will let you purchase MP3 versions of your favorite tunes, as well as streaming Internet "radio stations." Podcasts are still popular, too: they are MP3 files put together by news organizations or bloggers, which can be played on computer or portable MP3 players.

Let's start listening.

Playing CDs

Audio CDs, fortunately, are encoded with an Advanced Audio Coding format (AAC) that is a very open standard, so Fedora (and other Linux distributions) has no legal issues about playing them. Even better, AAC files are higher quality than MP3s, and Fedora includes some robust applications to actually enhance your music collecting experience.

There are two applications in Fedora that will play CDs: Sound Juicer and Rhythmbox. Sound Juicer is a music player and extractor that will play and copy a CD's contents.

Rhythmbox is a full-featured media application, analogous to Apple's iTunes or Real's RealPlayer. It will also play CDs for you, although not by default. It is designed for handling and organizing music files stored on your system or out on the Internet.

What many Fedora users usually do is use both applications in tandem. Sound Juicer is used to copy files from audio CDs and store them in a format that takes up less space on your hard drive. Rhythmbox can then be used to organize your music into playlists for your listening pleasure.

Of course, how you use these applications is up to you. Some users will just want to listen to music on one CD at a time—maybe their hard drive is nearly full with other files. In that case, the simple interface of Sound Juicer is perfect.

1. Insert an audio CD into your CD-ROM drive. The Audio Disc icon will appear on your desktop, and the Audio Disc dialog box will open (see Figure 13.1).

2. Select the Open Audio CD Extractor option and click OK. The Sound Juicer window will open and query the MusicBrainz Web site for the playlist and title information for this CD (see Figure 13.2).

The Brainz of the Outfit

MusicBrainz is a community music site that attempts to create a comprehensive music information database. Albums, artists, tracks, and a whole host of information are collected there by volunteers.

3. Click Play. The CD will begin to play (see Figure 13.3).

4. To move to another track, select the Disc menu and then the appropriate command. You can also double-click the desired track number to move right to that track of the CD.

5. Click Pause. The playback will stop.

If playing a CD is all you want to do, then at this point, you're all set. But if you have room on your hard drive and a little extra time, why not protect your CD from wear and tear and save the files to your PC? This will also give you the advantage of being able to play your music if the CDs aren't handy.

Figure 13.1
Decide how you want to handle the CD.

Figure 13.2
Getting track information for an audio CD.

Figure 13.3
Playing audio CD music.

To accomplish this, simply click the Extract button. The extraction process will begin with a status report displayed on the bottom of the Sound Juicer window (see Figure 13.4). After a few minutes, the CD's contents will be extracted.

Where to Put Your Music

Sound Juicer extracts CD files into your home directory in artist/album directories. If you want to change where extracted files are stored, select the Edit | Preferences menu command and change the Music Folder setting.

After extraction, the ripped files are now stored on your hard drive, initially in Ogg Vorbis format. If you have no more CDs to play or extract, you can close the Sound Juicer application and remove any CD from your CD-ROM drive.

Once you have a collection of music files on your Fedora PC, then Rhythmbox is the application to use.

Opening Rhythmbox

The first time you start Rhythmbox, you will see a wizard that asks if you want to import any music files on your computer into a centralized music library. If you have music on your computer, follow the instructions in the series of wizard dialogs to import the files into your library for the first time.

You can start by importing the music files you just extracted with Sound Juicer into Rhythmbox's library of music.

Figure 13.4
Extracting audio CD music.

1. Select the Applications | Sound & Video | Rhythmbox Music Player menu command. The Rhythmbox window will open (see Figure 13.5).

2. Select the Music | Import Folder menu command. The Import Folder into Library dialog box will open, as shown in Figure 13.6.

3. Navigate to the artist's folder for the extracted music and click Open. The music will be loaded into Rhythmbox's library.

To play a song or album or even all the songs by a particular artist, you can use the default Browse mode in Rhythmbox to narrow down the songs you want to play. At any time, just click Play, and the first song in the track list will be displayed.

■ Click the artist you have interest in listening to. All the tracks for the artist will be displayed in the track list.

■ Click the album you want to hear. All the tracks for the album will be displayed in the track list.

■ Double-click any individual track. The song will begin to play (see Figure 13.7).

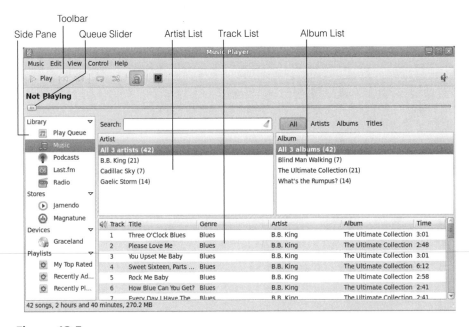

Figure 13.5
Getting into the Rhythmbox.

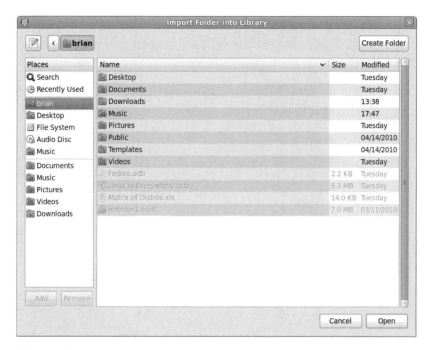

Figure 13.6
Importing music files.

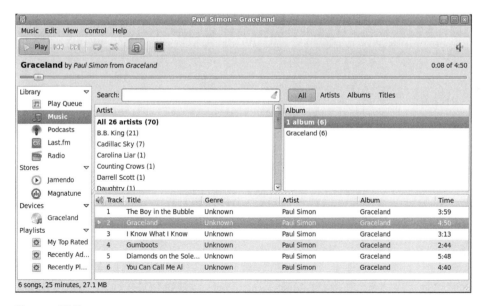

Figure 13.7
Playing music in Rhythmbox.

If you prefer to hear only certain songs in a certain order, you can create a playlist in Rhythmbox. Playlists are not only good for organizing music, but they also need to be created so you can burn an audio CD.

1. Select the Music | Playlist | New Playlist menu command. Rhythmbox will be configured to playlist mode (see Figure 13.8).

2. Type a name for your playlist and press Enter. The name will appear in the playlist list.

3. Click the Music option in the Library folder. Rhythmbox will shift to Browse mode, displaying the contents of the music library.

4. Click and drag an artist, album, or individual song to the new playlist and release the mouse button. The playlist will be populated with the selected songs.

Playing MP3s

As mentioned earlier in this chapter, Fedora's audio applications don't have the capability to play or create MP3 files. When music is extracted from CDs, for

Figure 13.8
Beginning the playlist creation.

example, Sound Juicer saves the files in the Ogg Vorbis format by default. If you only wanted to play that music on Fedora, you would be all set. But not all portable music players can handle Ogg files; they need MP3. Plus, many podcasts are still stored as MP3 files.

Clearly, it's in your best interest to make sure that your applications can deal with MP3 files. Here's how to do that.

1. Select the System | Administration | Add/Remove Software menu command. The PackageKit window will open (see Figure 13.9).

2. Type gstreamer in the Search field and click Find. The results will be displayed (see Figure 13.10).

Checking Where You Are

At this point, you should have the RPMFusion repositories added to PackageKit, so it will be able to find the files you need. Refer to the "Adding Repositories" section of Chapter 6 if you have not yet done this step.

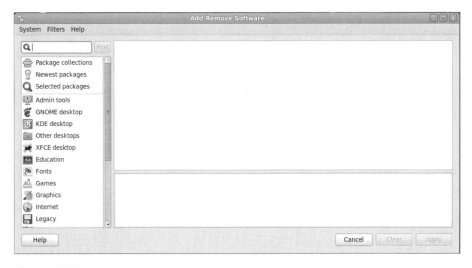

Figure 13.9
Application installation.

3. Click the following options to select them:

   ■ gstreamer

   ■ gstreamer-plugins-bad-free

- gstreamer-plugins-base

- gstreamer-plugins-good

- gstreamer-plugins-ugly

- gstreamer-python

- gstreamer-rtsp

- gstreamer-tools

- PackageKit-gstreamer-plug-in

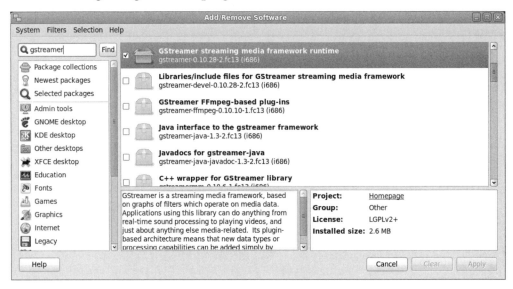

Figure 13.10
Narrowing down the list.

The Good, the Bad, and the Ugly

No, it's not a Clint Eastwood movie revival. "Good," "bad," and "ugly" refer to the levels of freedom each of these plug-ins has in terms of licensing. Codecs in the good plug-in are completely free, while the bad plug-in's codecs are more restrictive, and the ugly codecs are completely proprietary. It is not, it should be emphasized, a reflection of their performance.

4. Click Apply. You will be asked for your administrative password.

5. Type your password and click OK. PackageKit will install the software automatically.

The previous steps will enable Rhythmbox (and any other media application you might install later) to play MP3 files. Now you need to configure Sound Juicer to create MP3 files when it extracts music from CDs.

1. Select the System | Administration | Add/Remove Software menu command. The PackageKit window will open.

2. Type lame-libs and click Find. The results will be displayed in PackageKit.

3. Click the lame-libs package to select it.

4. Click Apply. You will be asked for your administrative password.

5. Type your password and click OK. PackageKit will install the software automatically.

Now, you are set to extract CDs into MP3 files, which you can play on any MP3 player. First, you need to specify this output format in Sound Juicer.

1. In Sound Juicer, select the Edit | Preferences menu command. The Preferences dialog box will open, as shown in Figure 13.11.

2. Click the Edit Profiles button in the Format section. The Edit GNOME Audio Profiles dialog box will open (see Figure 13.12).

Figure 13.11
Sound Juicer Preferences.

Figure 13.12
GNOME Audio Profiles.

3. Confirm the CD Quality, MP3 profile is in place. If it is, you are finished configuring Sound Juicer. If not, click New to open the New Profile dialog box.

4. Type MP3 and click Create. The New Profile dialog box will close, and the MP3 profile will appear in the list of GNOME audio profiles.

5. Click MP3 and click Edit. The Editing Profile dialog box will open.

6. Type the following command into the GSteamer Pipeline field.

```
audio/x-raw-int,rate=44100,channels=2 ! lame name=enc vbr=0 bitrate=192 !
id3v2mux
```

7. Type mp3 in the File Extension field.

8. Click the Active check box and click Close. The Editing Profile dialog box will close.

9. Close all dialog boxes and restart Sound Juicer. The MP3 option should now appear in the Output Format field.

Playing Podcasts

There are two things that make up a podcast: first is the audio file, usually in MP3 format. Second is the podcast's feed, which is essentially no different from the Web feeds discussed in Chapter 10, "Surfing the Web." A *feed* is a special Web page that lists new files on a periodic basis, allowing feed clients (such as Firefox's Live Bookmarks feature) to come along and check for new files.

Rhythmbox has its own feed reader, only it monitors feeds of podcasts. All you need to do is point Rhythmbox to the right place to pick up the feed, and it will do the rest.

Finding Podcasts

Finding podcasts on any subject matter that interests you is almost too easy. Visit Google and run a search on any subject that interests you and add "podcast" to the search terms. It should not take you long.

After you have found a podcast feed to link to, you will need to add the URL of the feed to Rhythmbox. Here's a way to do it with minimal typing.

1. In Firefox, find a page with a podcast link.

Recognizing Podcast Addresses

In case you aren't sure which URL to use, podcast feed URLs almost always end with an .xml extension.

2. Right-click the link and select Copy Link Location on the context menu that appears.

3. In Rhythmbox, click Podcasts in the Library list.

4. Click the Subscribe to a New Podcast Feed button. The New Podcast Feed dialog box will open.

5. Press Ctrl+V to paste the copied URL from Firefox in the URL of Podcast Feed field and click Add. The podcast will begin to load the most recent files (see Figure 13.13).

6. After a podcast is downloaded, click the appropriate podcast and click Play. The podcast will begin playback.

When you want to get the latest podcasts, click the Update All Feeds button.

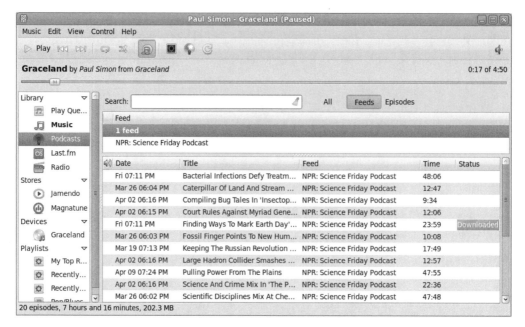

Figure 13.13
Downloading podcasts.

Tuning into Internet Radio

Streaming media is a fancy term for online multimedia content that is downloaded to your Fedora PC but not actually stored there. It is the primary method used by Internet radio to deliver content.

This method offers two big advantages. The first advantage is for the end user. As streaming media is sent to the client machine, it is processed immediately by the streaming media application, which gives the end user instant playback without having to wait for the entire file to download. After the file is played, the data is deleted, thus saving on precious hard drive space.

The second advantage to this approach is for the producer of the content. Because streaming media cannot be saved by the client, live events such as concerts can be broadcast without the fear of an unscrupulous end user bootlegging the material. Streaming media can also be sent out to many users simultaneously, which makes the broadcast of on-demand events and music possible.

One of the most popular applications of streaming audio is the live broadcast of radio station content on the Internet. Both standard and Internet-only radio stations are widely available on the Internet, many of which are suitable to listen to even on 56K dial-up connections. The sound quality of these radio broadcasts is not exceptionally sharp, but it's no worse than listening to a local station on a small radio. And, if you're listening to a station in Kenya from Wausau, you're doing pretty well already.

Rhythmbox (again) is the tool to use for playing Internet radio stations.

1. In Rhythmbox, click Radio in the Library list.

2. Click any station and click Play (see Figure 13.14).

3. To add a link, click the New Internet Radio Station button. The New Internet Radio Station dialog box will open.

4. Press Ctrl+V to paste the copied URL from Firefox into the URL of Podcast Feed field and click Add. The station will be added to the list of radio stations.

5. Click the station and click Play. The steaming broadcast will begin.

Figure 13.14
Listening to a radio station.

Formatting Station Names

When a station is added, its title appears as the actual URL, which is a bit cumbersome. To edit the entry, right-click the station entry and select Properties from the context menu. In the Properties dialog box that opens, edit the Title and Genre fields to something more manageable.

Backing Up CDs

If you want to protect your collection of original CDs, you can burn a copy onto another CD and use that instead. Rhythmbox can handle this, but it only burns playlists that you have already created. If you just want to burn a copy of an album, creating a playlist and then starting the copy process is a bit roundabout.

Instead, you can use Brasero to handle your CD burning chores.

1. Insert a blank CD-RW into your CD-ROM drive. The Blank CD Disc icon will appear on the desktop.

2. Select the Applications | Sound & Video | Brasero Disc Burner menu command. The Brasero window will open (see Figure 13.15).

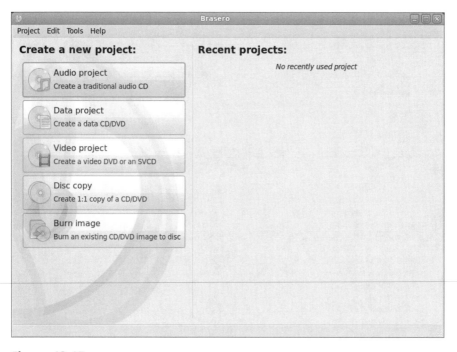

Figure 13.15
The Brasero application.

3. Click Audio Project. The New Audio Disc Project window will appear.

4. Click the Add button. The Select Files dialog box will open.

5. Navigate to the desired files, click to select them, and drag them to the Brasero window.

6. Rearrange the order of the music tracks by clicking and dragging the tracks in the list to a new position.

7. Click the Burn button. The Properties of your CD drive dialog box will open.

8. Click the Burn button. The Burning CD dialog box will open, detailing the progress of the task (see Figure 13.16).

Figure 13.16
Writing an audio disc.

Cancel Is Bad

Do not click Cancel in the middle of the disc-writing process. Your disc will be rendered unusable if the writing is interrupted.

9. When complete, the disc will be ejected from your drive. Click Close in the final message box to complete the process and close all dialog boxes.

Video on Fedora

Music is not the only thing you can find for entertainment on the Internet. You can find movie files in many places as well.

The video content on the Internet has exploded in recent years, thanks to the popularity of sites like YouTube and Hulu. Movies, TV shows, and home movies are just a few clicks away. But when you first install Fedora, you will discover that Firefox will need some help to play movies on these sites (see Figure 13.17).

When you see a screen like the one shown in Figure 13.17, you might be tempted to click the Install Missing Plugins button. Unfortunately, the Linux installation process for the missing Flash plug-in has not been perfected yet, so going this route is not a good idea. Instead, follow these very quick steps to get the Flash plug-in needed for most Internet video sites installed.

1. Select the Applications | System Tools | Terminal menu command. The Terminal window will open.

2. In the Terminal, type su. Enter your administrative password when asked.

Figure 13.17
YouTube movies can't be played without the Flash plug-in.

3. Now enter this command:

```
rpm -Uvh http://linuxdownload.adobe.com/adobe-release/adobe-release-i386-
1.0-1.noarch.rpm
```

This will add the Adobe repository to your Fedora machine.

4. Select the System | Administration | Add/Remove Software menu command. The PackageKit window will open.

5. Type Flash and click Find. The results will be displayed in PackageKit.

6. Click the Flash plug-in package to select it.

7. Click Apply. You will be asked for your administrative password.

8. Type your password and click OK. PackageKit will automatically install the software.

As you can see in Figure 13.18, Flash video playback will start to work immediately in Firefox.

Figure 13.18
A working Flash installation.

If Rhythmbox is the nerve center for audio files, then the VLC Media Player is the center for video files. It can handle many video formats, including DVDs. VLC is included in the RPMFusion repositories, so you can add it to Fedora after installation. You will also need to install a few additional codec files to accommodate DVD playback.

1. Select the System | Administration | Add/Remove Software menu command. The PackageKit window will open.

2. Type vlc and click Find. The results will be displayed in PackageKit.

3. Click the vlc package to select it.

4. Click Apply. You will be asked for your administrative password.

5. Type your password and click OK. PackageKit will automatically install the software.

6. Select the Applications | System Tools | Terminal menu command. The Terminal window will open.

7. In the Terminal, type su. Enter your administrative password when asked.

8. Now enter this command:

```
rpm -ivh http://dl.atrpms.net/all/libdvdcss2-1.2.10-5.fc12.i686.rpm
```

This will add the DVD codecs to your Fedora machine. You will need to restart your Fedora system to complete the installation.

Once the VLC Media Player and the proper codec are installed, you can play almost any movie file format you like, including DVDs.

1. Insert a DVD into your DVD drive. The movie's dialog box will open (see Figure 13.19).

2. Select the Open VLC media player option and click OK. The VLC Media Player control window will open, and the movie will begin to play (see Figure 13.20).

Figure 13.19
Choose how to handle a DVD.

Figure 13.20
Where Fedora users have gone before.

Conclusion

In this chapter, you learned how to use audio and video tools to play most of your favorite multimedia files.

But what if there's this one application on Windows that you just can't bear to part with? Do you have to keep a Windows partition sitting on your machine, taking up hard drive space? Answers to these questions can be found in the next chapter, "Working with Windows."

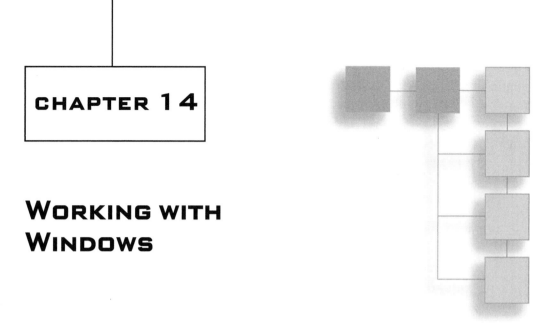

CHAPTER 14

WORKING WITH WINDOWS

One of the biggest fears for anyone moving to a new operating system is "Will my applications work?" For a long time, Windows users could sit back with a certain smugness and deride Linux as a platform that couldn't run the simplest Windows application. Those days are long gone, as many superior applications are available for Fedora natively (OpenOffice.org, Firefox, and Evolution to name a few).

But, let's be fair—sometimes, there's just that one application that you really have to have that has no Linux equivalent, or the Linux equivalent is something you just don't like.

There are three ways to go about solving this problem.

First, you can use an emulator to run Windows software. In software terms, an emulator is an application that mimics another software environment so certain apps can run on it. Emulators act as self-contained simulators of another operating system, and these days they run pretty well. However, there are some drawbacks. No emulator is perfect, and most do better with applications that they are prepared for rather than just any old application that comes along.

Second, you can install Fedora alongside Windows and boot into each of the operating systems separately. That has the advantage of running native Windows applications within a native Windows environment. (Well, if you can call that an advantage.) But, you can only run one operating system at a time: either you are running Fedora, or you are running Windows—not both.

Then there's a third, more attractive option, which will be examined in this chapter: using a virtual machine. With a virtual machine, you will be able to run Windows—or any other operating system for that matter—right inside Fedora. You can share files, cut and paste text from one operating system to another, and run any application you want inside the virtual machine.

In this chapter, you will learn about:

- How virtual machines work

- Where you can find and install a virtual machine free of charge

- The ins and outs of configuring a virtual machine

- How to install Windows on a virtual machine

- The best way to share information between Fedora and a virtual machine

Discussing Virtual Machines

In Chapter 2, "Before You Install Fedora," there was a technical discussion on how partitions work and how they are used to carefully separate one operating system's files from another's, even on the same hard drive.

But while that is true for most operating system installations, there's a different technology available that will allow you to install entire operating systems on the same partition as another operating system.

This technology is called *virtualization,* and it is one of the cutting-edge sectors of the IT world today.

Essentially, virtualization enables a guest operating system to run as a completely self-contained set of files inside a host operating system. All that is needed is a special virtual client application that acts as a "window" through which the guest operating system can be viewed and used.

What makes it even more useful is that, with the proper setup, the guest operating system can avail itself of the same devices that are available to the host operating system. In other words, if your Fedora computer has a DVD drive, the guest operating system can access it just like Fedora.

One of the simplest virtual clients to install for Fedora is VirtualBox from Oracle. VirtualBox comes in two versions: a commercial version and an open source version. The open source version has every feature of the commercial version except USB support and a remote display protocol server that enables users to connect remotely to a virtual machine.

Both versions of VirtualBox are free, but it's important to decide which one you are going to get beforehand, because virtual machines created for one version will not run in the other. The commercial version is free for personal evaluation, but if you need to deploy it commercially, you will need to get a $50/seat perpetual license. The open VirtualBox, known as VirtualBox OSE, is always free, however you use it.

For personal use, you should use the commercial version because the USB support is convenient to have.

Installing VirtualBox

With Fedora, only VirtualBox OSE is included, so you will need to download the packages directly from the VirtualBox site.

1. In Firefox, visit www.virtualbox.org/wiki/Linux_Downloads. The Download VirtualBox for Linux Hosts page will appear.

2. Click the link for the appropriate version of Fedora. The Opening VirtualBox dialog box will open.

3 2 - o r   6 4 - b i t ?

Computer processors may come in 32- or 64-bit versions. Usually when you install software on Fedora, the processor type doesn't matter because PackageKit already knows what software to get for you. When you install software from a third-party source, you will need to know what kind of processor you have. To find out, open a Terminal window and type uname -m. If i386 or i686 is reported back, you have a 32-bit machine and should use the i386 link. If amd64 is reported, you are using a 64-bit PC and should use that link for downloading VirtualBox.

3. Confirm the Open with Package Installer option is selected and click OK. The file will be downloaded, and the Do You Want to Install This File? dialog box will open.

4. Click Install. VirtualBox will be installed, but you will have to authenticate with the administrative password at least once.

After the installation is complete, it is important to make sure that your username is added to the vboxusers group so you can run and connect to the virtual machines.

1. In a Terminal window, type su. You will be promoted for your administrative password.

2. Enter your administrative password.

3. Type:

```
usermod -G vboxusers -a yourusername
```

where *username* is your username.

4. To make sure VirtualBox has all of the tools it needs to run, also type:

```
yum install make automake autoconf gcc kernel-devel dkms
```

This will enable better integration with Fedora and the VirtualBox system.

The first time you start VirtualBox, you will need to go through a very brief initial configuration routine.

1. Click the Applications | System Tools | Sun VirtualBox menu command. The VirtualBox License dialog box will open (see Figure 14.1).

2. Read the license and when you reach the end, click the I Agree button. The VirtualBox window will open (see Figure 14.2).

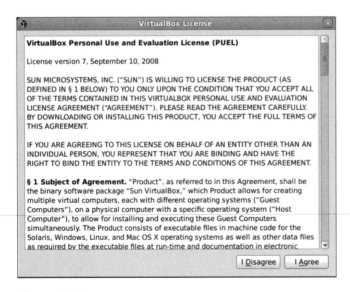

Figure 14.1
The VirtualBox license.

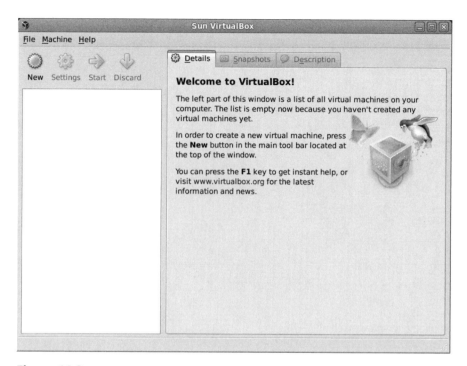

Figure 14.2
The VirtualBox window.

Configuring a Virtual Machine

Before you can install a guest operating system on a virtual machine, you first must build a virtual machine upon which to install the guest system. Don't worry, you're not going to have to get out the pliers and screwdrivers—remember, this is a virtual machine, and VirtualBox will do all the work for you.

1. Click the Applications | System Tools | Sun VirtualBox menu command. The VirtualBox window will open.

2. Click the New button. The Create New Virtual Machine dialog box will open (see Figure 14.3).

3. Click Next. The VM Name and OS Type page, shown in Figure 14.4, will appear.

4. Enter a name for your virtual machine. For this example, we are installing Windows 7, but set the operating system and version to whatever is appropriate for the OS you want to install.

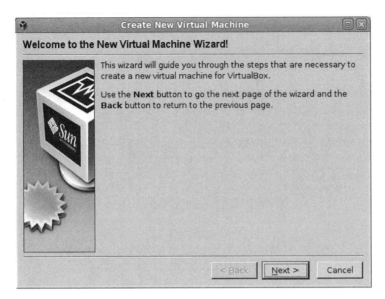

Figure 14.3
The first step to building a virtual machine.

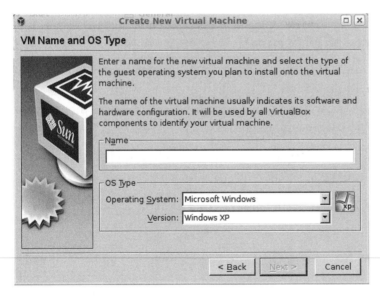

Figure 14.4
Giving your VM a name.

5. Click Next. The Memory page will appear (see Figure 14.5).

6. Use the slider to set the amount of RAM to devote to the virtual machine.

How Much RAM?

Typically, you will want to give your virtual machine enough RAM to operate efficiently yet not deprive your host operating system of the resources it needs. A good rule of thumb: give the virtual machine half the available RAM. You can change it later if either the guest or host operating system needs it.

7. Click Next. The Virtual Hard Disk page will appear, as shown in Figure 14.6.

8. Since you are installing Windows 7 (for this example) later, confirm the Create New Hard Disk option is selected and click Next. The Create New Virtual Disk dialog box will open.

9. Click Next. The Hard Disk Storage Type page will appear.

10. Confirm the Dynamically Expanding Storage option is selected and click Next. The Virtual Disk Location and Size page (see Figure 14.7) will appear.

11. Set the maximum size you want the hard drive to be.

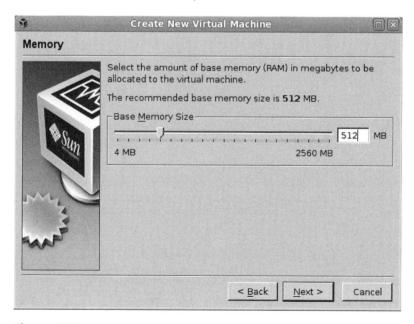

Figure 14.5
Setting the memory available to the virtual machine.

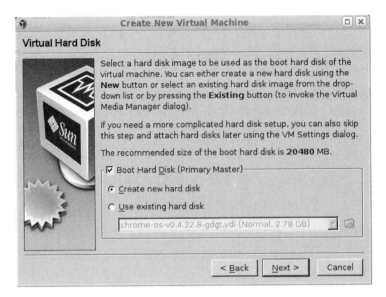

Figure 14.6
Establishing the hard disk space available to the virtual machine.

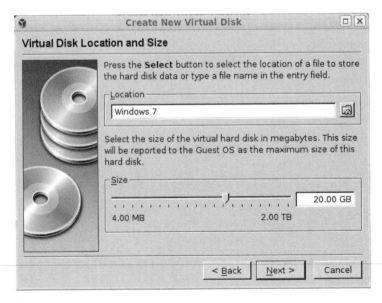

Figure 14.7
VirtualBox will recommend a size based on the type of operating system specified.

How Much Hard Drive?

Usually, a guest operating system does not need a lot of memory, since files can be stored on the host operating system and accessed from there by the guest operating system. With that in mind, don't feel like you need to give the host operating system more space than the recommended amount, unless your circumstances warrant a different approach.

12. Click Next. The Summary page will appear.

13. Review the settings and then click Finish. The Create New Virtual Disk dialog box will close, and the Summary page of the Create New Virtual Machine dialog box will appear.

14. Click Finish. The new virtual machine will appear in the Sun VirtualBox window (see Figure 14.8).

Installing Windows in VirtualBox

This may seem to be an odd section to have in a book about Fedora, especially when many of you have already used Windows and are well familiar with it. But,

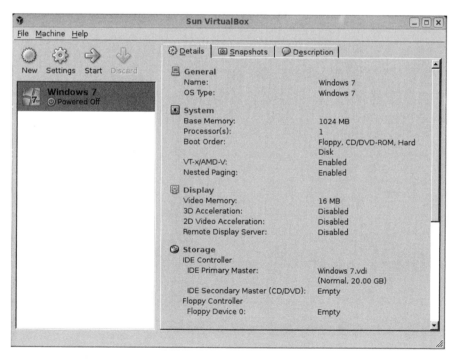

Figure 14.8
A new VirtualBox machine.

ask yourself this: When have you ever installed Windows on a machine? If you're like most people, you have purchased a machine that already has Windows installed on it—you never had to deal with installation.

Installing Windows is a lot like installing Linux: you set the disc in the drive and boot the machine to begin the installation process. Except in this case, the machine we will boot will be a virtual one.

Get the Right Windows

Be sure you have the right kind of Windows (whatever version) to install. Usually what you see online and in stores is an Upgrade version—that is, a version of Windows that is meant to replace an existing, older version of Windows. What you need is an OEM (original equipment manufacturer) version. Upgrades are less expensive than OEMs, so you might be tempted to get that instead. Don't—when you try to install an Upgrade version of Windows to a blank machine, even if it's virtual, the Windows install will fail.

1. Insert your Windows disc in your Fedora machine's DVD drive.

2. In VirtualBox, click the Windows virtual machine and then click Start. The First Run Wizard dialog box will open (see Figure 14.9).

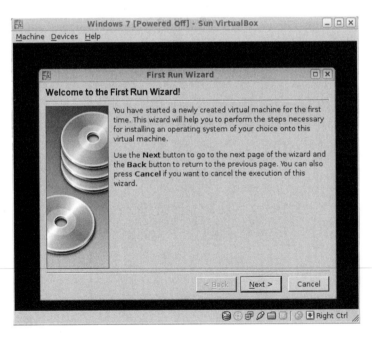

Figure 14.9
Getting prepped to install a new operating system.

3. Click Next. The Select Installation Media page will appear.

4. Confirm the CD/DVD-ROM Device option is selected and click Next. The Summary page will appear.

5. Confirm the settings and click Finish. The First Run Wizard dialog box will close, and the normal Windows installation boot process will begin, as shown in Figure 14.10.

6. After a lengthy boot process, the Install Windows dialog will appear within VirtualBox (see Figure 14.11).

7. Select your language and location settings and click Next. The Install Now page will appear (see Figure 14.12).

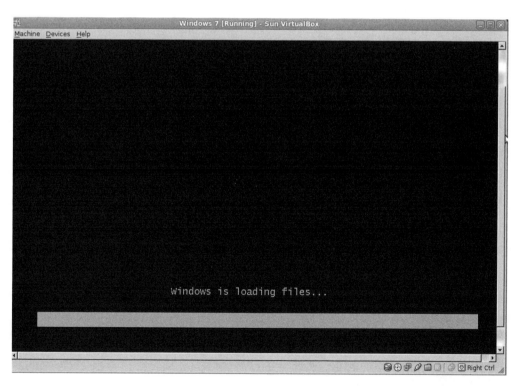

Figure 14.10
The start of the Windows installation boot.

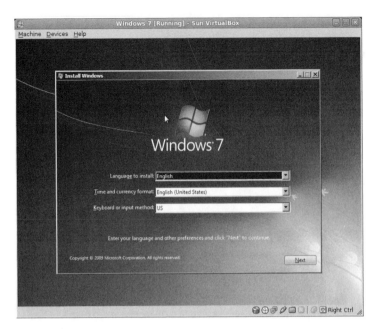

Figure 14.11
Installing Windows looks somewhat like installing Fedora.

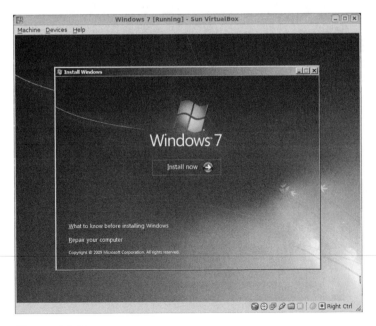

Figure 14.12
Start the install.

Mouse Trap

When a new virtual machine is installed, using the mouse within the guest operating system will capture the mouse within that window, not letting you use the mouse out in Fedora. To release the mouse, press the Right Ctrl key on your keyboard.

8. Click Install Now. The License Terms page will appear.

9. Click the I Accept the License Terms check box and click Next. The Type of Installation page will appear (see Figure 14.13).

10. Click the Custom (Advanced) option. The Where Do You Want to Install Windows? page will appear.

11. Confirm the location is Disk 0 Unallocated Space and click Next. The automated Windows installation process will begin (see Figure 14.14).

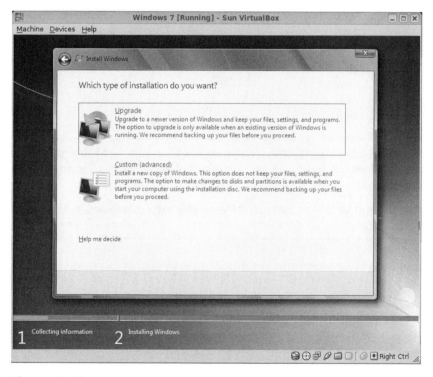

Figure 14.13
You can choose to upgrade or install fresh.

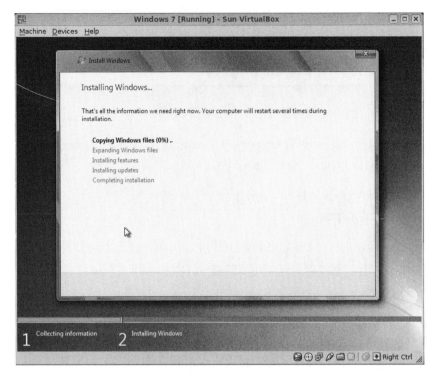

Figure 14.14
The installation will take a while.

So Slow...

It should be noted that Windows installations are very slow to begin with, and being on a virtual machine will cause a performance hit as well. During this part of the installation, feel free to walk away for a while and enjoy life.

Be aware that there will be at least one reboot during the installation (possibly more), but VirtualBox will handle that automatically.

12. After the installation process, the Set Up Windows dialog box will appear (see Figure 14.15).

13. Type your preferred username and computer name and then click Next. The Set a Password for Your Account page will appear (see Figure 14.16).

14. Type the password into the required fields, as well as a hint, and then click Next. The Type Your Windows Product Key page will appear.

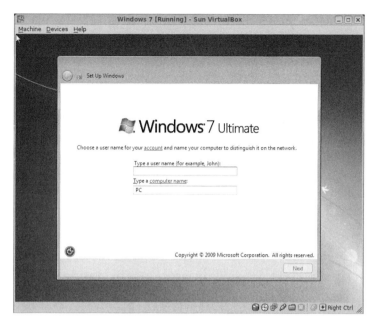

Figure 14.15
Finalizing Windows setup.

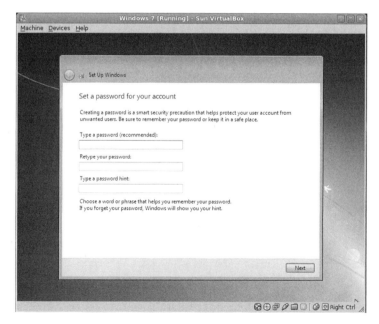

Figure 14.16
Set your passwords.

15. Type the Windows product key and click Next. The security settings page will appear (see Figure 14.17).

16. Click the Use Recommended Settings option. The time and date page will appear.

17. Set your current time zone, date, and time settings; then click Next. The current location page will appear (see Figure 14.18).

18. Click the option that is appropriate. Windows will search for your network (which VirtualBox will supply) and once found, Windows will start, as shown in Figure 14.19.

Sharing Between Host and Guest Machines

One of the first things you should do after installing any guest operating system, Windows or otherwise, is to establish a smoother interface between the guest and host operating systems.

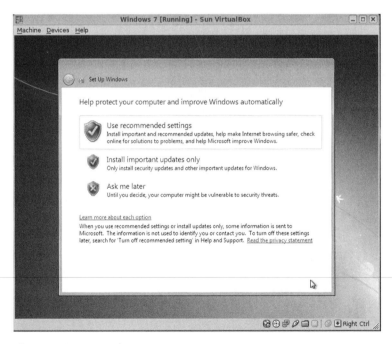

Figure 14.17
Confirm your security settings.

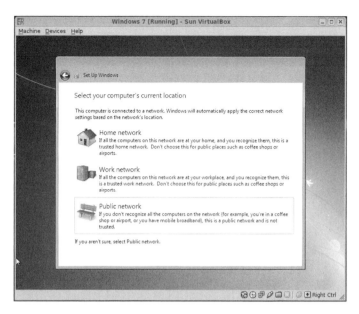

Figure 14.18
Confirm your network location.

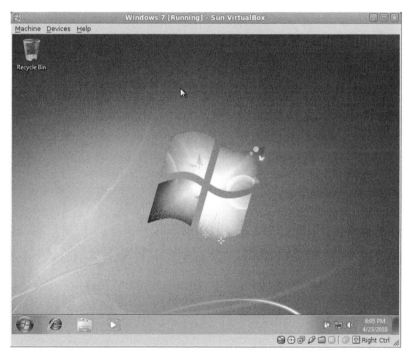

Figure 14.19
Windows inside Fedora.

Such smoothing will allow, for example, the mouse cursor to roam freely between the two operating systems, as well as allow easier file transfers between one and the other. This is accomplished by the Guest Additions, which need to be installed on the guest operating system after it is properly installed and running.

Making Room for a New CD

Even though the Guest Additions CD is "virtual," it's still a good idea to remove the Windows 7 installation disc from the drive before beginning the next set of steps.

1. In the VirtualBox menu for the virtual machine, click Devices | Install Guest Additions menu command. The Question dialog box, shown in Figure 14.20, will open.

2. Click Yes. A confirmation dialog box will appear.

3. Click Yes. The Guest Additions file will be downloaded, and a final confirmation dialog box will appear (see Figure 14.21).

4. Click Mount. The AutoPlay window will open inside Windows, as shown in Figure 14.22.

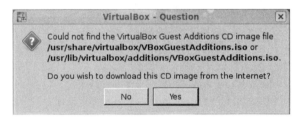

Figure 14.20
Do you want to download the Guest Additions?

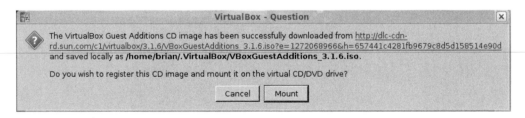

Figure 14.21
Mount the virtual CD in your Windows operating system.

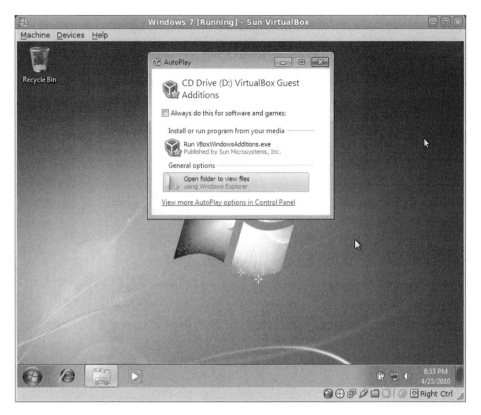

Figure 14.22
Once mounted, Windows will load a virtual CD just like a real one.

5. Click the Run VboxWindowsAdditions.exe option. The User Account Control dialog box will open.

6. Click Yes. The Sun VirtualBox Guest Additions Setup dialog box will open (see Figure 14.23).

7. Click Next. The License Agreement page will appear.

8. Click I Agree. The Choose Install Location page will appear.

9. Click Next. The Choose Components page will appear.

10. Click Install. The Guest Additions will be installed. Accept any verification questions that might occur, based on your Windows settings.

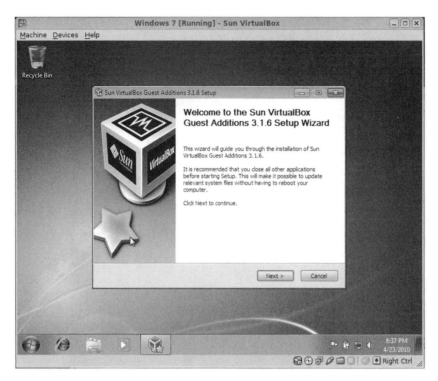

Figure 14.23
Install the Guest Additions like any other Windows application.

11. When the Completing page appears, confirm the Reboot Now option is selected and click Finish. The virtual machine will be restarted.

After the system restarts, you will be able to cut and paste text and images from Fedora to Windows, and vice versa, as well as have a more seamless interface.

There is one more level of integration you need to truly get Fedora working with its Windows guest: file sharing. To do that, you need to map a Windows network drive to a Fedora directory. From that folder, you can share files from within either operating system.

After you install the Guest Additions, you can create a Shared Folder.

1. With the Windows virtual machine powered off, select the machine and click Settings. The Settings dialog box will open.

2. Click Shared Folders. The Shared Folders page will appear (see Figure 14.24).

3. Click the small Add Shared Folder icon. The Add Share dialog box will open.

4. Click the Other option in the Folder Path field. The Find Directory dialog box will open.

5. Navigate to the folder you want to share and click Choose. The Find Directory dialog box will close, and the folder path and the folder name will be set in the Add Share dialog box. Make a note of the folder name.

6. Click OK. The Add Share dialog box will close.

7. Click OK. The Settings dialog box will close.

8. Start the Windows virtual machine and log into Windows.

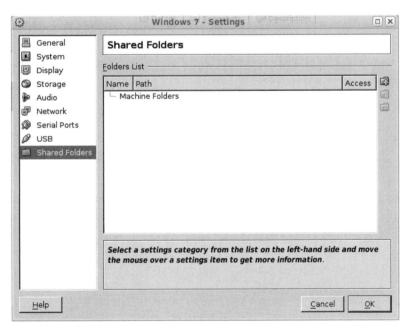

Figure 14.24
Create a connection to share a folder with Windows.

9. In Windows, click the Start button and then Computer. Windows Explorer will open.

10. Click Map Network Drive. The Map Network Drive dialog box will open (see Figure 14.25).

11. In the Folder field, type \\vboxsvr*folder name*, where *folder name* is the name of the shared folder you set up in the VirtualBox settings. Or browse for it to find the shared vboxsvr folder in Windows Explorer.

12. Click Finish. The new drive will appear in Windows Explorer with all of the contents of the Linux directory you specified visible (see Figure 14.26).

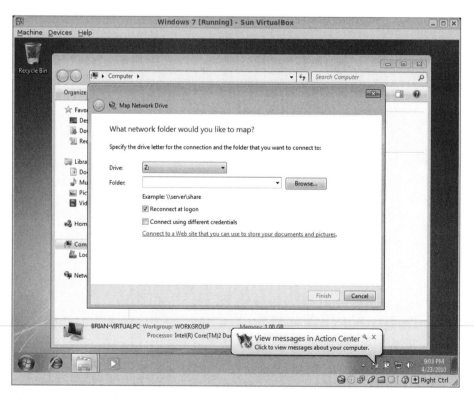

Figure 14.25
Mapping a network drive.

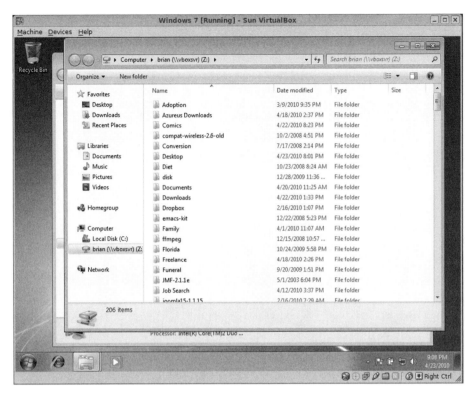

Figure 14.26
Sharing files with Fedora.

Conclusion

In this chapter, you learned how to get the best of both worlds, should you not be able to leave Windows completely behind. By using virtualization technology, it is easy to get a fully functional Windows installation running right inside Linux.

While hanging on to Windows is all well and good, let's not forget, Fedora has some serious native tools of its own. In the remaining chapters of this book, you'll get to dive into the major components of this powerful office suite to complete your journey into Fedora.

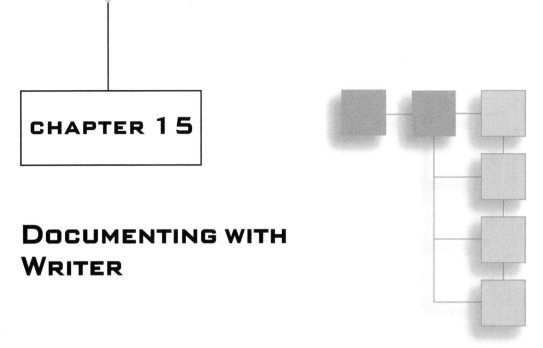

CHAPTER 15

DOCUMENTING WITH WRITER

It was a dark and stormy night...

The urge to put words on paper is very strong in most cultures. Paper and ink lend a sense of permanence that we don't seem to have in our own brains. Scientists speculate that we do indeed remember everything we have experienced, perhaps all the way back to Minute One. But, until we can figure out how to *recall* all of that detail, we still need to write it down.

The written word has more uses than just archiving memories and events. It's still the most pervasive form of communication in the world. Every type of media uses writing as its basis, even television (though some writing there is a bit shaky). The Internet has been the fastest growing medium in the world, and even with the advent of streaming audio and video, people mostly read the written works of others.

Either on paper or on an e-reader device, this writing thing will be around for some time, and it's important that you have the right tools to put your words together so you can worry about what to write, as opposed to how to write it.

The Writer component of OpenOffice.org makes a great tool to get your words on paper or on computer screens around the planet. In this chapter you will:

- Explore the basics of the Writer interface

- Create and edit documents

- Insert special elements in a document

The Writer Interface

Contrary to what you might think, Writer is not a separate application in the OpenOffice.org suite. Think of it more as a set of clothes that OpenOffice.org puts on to go to work building a document. It's still OpenOffice.org and shares many of OpenOffice.org's functions, but with the new outfit on, it's Writer.

Part word processor, part desktop publisher, Writer is jammed with tools and functions to put a document together. This section will detail the tools found in the toolbars, menus, and shortcut keys that make up the Writer outfit.

Exploring the Toolbars

When Writer appears on the screen, you can get a good look at its interface and see how closely it resembles other word processing programs (see Figure 15.1).

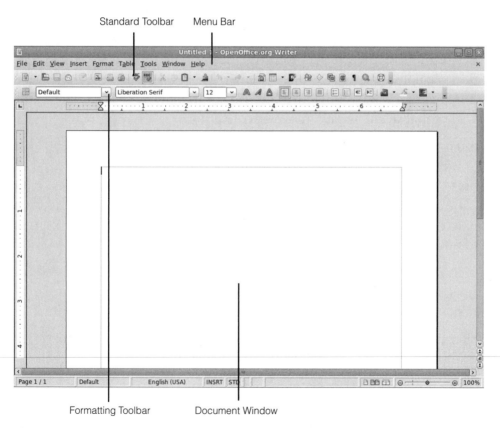

Figure 15.1
The Writer interface.

First, the Standard toolbar appears on the top of the window, and the Formatting toolbar adds even more functionality. Since the toolbars are a great resource while you work in Writer, let's examine them more completely.

Standard Toolbar

The first set of tools to examine is the Standard toolbar, a toolset tightly configured for Writer. Typically, the Standard toolbar appears at the top of the screen, although it can be repositioned (see Figure 15.2).

Table 15.1 describes the basic functions of each of the buttons on the Standard toolbar.

Formatting Toolbar

As you would expect, the Writer version of the Formatting toolbar primarily focuses on the manipulation of text and paragraph styling (just as the Calc Formatting toolbar concerns itself with row and cell manipulation).

Figure 15.3 shows the Formatting toolbar for Writer. Table 15.2 describes the functions of the same set of tools.

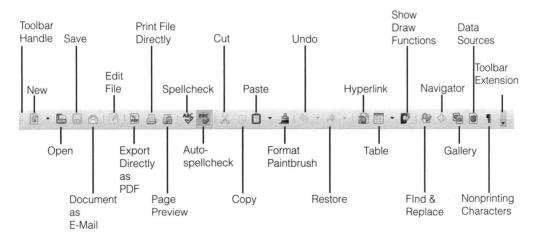

Figure 15.2
The Standard toolbar.

Table 15.1 The Standard Toolbar Buttons

Name	Function
Toolbar Handle	A toolbar control that allows users to move any docked toolbar to any position within OpenOffice.org and undock a toolbar as well.
New	A single click opens a new Writer window and document. Clicking the drop-down control displays a list of OpenOffice.org documents that can be created.
Open	Opens the Open dialog box, where existing documents can be opened.
Save	Saves the current document.
Document as Email	Starts the default Fedora email program (usually Evolution) and creates a new email with the current document as an attachment.
Edit File	Turns the read-only status for the document on and off.
Export Directly as PDF	Opens the Export dialog box, set to convert the document to a PDF file.
Print File Directly	Prints the document to the default Fedora printer.
Page Preview	Toggles between Preview and Edit modes.
Spellcheck	Opens the Spellcheck dialog box and runs a spelling check on the document.
AutoSpellcheck	Toggles the "check as you go" status for the document on and off.
Cut	Cuts selected text from the document.
Copy	Copies selected text in the document.
Paste	Pastes cut or copied text into the document.
Format Paintbrush	Enables the application of a format to selected text.
Undo	Regresses to the last editing change made to the document.
Restore	Returns any undone changes.
Hyperlink	Opens the Hyperlink dialog box, where you can insert an HTML hyperlink to selected text.
Table	Opens the Insert Table dialog box with a single-click. A click-and-hold action reveals the row-by-column table creator.
Show Draw Functions	Toggles the Drawing toolbar on and off.
Find & Replace	Opens the Find & Replace dialog box, which enables users to search for and replace text in a document.
Navigator	Opens the Navigator tool, which displays various elements of the document in one location, allowing users to view and navigate to different sections of the document.
Gallery	Opens the Gallery pane, which contains backgrounds, bullets, sounds, and other elements to insert in your document.
Data Sources	Opens the Data Sources pane that allows users to create form letters from various sources.
Nonprinting Characters	Toggles nonprinting character visibility in the document.
Toolbar Extension	Allows users to see the rest of the toolbar's buttons if the OpenOffice.org window is not wide enough.

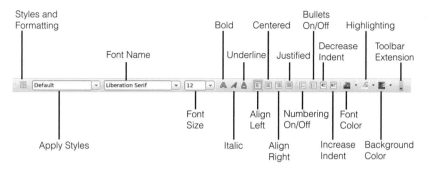

Figure 15.3
The Formatting toolbar.

Table 15.2 The Formatting Toolbar Buttons

Name	Function
Styles and Formatting	Toggles the Styles and Formatting window, which displays the styles and formats within an open document.
Apply Style	Applies the selected style to selected text.
Font Name	Changes the font of selected text.
Font Size	Changes the font size of selected text.
Bold	Applies the bold style to selected text.
Italic	Applies the italic style to selected text.
Underline	Underlines selected text.
Align Left	Aligns selected paragraphs to left margin.
Centered	Centers selected paragraphs on page.
Align Right	Aligns selected paragraphs to right margin.
Justified	Justifies selected paragraphs to fill all space between margins.
Numbering On/Off	Changes selected paragraphs to a numbered list.
Bullets On/Off	Changes selected paragraphs to a bulleted list.
Increase Indent	Indents selected paragraphs.
Decrease Indent	Shifts selected paragraphs toward left margin.
Font Color	Click applies displayed color to selected text. Click and hold reveals more colors to apply.
Highlighting	Click applies displayed highlight color (or fill) to selected text. Click and hold reveals more fills to apply and the capability to remove fills.
Background Color	Applies background color (or fill) to document.
Toolbar Extension	If the OpenOffice.org window is not wide enough, clicking this extension allows users to see the rest of the toolbar's buttons.

Customizing Toolbars

The Standard and Formatting toolbars are not the only two sets of tools available in Writer, not by a long shot. In fact, as of OpenOffice.org 3.2, the version that ships with Fedora 13, there are a total of 22 available toolbars in Writer. Most of these toolbars will pop up as needed. For instance, when you begin to insert a table, the Table toolbar will appear as a floating window.

To make a toolbar visible at any time, a quick procedure is all you need.

1. Click the View | Toolbars menu. The Toolbars submenu will appear (see Figure 15.4).

2. Click Picture. The Picture toolbar will appear as a floating toolbar (see Figure 15.5).

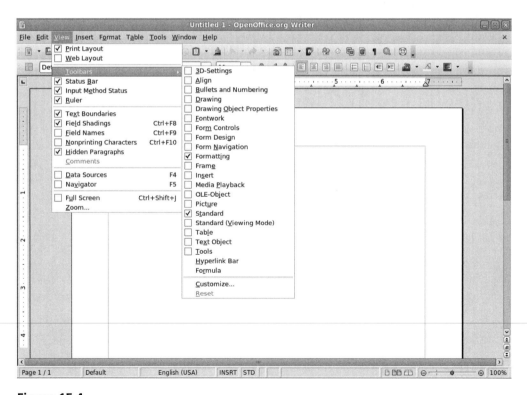

Figure 15.4
Your choice of toolbars.

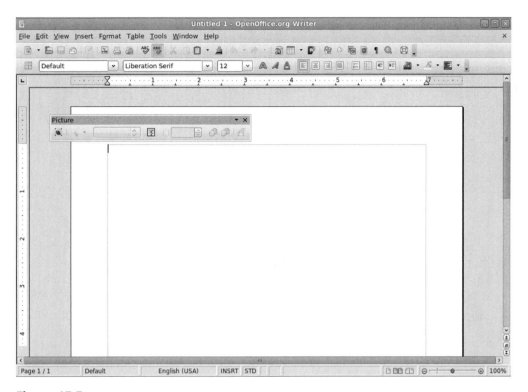

Figure 15.5
New toolbars float.

3. To dock, or attach, a floating toolbar so that it no longer blocks the document window, carefully click and drag the toolbar's title bar toward the part of the window where you want the toolbar to be docked. A gray outline will appear, marking the planned position of the toolbar. Use a light touch.

4. Release the mouse button. The toolbar will be dropped into the desired space on the border of the document window (see Figure 15.6).

5. To undock or move a toolbar to another position, click the toolbar handle (refer to Figure 15.2) and drag the cursor toward the part of the window where you want the toolbar to be. A gray outline will appear, marking the planned position of the toolbar.

6. Release the mouse button. The toolbar will be dropped into the desired space.

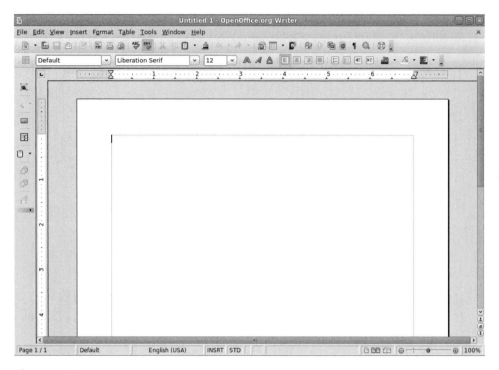

Figure 15.6
Docking toolbars is easy.

You can also make any button in a toolbar's toolset visible or hidden, as demonstrated in the following steps.

1. Click the toolbar extension button on the Formatting toolbar. The extension menu will appear.

2. Select the Visible Buttons command. A submenu of the available buttons will appear (see Figure 15.7).

3. Checked menu commands represent visible buttons. Click any unchecked button. The selected icon will appear in the Formatting toolbar.

4. Click the toolbar extension button on the Formatting toolbar again. The Extension menu will appear.

5. Select the Visible Buttons command.

6. Select a checked icon option. The selected icon will disappear from the Formatting toolbar.

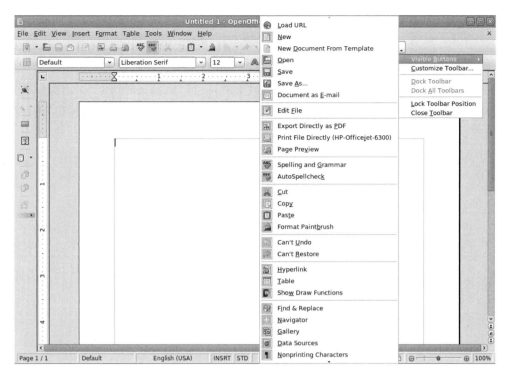

Figure 15.7
Choose which buttons to see and which to hide.

What Do All These Menus Mean?

The toolbars contain a voluminous amount of functions to assist in the creation of documents. Yet, they pale in comparison to the depth of the menu commands found in Writer. The menus represent every toolbar command, plus many additional commands. In theory, you could put every menu command on the toolbars, but that would add so much clutter to the screen that you'd only have a two-inch-tall space in which to type your document.

Because of the sheer number of menu commands, this section of the chapter will not detail every available command. Instead, the more commonly used menu commands will be explained.

Editing Your Document

Of all of the available menus in Writer, the Edit menu is perhaps the most useful. It contains the most pervasive commands in Writer, except for the Open and Save commands in the File menu.

In this menu, you'll find the ubiquitous Cut, Copy, and Paste functions, as well as the Undo, Redo, and Repeat commands. You can open the Find & Replace dialog box from here, as well as track changes to the document.

The examples in this section will highlight the most basic of these commands, starting with cutting and pasting any document object using the Edit menu commands.

1. In an open Writer document, select a passage of text, a graphic, or a form field.

Click Mania

You can select an entire paragraph of text by quadruple-clicking anywhere within the paragraph. Double-clicking selects a word. Triple-clicking selects an entire sentence in a paragraph.

2. From the Edit menu, click Cut.

3. Move the cursor to another area of the document.

4. Again from the Edit menu, click Paste. The cut text will appear in the new spot.

You can create copies of document items such as text or graphics in just a few steps.

1. To copy an item, select the desired item.

2. From the Edit menu, click Copy.

3. Move the cursor to another area of the document.

4. From the Edit menu, click Paste. A copy of the text will appear in the new spot.

Here is how the Undo, Redo, and Repeat functions of the Edit menu can help you work.

1. After performing any edit within a document, click Edit | Undo. The most recent change to the document will vanish.

Undo Actions

The Undo, Redo, and Repeat commands will always be followed by a one-word description of the action that will be performed.

2. Click Edit | Redo to put the change back on-screen.

3. Click Edit | Repeat to repeat the most recent change.

Viewing Your Document

The way you look at things influences how you treat them. For example, look at a bug down on the ground, and you will likely feel indifferent. Look at the same bug through an electron microscope, and you may shudder in revulsion.

How you view a document is important to your work. When you have a document with a lot of graphics, seeing the whole page at once helps you balance the look of the page. Conversely, those with vision problems may want to make the print appear really big without increasing the font size. Follow these steps to change your outlook on your document.

1. In an open document, click View | Zoom. The Zoom & View Layout dialog box will appear (see Figure 15.8).

2. Select the option that matches your desired view choice.

   ■ If you want a precise zoom percentage, click the Variable option and enter the numeric value (see Figure 15.9).

Zoom-a-Zoom!

The minimum zoom percentage is 20% and the maximum zoom percentage is 600%.

   ■ To see an entire page, select the Fit Width and Height option in the Zoom & View Layout dialog box.

   ■ For the best size for your current screen dimensions, select the Optimal option.

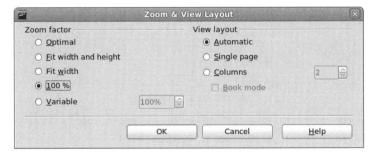

Figure 15.8
Decide how close up you want to see the document.

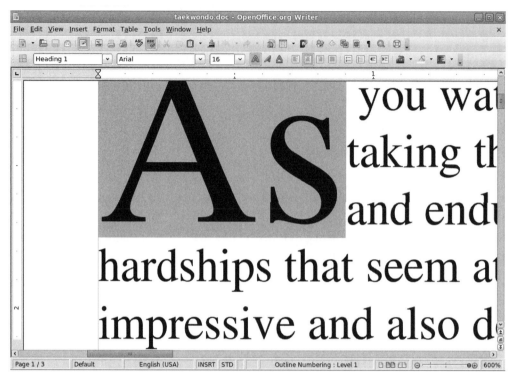

Figure 15.9
At 600%, things get really big.

We've already discussed the capability of OpenOffice.org to change its own interface by moving toolbars and changing menus. You can make other subtler interface changes that can be just as important. To see the various interface add-ons that can assist you in working with your documents, follow these steps.

1. In an open document, open the View menu.

2. Click the Text Boundaries command.

3. Click the Ruler command.

4. Click the Field Shadings command.

5. Click the Status Bar command. Note the screen changes after implementing each of these commands. You can experiment to decide which combination is most efficient for the way you work.

Inserting Cool Stuff

In the early days of electronic document creation, there was text. That was it. Things got rather exciting when italic text came on the scene. Underlining caused a huge ruckus. But then things sort of calmed down.

That lasted for a few years (eons in computer time), until someone got the idea to put real-time artwork in documents. Now, if you don't have graphics in your document, people look at you funny.

Writer's Insert menu contains the commands to insert artwork quickly and easily into your document, as explained in the following steps.

1. In an open Writer document, select Insert | Picture | From File. The Insert Picture dialog box will appear (see Figure 15.10).

2. In the Insert Picture dialog box, navigate through the directories to select the desired image.

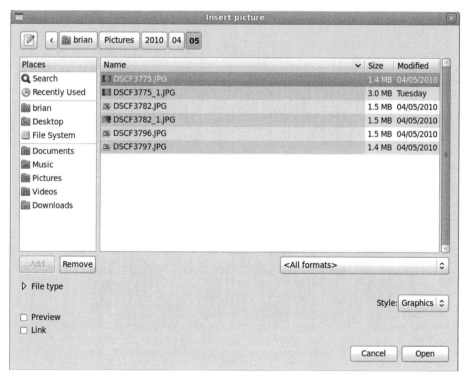

Figure 15.10
Preview the art you want to insert in the Insert Picture dialog box.

3. Check the Preview check box to see the graphic files as you select them in the file list.

4. When you have selected the image you want to insert, click the Open button.

In the document, the graphic appears surrounded by a box comprised of green squares (see Figure 15.11). These are the graphic handles. The following steps show you how to size, move, and anchor the graphic in your document.

1. Place the pointer over the left center handle. The pointer will change to a left-right arrow. Drag the handle to the left to stretch the graphic horizontally. You can repeat this action with any of the graphic handles.

Copying Graphics

Holding the Ctrl key while dragging any graphic handle immediately produces a copy of the graphic.

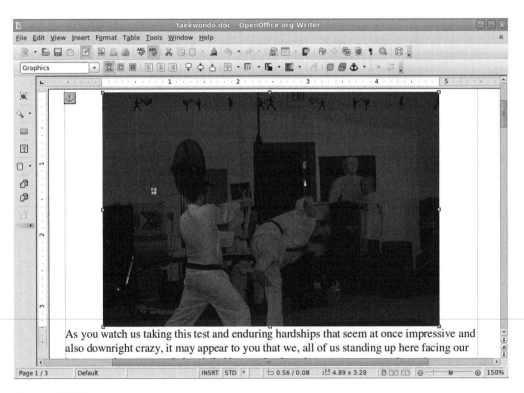

Figure 15.11
An inserted graphic, ready for placement.

2. Place the pointer within the graphic and drag it across the screen. The graphic will move with the pointer.

3. To wrap text around the graphic, right-click the graphic. A context menu will appear.

4. Select Wrap | Optimal Page Wrap. The text of the document will now wrap around the graphic (see Figure 15.12).

Cool Wraps

For a cool effect, choose Wrap | In Background from the context menu. Text flows *over* the graphic.

5. To keep graphics close to a particular section of the document, select the appropriate Anchor command from the context menu.

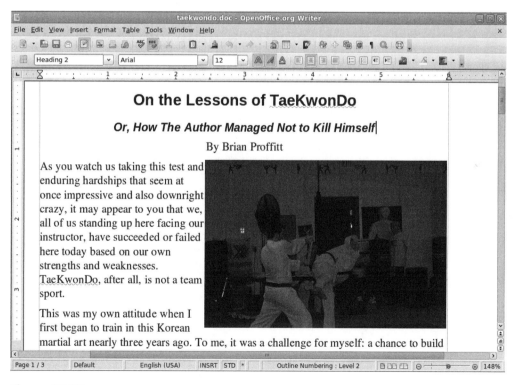

Figure 15.12
A neatly wrapped graphic in a document.

Absolute Positioning

For absolute positioning, choose the Anchor | As menu command from the image's context menu. The graphic remains exactly where placed in the document.

Umlauts, grave marks, Dingbats. Terms that sound like they belong in a dark, spooky cemetery. Believe it or not, these are descriptions of special characters that Writer can place in your document.

Because the standard 101- or 103-key U.S. PC keyboards have no room for them, OpenOffice.org has an easy-to-use dialog box to find and insert special characters.

1. Place the cursor at the spot in the document where you want the special character inserted.

2. In the Insert menu, click Special Character. The Special Characters dialog box will open (see Figure 15.13).

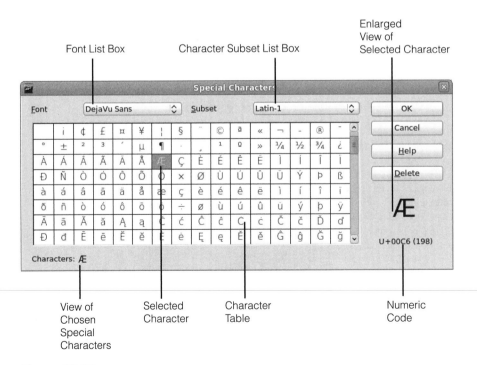

Figure 15.13
The Special Characters dialog box.

3. Select the Dingbats font in the Subset list box.

4. Select any desired character. The character will appear in the Characters field at the bottom of the dialog box.

5. Click OK. The character will be placed within the document.

Key Combinations

Key combinations are the quickest way to execute commands. As fast as a mouse is, anytime you have to lift your fingers and grab a mouse, it slows down your typing.

Accelerator keys do a good job of emulating menu commands, but often key combinations are even shorter, and therefore faster.

Table 15.3 lists the key combinations found in Writer's default menus. Although this is not all of the available key combinations, these tend to be used most often.

Key Listing

For a complete listing of all of the key combinations available in Writer, click any toolbar's extension control, choose Customize from the menu, and then click the Keyboard tab in the Customize dialog box.

Creating Documents

Flight school offers two kinds of lessons: those on the ground and those in the air. In ground school, students learn how a plane flies and what all of the instruments do. In the airplane, student experience how everything works together to perform the miracle of flight.

The tools of Writer have been described with some detail in the previous sections of this chapter. Ground school is over. Now it is time to fly and experience how to use those tools to accomplish basic tasks for your document.

Formatting Text

Formatting a document is essential in today's world. No longer are readers content to see a page with plain-looking letters. Even a large fiction novel, which is nothing but words, has been formatted with the font that the publisher feels is most attractive and at the same time most legible.

Table 15.3 Writer Key Combinations

Key Combination	Equivalent Menu Command
Ctrl + A	Edit | Select All
Ctrl + C	Edit | Copy
Ctrl + F	Edit | Search & Replace
Ctrl + N	File | Text Document
Ctrl + O	File | Open
Ctrl + P	File | Print
Ctrl + Q	File | Exit
Ctrl + S	File | Save
Ctrl + V	Edit | Paste
Ctrl + X	Edit | Cut
Ctrl + Z	Edit | Undo
Ctrl + Shift + J	View | Full Screen
F4	View | Data Sources
F5	View | Navigator
F7	Tools | Spelling and Grammar
F9	Tools | Update | Fields
F11	Format | Styles and Formatting
Ctrl + F2	Insert | Fields | Other
Ctrl + F3	Edit | AutoText
Ctrl + F7	Tools | Language | Thesaurus
Ctrl + F8	View | Field Shadings
Ctrl + F9	View | Field Names
Ctrl + F10	View | Nonprinting Characters
Ctrl + F12	Insert | Table

Writer has three levels of formatting: characters, paragraphs, and pages. The Format menu holds the starting point for all of these levels.

When you format these items, you apply new fonts, change font sizes and colors, and set tab stops, indent lengths, and page margins—and that's just for starters.

The following two examples will guide you through the basics of formatting at the character and paragraph levels.

1. In an open Writer document, select a passage of text.

2. Click the Format | Character menu command. The Character dialog box will appear (see Figure 15.14).

3. In the Font list, choose a desired font.

4. In the Typeface list, select Bold Italic.

5. In the Size list, select 14 pt.

6. Click the Font Effects tab. The Font Effects tab will open.

7. In the Effects area, select the Outline check box.

8. Choose a different color from the Font Color list.

9. Click OK to see the results of your setting changes (see Figure 15.15).

Not only can you alter the look of characters, but you can also make hyperlinks out of them.

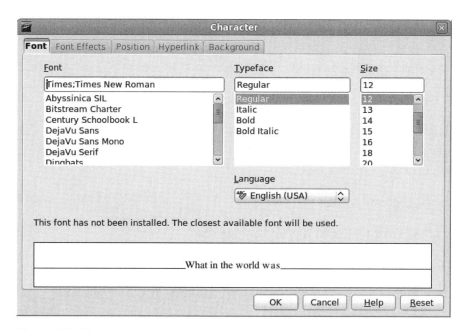

Figure 15.14
Format text with the Character dialog box.

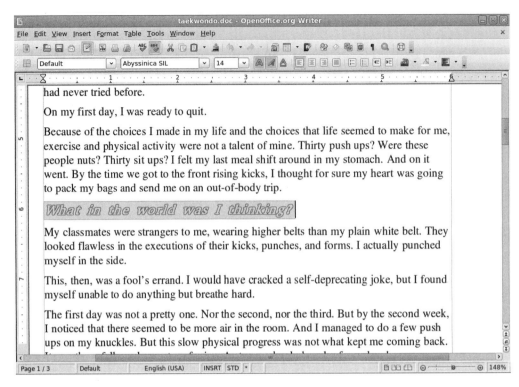

Figure 15.15
Altered text, courtesy of the Character dialog box.

1. With text selected, click Format | Character once more.

2. In the Character dialog box, select the Hyperlink tab.

3. In the URL field, type the Web address of the file you want to link to. (Use the Browse button to locate a file on your Fedora system.) Your selected text should be in the Text field.

4. Click the Background tab.

5. Select a color with which to highlight your text.

6. Click OK to check your work.

Paragraphs can also be formatted with different margins and line spacing.

1. With your cursor within any paragraph in the document, click Format | Paragraph. The Paragraph dialog box will appear (see Figure 15.16).

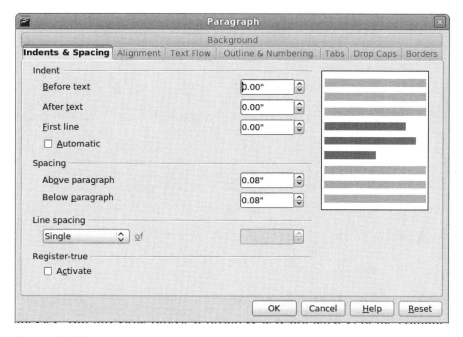

Figure 15.16
Use the Paragraph dialog box to format similar blocks of text.

2. Using the arrows, change the measurement in the Before Text field to 1.00".

3. In the Line Spacing field, change to the Double option.

4. Click OK to see the results of the changes.

Paragraphs can be justified to fill the width of a page, as shown in the following steps.

1. With the cursor in another paragraph, click Format | Paragraph.

2. Click the Alignment tab.

3. Click the Justified radio button. Leave the other settings as is.

4. Click OK to see the results of the changes.

The qualities of paragraphs can be changed in this dialog box, too.

1. With the cursor at the beginning of another paragraph, click Format | Paragraph again.

2. Click the Tabs tab.

3. In the Position field, change the 0.00" setting to 2.50".

4. In the Type section, select the Right radio button.

5. In the Fill character section, select the series of periods (........) radio button.

6. Click OK.

7. Press the Tab key to see the results of your settings.

You can even create a large drop cap at the beginning of your paragraph.

1. With the cursor in another paragraph, click Format | Paragraph again.

2. Select the Drop Caps tab.

3. Select the Display Drop Caps check box.

4. Select the Whole Word check box.

5. Click OK to see the results of your changes (see Figure 15.17).

Formatting Pages

Formatting a document can be tricky work. You have probably already noticed in your wanderings through the various tools that Writer has quite a few potential settings to tweak.

First, don't panic. Most likely, you won't need to use many of these settings except in very specialized documents. They are just there when you need them.

You'll use some settings, though, more often than others. Perhaps not every day, but certainly every once in a while, particularly in a business setting that uses specialized stationary. These settings include page margins, headers and footers, and multiple columns. This section explains how to accomplish these tasks, starting with setting page margins.

1. Create a new text document in OpenOffice.org.

2. Click the Format | Page menu command. The Page Style: Default dialog box will open.

3. Click the Page tab (see Figure 15.18).

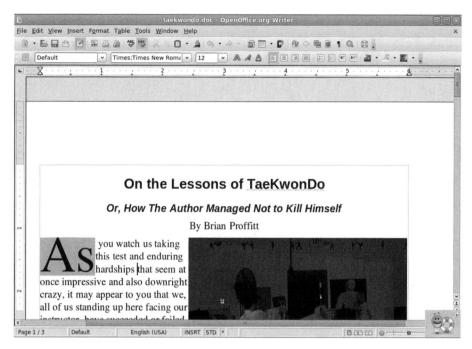

Figure 15.17
Drop caps lend a more literary look to your document.

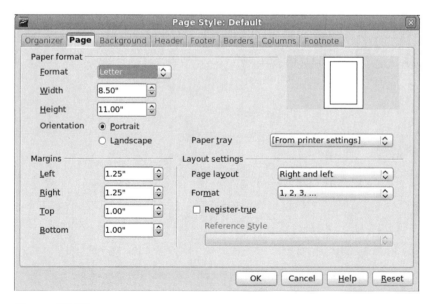

Figure 15.18
The Page tab contains the settings for page margins and size.

4. In the Format field, select the Legal option. Note the changes in the Pre-view area.

5. Try to even out the margins by changing the Left, Right, Top, and Bottom settings to 1.50".

6. Click OK to complete.

View Margins

To see the margins of the document on-screen, click View | Text Boundaries.

Organizing Styles

In the Organizer tab of the Page Style dialog box, you can change the style of pages by selecting from preset categories.

This task shows how to add headers and footers to a document.

1. In the legal-sized document, click the Format | Page menu command.

2. In the Page Style: Default dialog box, click the Header tab (see Figure 15.19).

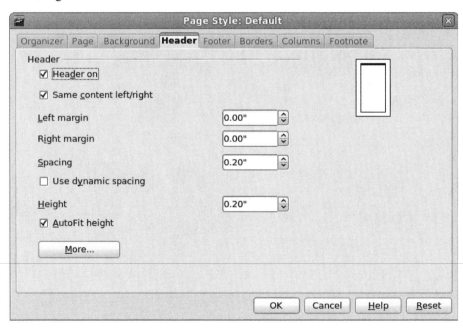

Figure 15.19
Build a header on this tab of the Page Style dialog box.

3. Select the Header On check box to make the rest of the options on the tab available.

4. Increase the Spacing value (which is the space between the header and document) to 0.25".

5. Select the AutoFit Height check box.

6. Clear the Same Content Left/Right check box, which allows for different headers on facing pages.

7. Click the Footer tab.

8. Repeat the settings from the Header tab, except this time leave the Same Content Left/Right check box selected.

9. Click OK to close the dialog box.

Documents are made up of different kinds of pages. The first page is one such type and is generally configured differently, as seen in the following steps.

1. In the document, place the cursor in the header area of the first page. In case you don't have a header in the current document, select Insert | Header.

2. Select the Insert | Fields | Page Number menu command.

3. Click the Align Right icon on the Formatting toolbar. (Odd-numbered pages are always right pages.)

4. Create enough dummy text to make the document at least four pages long.

5. Look at the header on Page 3. It has a right-aligned number 3.

6. Place your cursor in the header area of Page 2.

7. Choose Insert | Fields | Page Number.

8. Look at Page 4 to see that the even-numbered page headers now contain left-aligned numbers.

9. Place your cursor in any footer area.

10. Click Insert | Fields | Date.

11. Click the Centered icon on the Formatting Toolbar.

12. All the footers in the document will now contain the present date (see Figure 15.20).

These steps highlight the method used to create columned text in Writer.

1. Create a new text document in OpenOffice.org.

2. Click the Format | Page menu command.

3. Click the Columns tab in the Page Style: Default dialog box (see Figure 15.21).

4. If you want two or three equal-width columns, click the appropriate preset in the Columns area.

Off-Center Columns

The Columns area also presents two off-center column options. Use them if you want a one-third/two-thirds look to your page.

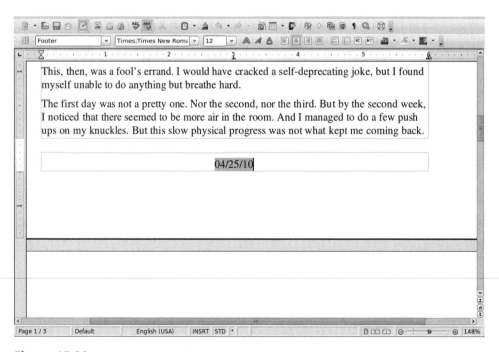

Figure 15.20
It's easy to create headers and footers.

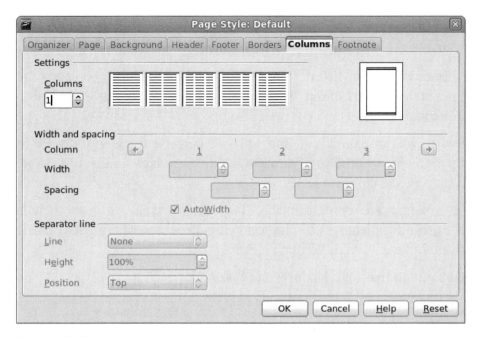

Figure 15.21
The Columns tab reveals a powerful interface for column creation.

5. If you need more than three columns, select the desired value in the Columns field.

Limit Column Numbers

Unless you are creating an index-like document, it is recommended that you stay to four or fewer columns, because more columns make text harder to read.

6. If you need unequal columns, clear the AutoWidth check box.

7. Adjust the Widths and Spacings between columns to your specifications.

Viewing Off-Screen Columns

If you have more than three columns, use the left and right arrow navigation buttons to view the off-screen column settings.

8. Select a separator line width in the Line field, if desired.

9. Click OK.

Making Lists

If you want to remember something, write it down.

We all do it every day: create lists of things to do, groceries to buy, people to send cards to. Lists are a big part of our lives, if only because our brains are wired to think in sequential terms.

We like it when we can plan ahead, and since we perceive the world around us moment by moment, we tend to organize our thoughts sequentially, too. So we use lists to plan and to communicate.

Lists in documents are commonplace. Two major types of lists include numbered lists and bulleted lists. The following steps describe how to create numbered and bulleted lists in Writer.

1. Type a four- to five-item list, pressing Enter after each item.

2. Select the entire list.

3. From the Format menu, click Bullets and Numbering.

4. In the Bullets and Numbering dialog box, click the Numbering Type tab (see Figure 15.22).

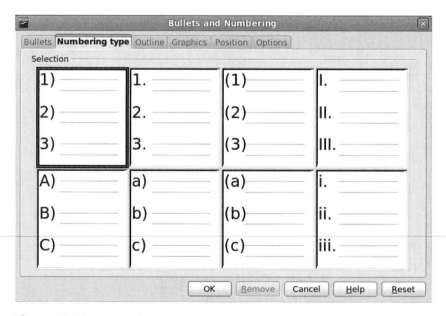

Figure 15.22
Select the style of numbering here.

5. Choose any of the eight options.

6. Click OK. Figure 15.23 shows a numbered list example.

Numbering Lists

Click the Numbering On/Off button on the Formatting toolbar to create a list with the default numbering style.

Now we'll walk through the creation of a bulleted list.

1. Type a four- to five-item list, pressing Enter after each item.

2. Select the entire list.

3. From the Format menu, click Bullets and Numbering.

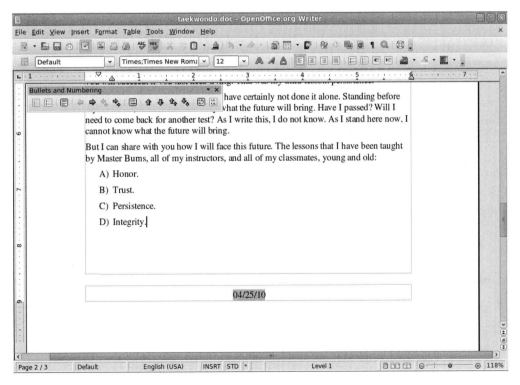

Figure 15.23
A sequential list should always be in the right order.

4. In the Bullets and Numbering dialog box, click the Bullets tab
   (see Figure 15.24).

5. Choose any of the eight options.

Graphical Bullets

For more options, click the Graphics tab to choose from several graphics-based bullets.

6. Click OK. Figure 15.25 shows a bulleted list example.

Bulleting Lists

Click the Bullets On/Off button on the Formatting toolbar to create a list with the default bullet style.

Building Tables

The final basic document element to be explored is the table. More complete than lists, tables provide a fast, compact way of getting information across to readers.

Creating a table in Writer is a fairly automated process, although it is not a full-fledged AutoPilot, as the following steps will show.

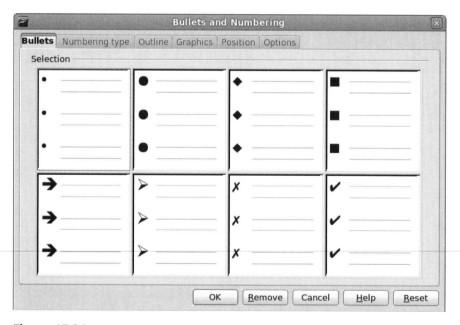

Figure 15.24
Select bullet styles in this tab.

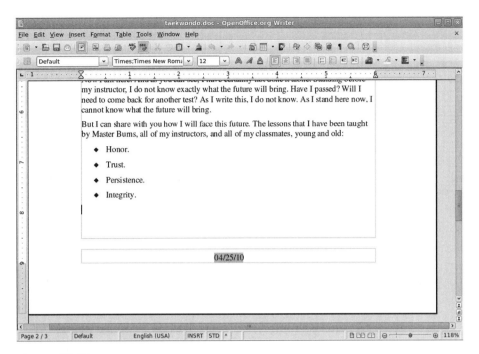

Figure 15.25
Bulleted lists present items in no particular order.

1. In an open Writer document, place the cursor at the point where you want to insert the table.

2. From the Insert menu, click Table.

3. In the Name field of the Insert Table dialog box, type in a one-word name for the new table (see Figure 15.26).

4. In the Size area, enter the number of rows and columns desired.

5. If the table needs a header, be sure to select the Heading check box. If the rows and columns should be outlined, select the Border check box.

Repeating Headings

If a table may lie on more than one page, select the Repeat Heading check box.

6. Click OK. Figure 15.27 shows a five-column, three-row table.

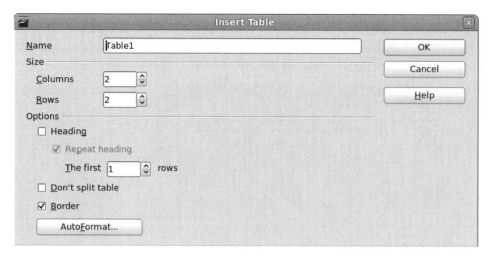

Figure 15.26
Begin building a table.

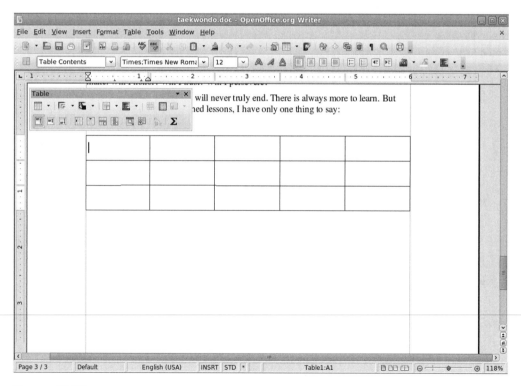

Figure 15.27
The newly designed table.

Conclusion

This introduction to Writer and its many tools covered a lot of material, but there is more to OpenOffice.org than just a word processor.

Chapter 16 will focus on the spreadsheet of OpenOffice.org, the venerable Calc application.

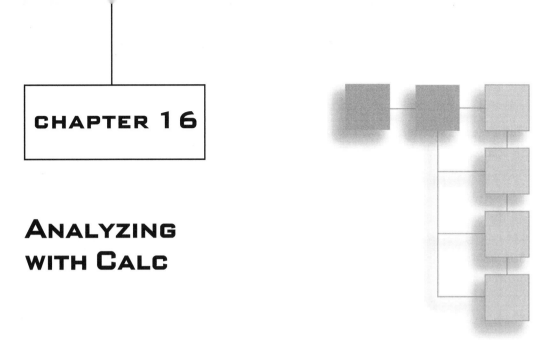

CHAPTER 16

ANALYZING WITH CALC

Accountants aren't the only ones using spreadsheets these days. With online banking, online trading, and online loan applications available to the average consumer, more and more people use spreadsheets to track their rapidly changing finances.

This new demand, coupled with the already present needs of the business world for clearer, faster reporting, requires a spreadsheet program that is pretty powerful. Calc delivers the spreadsheet power you need to your Fedora desktop. This component of OpenOffice.org delivers many of the same functions found in Microsoft Excel or Lotus 1-2-3 and maintains interoperability with these applications and the rest of OpenOffice.org.

In this chapter, you will learn about:

- The basics of spreadsheets and Calc

- Formatting data in Calc

- Building basic spreadsheets

A Spreadsheet Primer

You have likely used a spreadsheet before, at one time or another. Many spreadsheet users, however, often do not create or modify the basic workings of the spreadsheets they use. They just plug in the numbers and print the assigned reports like they're supposed to.

There comes a time in computer users' lives when they need to create a spreadsheet for themselves. At that time, it's a good idea to know how these spreadsheet doodads work.

It all comes down, more or less, to cells. A familiar type of cell is the basic building block of your body. There are many different types of cells: muscle cells, skin cells, liver cells—the list goes on and on. But no matter what kind of cell you look at, they all have pretty much the same basic structure: nucleus, plasmalemma, cell wall, mitochondria, and other hard-to-pronounce components. Even though they have the same overall structure, cells can have vastly different jobs because of the specialized way they have been put together.

The same theory applies to spreadsheet cells. They are all rectangular, and they all can contain data. But each cell in a spreadsheet can have a different task. One cell may sit empty, filled in with an attractive shade of purple. Another cell may contain the number 42. Still another may contain a formula that refers to the number 42 in another cell and displays something completely different.

Cells are all the same, but they can be used in many different ways.

Cells are typically positioned and referred to in rows and columns. By universal convention, spreadsheet rows are denoted with numbers, and columns are denoted with letters. Because spreadsheets sometimes need more than 26 columns, the columns after the letter Z move to a two-letter notation (AA, AB, AC, and so on). This lettering convention continues to column IV, which makes 256 the maximum number of columns a Calc spreadsheet can have. A spreadsheet can contain 65,536 rows, giving you the potential to fill 16,777,216 cells. With over 16 million cells to fill, you probably won't run out of space to perform the needed calculations, unless, maybe, you work for NASA.

You identify cells by their row and column position in the spreadsheet. The cell that's four rows down and eight columns across is identified as cell H4. Find the cell reference by looking at the bold column and row headings or reading the coordinates (C4) from the Name Box field in the Formula Bar, as seen in Figure 16.1.

Multiple cells are called *ranges.* An inverted color fill denotes a selected range of cells. The coordinates of a range include the cell in the upper-left corner of the

Name Box   Bold Column Heading

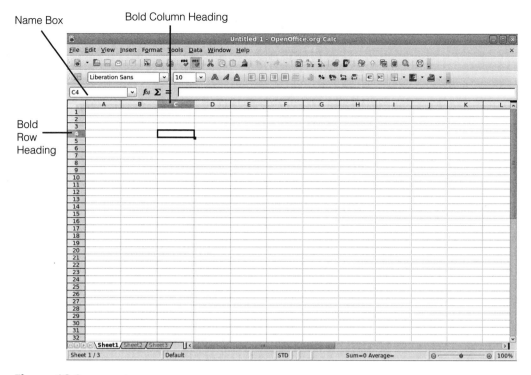

Bold
Row
Heading

Figure 16.1
Reading a cell's coordinates.

range and the cell in the lower-right corner of the range. Thus, you would reference the range selected in Figure 16.2 as D2:G14.

Now you've got the basics down. As you progress through the chapter, you will start to see how the cells of a spreadsheet fit together to make a body of data.

Learning the Calc Interface

When you start cooking, you want to have all of your ingredients out on the counter before you begin. Nothing is so frustrating as having to stop to find the jar of saffron when your hands are covered in flour. Even better, have your ingredients chopped, cut, and measured before you begin for true speed.

The same concept applies when building a spreadsheet. You need to have all of your tools before you begin. In this section, the Calc tools will be examined, with special emphasis on those tools unique to Calc.

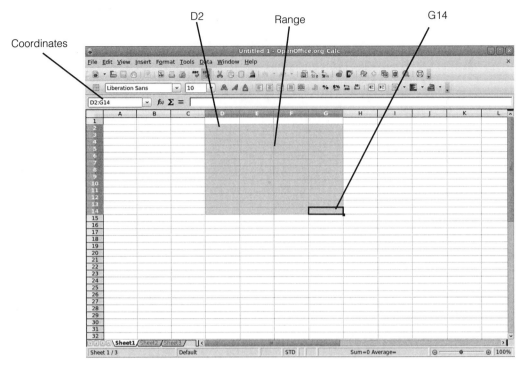

Figure 16.2
Reading a range's coordinates.

Working with Calc Tools and Menus

You will have probably noticed that the Calc and Writer interfaces have many similarities (see Figure 16.3).

Calc, of course, makes use of the ubiquitous Standard toolbar. As in all of the OpenOffice.org components, its toolset remains mostly the same. If you need to review the core Standard and Formatting toolbar functions, refer back to Chapter 15, "Documenting with Writer." For now, let's look at what's different for each of these toolsets.

Standard Toolbar

The Calc Standard toolbar deals mostly with file and data manipulation.

Figure 16.4 illustrates the Standard toolbar for Calc. Table 16.1 lists the functions of the new or changed buttons on the Standard toolbar.

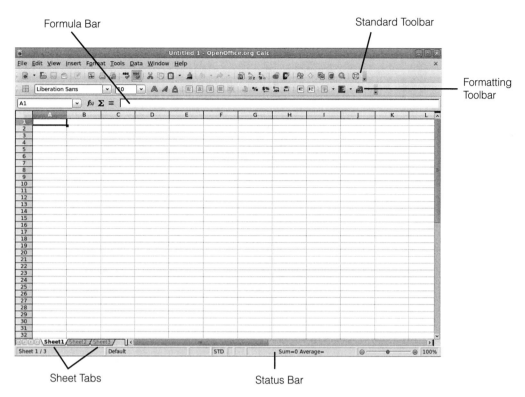

Figure 16.3
The primary toolsets of the Calc interface.

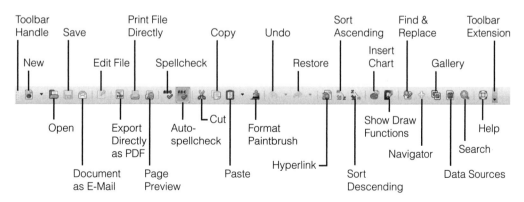

Figure 16.4
The Calc Standard toolbar.

Table 16.1 Calc-Specific Standard Toolbar Buttons

Name	Function
Sort Ascending	Allows users to move any docked toolbar to any position within OpenOffice.org.
Sort Descending	Opens a new Writer window with a single click. Clicking the drop-down control displays a list of OpenOffice.org documents that can be created.
Insert Chart	Opens the Open dialog box, where existing documents can be opened.

Formatting Toolbar

The Calc Formatting toolbar primarily focuses on the manipulation of data values and their presentation.

Figure 16.5 illustrates the Formatting toolbar for Calc. As with the Standard toolbar, many of the functions in this Formatting toolbar duplicate the functions in Writer. Table 16.2 lists the functions of the new or changed buttons in the Formatting toolbar.

The use of these buttons will be explored in the section "Good-Looking Data" later in this chapter.

Formula Bar

The Formula Bar is a toolbar only found in Calc. It is small in terms of the number of functions it contains, but it is probably the most important toolbar in

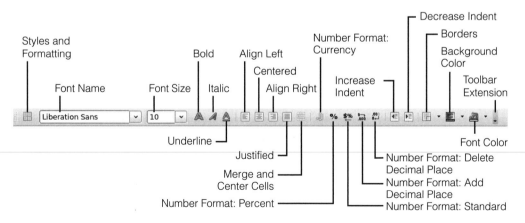

Figure 16.5
The Calc Formatting toolbar.

Table 16.2 Calc-Specific Formatting Toolbar Buttons

Name	Function
Merge and Center Cells	Centers data horizontally in selected cells.
Number Format: Currency	Applies currency format to numeric data in selected cells.
Number Format: Percent	Applies percentage format to numeric data in selected cells.
Number Format: Standard	Applies standard format to numeric data in selected cells.
Number Format: Add Decimal Place	Adds a decimal place to the significant value of data in selected cells.
Number Format: Delete Decimal Place	Removes a decimal place from the significant value of data in selected cells.
Decrease Indent	Decreases the amount of indent space for data in a specific cell.
Increase Indent	Increases the amount of indent space for data in a specific cell.
Borders	Applies borders to selected cells.

this component. Here is where you enter all of the functions and formulas used in your spreadsheet.

The Formula Bar has two distinct modes: the Cell Edit mode and the Data Input mode. The distinction may seem a bit too fine, but you'll pick up on it quickly.

In the Cell Edit mode, the Formula Bar's tools deal with the selected cell or cells as they relate to other cells. When in Data Input mode, the functions of the Formula Bar apply to data or formulas within *one* cell.

Figure 16.6 shows the Formula Bar in the Cell Edit mode, and Figure 16.7 shows the same bar in the Data Input mode.

Table 16.3 lists the functions of all of the buttons in either mode of the Formula Bar.

Putting Styles and Formatting and Navigator Tools to Work

The Styles and Formatting window is an underrated tool in OpenOffice.org. In Writer, it hardly seems necessary, given the presence of the Apply Styles field in the Formatting toolbar.

In Calc, the Formatting toolbar doesn't contain such a field, so the Styles and Formatting window becomes more important.

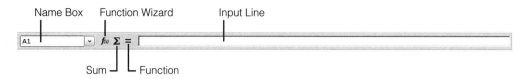

Figure 16.6
The Calc Formula Bar in the Cell Edit mode.

Figure 16.7
The Calc Formula Bar in the Data Input mode.

While the appearance of the Styles and Formatting window varies between OpenOffice.org components, its functionality remains the same. The Styles and Formatting window catalogs all available styles in each OpenOffice.org component and lets you apply those styles in the active file.

Figure 16.8 displays the Styles and Formatting window in its Calc incarnation.

The Styles and Formatting window has two sections: a style section on the left and a tool section on the right. The contents of the style section vary in different

Table 16.3 Formula Bar Buttons

Name	Mode	Function
Name Box	Both	Displays coordinates of selected cell or cell range. Entering coordinates into this field and pressing Enter navigates the cursor to the input cell or cell range.
Function Wizard	Both	Opens the Function Wizard.
Sum	Edit	Activates the SUM function, which adds the values of selected cells and displays the total in an adjacent cell.
Function	Edit	Activates the data input mode and begins the entry of a formula into the selected cell and its input line.
Cancel	Input	Removes input value and restores cell to last value.
Accept	Input	Copies value in input line to selected cell.
Input Line	Both	Displays or enables entry of data values and formulas into selected cell.

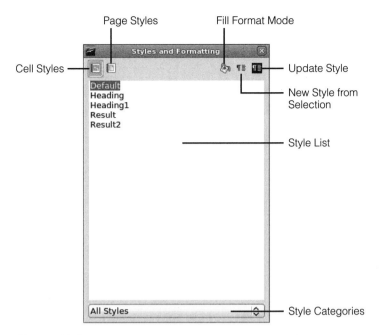

Figure 16.8
The Calc Styles and Formatting window.

OpenOffice.org components. In Calc, for instance, there are only two style buttons, where Writer has five buttons. These style buttons control the contents of the Style list in terms of the object type to which the styles apply. This differs from the Style Category list at the bottom of the Styles and Formatting window. This list controls the Style list as well, by further categorizing the available styles. Table 16.4 details the functions of the buttons within the Calc Styles and Formatting window.

The best way to understand how the Styles and Formatting window works is to see it in action.

1. In an open Calc spreadsheet, open the Styles and Formatting window by clicking the Styles and Formatting button on the Formatting toolbar.

2. Select any cell with data in the spreadsheet.

3. Double-click the Heading style in the Styles and Formatting window. The Heading style will format the cell.

4. Click the Fill Format Mode button in the Styles and Formatting window.

5. Select the Default style in the Styles and Formatting window.

6. With the cursor now appearing as a paint can, click the cell with Heading style. The style of the cell will change to Default.

7. Select a cell that contains data with your preferred default style of text.

8. Click the New Style from Selection button in the Styles and Formatting window.

9. In the Create Style dialog box, enter Cell Text as a style name.

10. Click OK.

11. Apply the new Cell Text style to the Default style cell created in Step 6 using either the double-click or Fill Format Mode methods.

The Navigator window is also nice to have around in Calc. As in Writer, the Navigator lists all of the objects within a spreadsheet and allows you to navigate to them with a few clicks of the mouse.

Figure 16.9 shows a typical Calc Navigator window. Right away you can see it is not as complex as the Navigator in Writer. It is no less useful, however.

Table 16.5 lists the functions of each of the buttons within the Navigator.

Table 16.4 The Calc Styles and Formatting Window Buttons

Name	Function
Cell Styles	Changes the Style List display to available cell styles.
Page Styles	Changes the Style List display to available page (or sheet) styles.
Fill Format Mode	Changes the cursor to fill mode. Clicking a cell or page applies the selected style to that object.
New Style from Selection	Records the style of the current cell or page and activates the Create Style dialog box to name the new style.
Update Style	If you change an existing style, updates all instances of that style in the document.

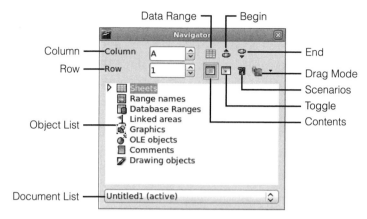

Figure 16.9
The Navigator in Calc is more streamlined than some of its OpenOffice.org counterparts.

Table 16.5 The Calc Navigator

Name	Function
Column	Lists the column letter of a selected cell. Values entered in this field (either directly or with the spin box controls) move the cursor to that column.
Row	Lists the row number of a selected cell. Values entered in this field (either directly or with the spin box controls) move the cursor to that row.
Data Range	Selects entire data area in the active spreadsheet.
Begin	Selects cell in upper-left corner of data area.
End	Selects cell in lower-right corner of data area.
Contents	Turns Object List in the Navigator on or off.
Toggle	Shifts Object List view to show only the current object type selected.
Scenarios	Changes Object List to a list of all scenarios associated with the active spreadsheet.
Drag Mode	Chooses the end result of click-and-drag actions of moving objects between documents.
Object List	Lists all elements contained within the active document.
Document List	Lists all open documents in Calc, distinguishing between active and inactive documents.

Not Just One Sheet

The perceived universe has three dimensions: length, height, and depth. Some people define time as the fourth dimension, and scientists have theorized about the existence of objects called superstrings that may vibrate through as many as 11 dimensions, which is enough to make nonscientists' heads hurt.

For now, we'll apply just the three-dimension analogy to Calc. Because now that you have mastered the existence of the two-dimensional spreadsheet, it's time to venture into the third dimension: multiple spreadsheets.

The origin of multiple spreadsheets goes all the way back to the paper spreadsheets we talked about earlier in the book. When the early spreadsheets grew so large—with hundreds and thousands of rows and columns—some accountant-types got the idea to start layering some of the calculations onto other sheets. In this manner, spreadsheets didn't grow to huge sizes, but still maintained the detail the accountants wanted.

When electronic spreadsheets were created, this methodology carried over. Even though size is a less pressing issue on a computer screen thanks to scrolling, most people still find it cumbersome not to see all of the data in a reasonable area. And, because we often print electronic spreadsheets, they still relate to the old paper medium.

When using multiple spreadsheets, it is important to remember how the sheets interconnect (if at all). Some people simply place unrelated datasets on each sheet, while others use related data with many cross-references. If you do use cross-references between multiple sheets, be careful that you don't inadvertently erase or change a piece of data that a cell on another sheet needs.

The use of multiple sheets is pretty simple. To view another sheet, simply click its sheet tab near the bottom of the screen. If you want to select more than one sheet (useful for printing), click a tab and hold the Shift key while clicking another tab. The two tabs and any in between them become selected. To select nonadjacent tabs, hold the Ctrl key while clicking.

New Calc documents have three sheets by default. Sometimes, you may need more (or fewer) sheets. The next steps guide you through this procedure.

1. In an open Calc document, right-click the sheet tab adjacent to the location where you want to insert a new sheet.

2. Choose Insert Sheet from the context menu. The Insert Sheet dialog box will open.

3. In the Position area of the Insert Sheet dialog box (see Figure 16.10), select the After Current Sheet radio button.

4. Select the New Sheet radio button.

5. Leave the No. of Sheets value at 1 and enter a new name for the sheet in the Name field.

6. Click OK. The new sheet will appear, as seen in Figure 16.11.

7. Right-click another sheet tab.

8. Choose Delete Sheet from the context menu.

9. When asked if you are sure you want to delete the selected sheet, click Yes. The sheet will be removed from the spreadsheet document.

Besides being able to create new sheets from scratch, Calc can import whole sheets from other documents. This is more effective and faster than cutting and pasting a data area from one document to another.

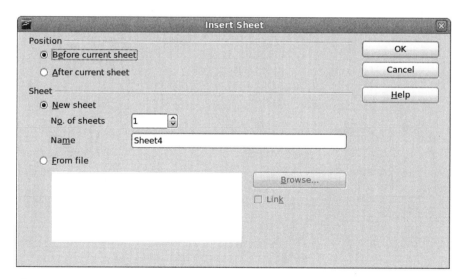

Figure 16.10
This dialog box allows you to create new sheets or borrow sheets from other documents.

1. In an open Calc document, right-click the sheet tab adjacent to the location where you want to insert a new sheet.

2. Choose Insert Sheet from the context menu.

3. In the Position area of the Insert Sheet dialog box, select After Current Sheet radio button.

4. Click the From File radio button.

5. Click the Browse button to locate the correct file in the Insert dialog box.

6. Click Open in the Insert dialog box. The Insert Sheet dialog box will now display a list of the available sheets in the second file in the From File list (see Figure 16.12).

7. Select the desired sheet.

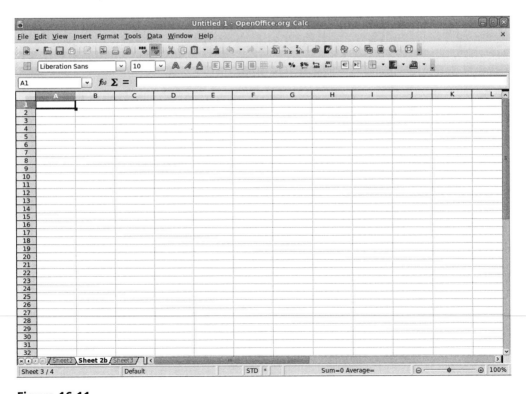

Figure 16.11
The new sheet, ready for data entry.

8. Click OK. The new sheet from the other document will appear within the active document.

Cross-Reference Check

If your newly imported sheet has any cross-references to other sheets, particularly in its former home, those cross-references will become invalid. Check your new sheet thoroughly.

With all of these sheets flying around in the document, you likely need to perform some of the usual housekeeping functions to keep your documents looking neat and orderly.

Moving, copying, and renaming sheets is a piece of cake in Calc, as you will see in the next steps.

1. In an open Calc document, right-click the sheet tab you would like to move.

2. Click Move/Copy Sheet on the context menu.

3. In the Move/Copy Sheet dialog box (see Figure 16.13), be sure that the active document appears in the To Document field.

4. In the Insert Before list, select the sheet that you want to put your selected sheet in front of.

5. Click OK. The sheet will move to its new location.

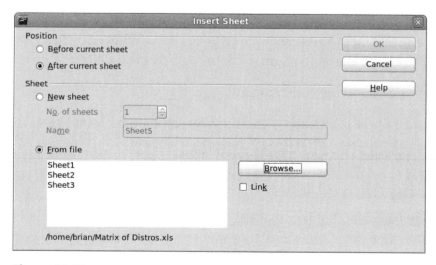

Figure 16.12
Choose from a list of sheets to place in your document.

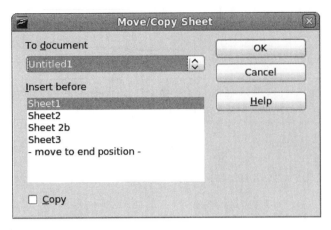

Figure 16.13
The Move/Copy Sheet dialog box.

To copy a sheet to another location in the spreadsheet, repeat Steps 1–4 and then continue with the following procedure.

1. Select the Copy check box.

2. Click OK. A copy of the sheet will move to its new location.

Sending Spreadsheets

To send a sheet or a copy of a sheet to another document, select the destination spreadsheet document in the To Document list and then complete the steps to move or copy a sheet.

3. A copy of a sheet takes the name of the original sheet, followed by the copy number. To rename this copy, right-click the copied sheet's tab.

4. Click Rename Sheet in the context menu.

5. In the Rename Sheet dialog box, enter the new name in the Name field.

6. Click OK. The sheet will now have the new name.

Good-Looking Data

The human body has several quirks that we have to put up with daily. One of them is the wandering eye. This is not the wandering eye that gets people in trouble. Rather, it is the inability of our eyes to stay focused in any one place for almost any length of time.

Our eyes, it seems, always have to be moving, soaking up the world around us. This translates into the need to create documents that attract our eyes so that they naturally want to look at the words on the page. It helps that in most cultures, lettering attracts the eye, even if we can't figure out the words. Though this is a learned response, the attraction doesn't keep the eyes there for long. It becomes necessary, therefore, to keep the interest with something other than just letters. Sometimes it's done by using outstanding content, other times by eye-catching colors (yellow fire trucks get more attention, for example, than red ones).

One thing that eyes—and the brain behind them—detest is confusion. Place a jumbled document or spreadsheet before someone, and the frustration level goes through the roof. At that point, the person will most likely ignore the document. Our visual system wants things to be simple and consistent.

You can establish consistency in a Calc spreadsheet in many different ways beyond the obvious use of colors and fills. One method is to use consistent formatting of data. In this context, the format of data refers to the way it appears.

For instance, time can be expressed in many different ways. Right now, as I write these words, it is Monday, April 26, 2010, 8:46 in the evening, Eastern Daylight Time. Or is it 2046 hrs on 26/04/10? Time can be presented in thousands of different formats. You are free to choose whichever kind of format you want, but it is important to maintain consistency. If you use a 12:34 p.m. format in one cell with time data, then you should use the same format in other time data cells.

Time is just one of the values in Calc that can have different formats. Dates, text, numbers, and currency can all be displayed in different ways, as you will learn in the next sections.

Formatting Text

Text formats are perhaps the simplest to understand. Calc handles text in much the same way as Writer. Each cell can hold over 64,000 characters of text, so you can create whole documents within cells. But why would you want to?

You accomplish text formatting using the same tools found within Writer, with some additional functions designed specifically for cell use.

1. Within an open Calc spreadsheet, select a cell with data.

2. Click the Bold button on the Formatting toolbar.

3. Enter 24 into the Font Size field.

4. Choose Format | Cells.

5. Click the Alignment tab in the Format Cells dialog box (see Figure 16.14).

6. In the Text Orientation area, click the Vertically Stacked check box.

7. Click OK. Figure 16.15 shows the newly formatted text.

You can also have text auto-wrap within a cell.

1. In an empty cell within the spreadsheet, enter a lengthy text passage. A small red triangle will indicate the presence of overflow text.

2. Choose Format | Cells.

3. Click the Alignment tab in the Format Cells dialog box.

4. Select the Wrap Text Automatically check box.

5. Click OK. The lengthy text passage will appear in full within the cell.

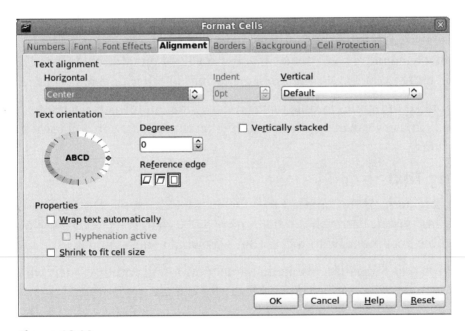

Figure 16.14
The Format Cells dialog box lets you choose the alignment of text within a cell.

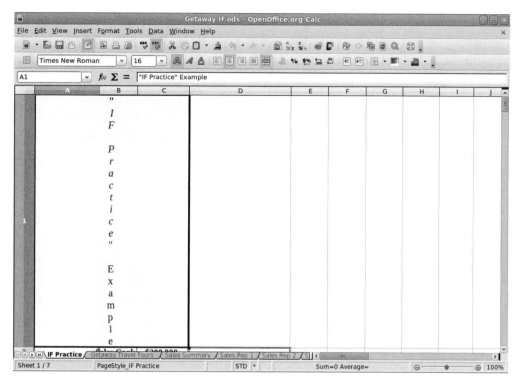

Figure 16.15
Vertical text in a spreadsheet.

Formatting Values

Politicians love to talk about values. We need to get back to traditional values, they say. But whose tradition? European? Asian? African? There is no one answer.

Nor is there one way to display data values. The different time formats have already been shown. Numbers, too, can be expressed in different ways. One dataset may project a significant value to the hundredths place, while another projects it to the thousandths place.

Even in the English-speaking cultures, numbers carry different names. In the United States, citizens refer to 1,000,000,000 as a billion. In the United Kingdom, a billion is officially 1,000,000,000,000,000,000. Advocates of the Queen's English refer to this as yet another example of the insidious U.S. corruption of the English language. Quite.

Within a spreadsheet, it may not be obvious to readers what is a data value and what is text. Is that 1999 in cell C3 indicative of a year, one short of 2,000 items, or the brand-name of a new company? The next steps show one quick way to find out.

1. With a Calc spreadsheet open, click Tools | Options.

2. In the Options dialog box, select the OpenOffice.org Calc | View menu tree options (see Figure 16.16).

3. Select the Value Highlighting check box in the Display section of the dialog box.

4. Click OK. The spreadsheet will now display all data values in a new color.

Formatting Numbers

"Mathematics," Galileo Galilei once said, "is the alphabet with which God has written the universe." This means that we had better be really careful how we present our numbers. You never know who might be checking your work.

One other thing: number formats vary from nation to nation, so if you create a spreadsheet for readers in another country, try to accommodate their

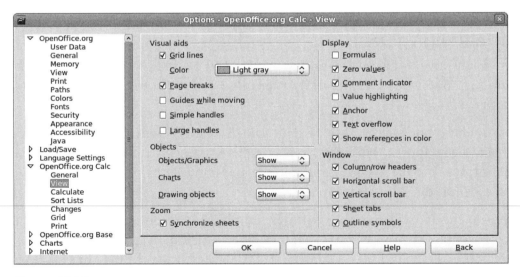

Figure 16.16
The View page of the Options dialog box.

conventions as a courtesy. These steps demonstrate how to modify the format of a numeric value within a spreadsheet.

1. In an open Calc spreadsheet, select a cell with a numeric data value.

2. Choose Format | Cells.

3. In the Format Cells dialog box, click the Numbers tab (see Figure 16.17).

4. Select Currency in the Category list.

5. Select the –$1234.12 option in the Format list. A preview of the selected number will appear in the Preview window, and the values in the Options area will change to correspond to the selected format.

6. Click OK.

Formatting Date and Time

Most people over the age of 30 remember the way they were taught to tell time. The little hand on the three, and the big hand on the twelve meant 3:00.

These days, you can hardly find a clock that tells time in analog fashion.

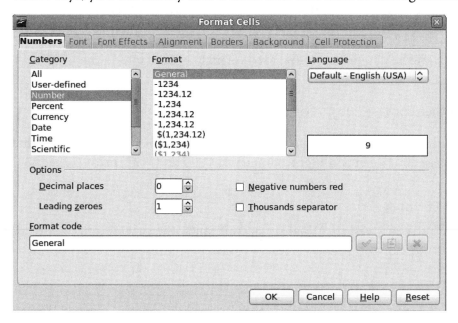

Figure 16.17
Setting numeric value formats.

Agreement on timekeeping is still a hot issue in international circles. While most countries have adopted the Gregorian calendar for trade purposes, many countries still have their own calendars and dates. And, to make it more confusing, dates displayed from the same calendar can be shown in different ways. In the U.S., 4/27/10 translates to 27.4.10 in Europe.

Calc takes this all in stride and lets you choose your preferred method of displaying dates and times—at least those based on the Gregorian calendar. These steps show how to modify the format of date and time values within a spreadsheet.

1. Enter your date of birth into an empty cell within any open Calc document. Use any number-based format.

2. Select the cell.

3. Choose Format | Cells.

4. In the Format Cells dialog box, click the Numbers tab.

5. Select Date in the Category list.

6. Select the Friday, December 31, 1999 option in the Format list. In the Preview window, you can see the day of the week on which you were born.

7. To convert the date to an hour-based format, select Time in the Category list.

8. Select the 876613:37:00 option in the Format list.

9. Click OK. Now you can see the number of hours, minutes, and seconds that have passed between Midnight, January 1, 1900 and your birthday.

Formatting Currency

Now for the nitty-gritty stuff. What do accountants, the originators of spreadsheets, count most of all?

Money.

The next steps show how Calc not only formats currency values, but also does so in a very cosmopolitan manner.

1. In an open Calc spreadsheet, select a cell with a numeric or currency data value.

2. Choose Format | Cells.

3. In the Format Cells dialog box, click the Numbers tab.

4. Select Currency in the Category list.

5. The Format list has two fields: a list of nations and a list of available formats for that nation. Select € Italian (Italy) in the top drop-down list.

6. Select the –€1234.- - option.

7. Click OK. The value will now appear in euros.

Even though Calc offers a plethora of both common and esoteric formats, someday you may need to create your own, as the following steps demonstrate.

1. With any Calc spreadsheet open, select Format | Cells.

2. In the Format Cells dialog box, click the Numbers tab.

3. Select Percent in the Category list.

4. Select the –12.95% option in the Format list.

5. Select the Negative Numbers Red check box. Information will now appear in the Format code field.

6. Click the Edit Comment button, which has a note icon and is immediately to the right of the Format code field.

7. Change the User-Defined value to Red Percent.

8. Click the Add button. You have now added the format to the Percent and User-Defined categories.

Formatting Cells

Thus far, the previous sections in this chapter have concerned themselves with formatting the data contained within a cell, but not the cell itself.

Formatting cells goes beyond just making the data look pretty. Recall that the human eye needs to have something to keep it focused. Following a long row of data across a screen is very difficult if nothing keeps the eye from wandering up or down into the adjacent rows.

With the judicious addition of fills and borders, you can help the eye track data across a screen.

All cells have borders. Sometimes, the borders are invisible, but they are always there, like the air we breathe.

Cell borders can come in all of the available OpenOffice.org colors and can be as thick as 9 pts. I don't recommend that you use such an extreme width on individual cell borders, as you will obscure the cell's contents. But you may find uses for all of the various thicknesses.

Cell fills are also referred to as backgrounds for cells. These, too, come in a vast variety of colors. Care should be taken, however, to avoid the darker shades, as these obscure the text as well. But if you do use a dark fill color, you can change the text color to increase the contrast between text and background.

As you create your own fills, try to keep the number of different colors to a maximum of three shades. More than that could lead to confusing data representation and a frustrated brain.

1. Open a Calc document.

2. Select a range of cells one column wide.

3. Choose Format | Cells.

4. In the Format Cells dialog box, click the Borders tab, as seen in Figure 16.18.

5. In the Preview window, click the areas immediately to the right of and below the gray box. Solid lines will appear in the Preview window.

6. In the Style list, select the 2.50 pt option.

7. In the Color field in the Line group, select Blue.

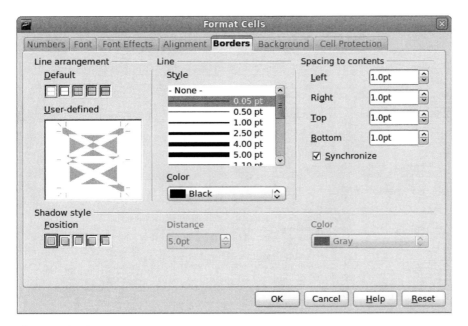

Figure 16.18
Making a run for the border.

8. In the Shadow Style group, click the second Position preset button.

9. In the Color field in the Shadow group, select Orange 4.

10. Click OK. A partially blue box with an orange shadow will appear around the selected range, as shown in Figure 16.19.

11. With the same range selected, repeat Steps 3 and 4, except this time click the Background tab.

12. Select Yellow.

13. Click OK. The background will be changed.

Formatting Ranges

To quickly apply borders and fills, click and hold the respective buttons on the Formatting toolbar.

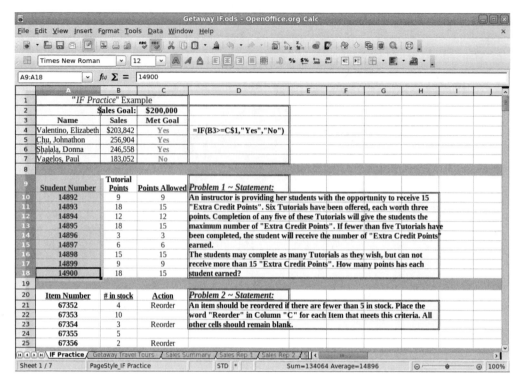

Figure 16.19
Interesting shadow effects can be achieved.

Conclusion

Calc is an effective tool for the creation and management of data spreadsheets. This chapter reviewed many of the basic concepts of Calc, and as you explore this application in your continued use of Fedora, you will find it to be a very powerful tool.

Chapter 17 will move on to review an OpenOffice.org component that will enable you to present your ideas to the world in new and attractive ways: Impress.

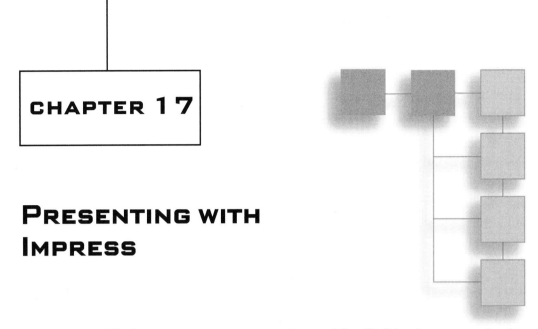

CHAPTER 17

PRESENTING WITH IMPRESS

They're not called meetings anymore, you know. The "in" business crowd refers to them as *collaboration sessions* or *community meet-ups*.

Nor are these discussions held in traditional conference rooms. More and more, corporations are turning away from the same old long table and swivel chairs in favor of more comfortable surroundings.

Corporations around the world have begun to recognize that how we meet is at least as important as why we meet.

Why we meet is to trade new ideas and improve the condition of the environment we share with others. (That, and free donuts.) And fancy collaborative fads aside, meetings work better when the *many* settle down and listen to *one* person every once in a while.

Which means that one person has to get up and speak before the many. Oftentimes, this person speaks with informal, impromptu statements. But sometimes, the person will give a full-fledged presentation. And that is where OpenOffice.org's Impress application comes into play.

In this chapter, you will:

- Explore the Impress interface

- Learn how to organize ideas for a presentation

- Create an Impress presentation

The Second Greatest Fear

Some people are good at presentations. They stand up in front of everyone else and mesmerize us with their logic, charisma, and charm. No notes, no slides—just the person and his or her vision.

The rest of us may require a little assistance. In a public speech, the power of the speaker's words is the only thing that can help people remember the speaker's message. Have you ever noticed how politicians always work some sort of catch phrase into their speeches? They are not trying to be trite—they're trying to give their audiences something to remember, because our memory and sense of hearing do not always work well together.

In a private business setting, where a lot of detail may be required, entirely verbal presentations would be impossible for others to remember later. So speakers have two choices: reduce the presentation to its mere essence to get the overall points across, or rely on some other form of communication to get the finer points of the message to the audience.

Since many people fear public speaking second only to death, most would rather not become fiery orators in order to get their points across. Which leaves the second option: use another way to communicate. We simply remember things better if we have seen them with our own two eyes.

Thus, the corporate slide show was born.

It started off with placards at first, showing charts created by people whose job was to do nothing but show the charts. Overheads were used next, lending presenters the ability to support their points on the fly. Then came slides, which added color and speed to presentations. Finally, the slides were created directly on a computer and projected from there, as well.

Which brings us to the component in OpenOffice.org that gets this job done for you: Impress.

Learning the Tools to Use

The makers of Impress have loaded it with dozens of interesting tools that help you build incredible presentations with ease. This is readily apparent when looking at the Impress interface (see Figure 17.1).

Standard Toolbar

Line and Filling Toolbar

Slide Pane

View Controls

Presentation Toolbar

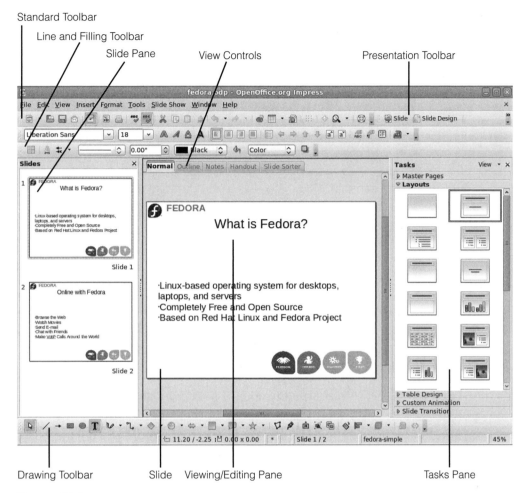

Drawing Toolbar   Slide   Viewing/Editing Pane   Tasks Pane

Figure 17.1
The Impress interface in Normal view.

Within Impress, you can choose from six views when working with your presentation. Five of these views enable you to edit your presentation in different ways. The sixth lets you view your presentation from start to finish. Figure 17.1 highlights the view controls in the center of the interface. Table 17.1 outlines the different views and their purposes.

Each of the five Edit views in Impress has a different set of tools to use. The following sections will examine these tools.

Table 17.1 The Impress Views

View	Function
Normal	The default (and primary) view in Impress where you edit slides on an individual level.
Outline	This view enables the creation and editing of the presentation's outline, which the slides directly reflect.
Notes	Many presenters need notes to guide them through their presentation. Use this view to create such notes.
Handout	Sometimes handouts accompany presentations so the audience can follow along and create their own notes. This view enables the creation of presentation handouts.
Slide Sorter	Use the Slide Sort view to shift the slide order in a presentation, if needed.
Slide Show	This read-only view shows the presentation in its entirety.

Normal View

If any view could be called the center of Impress, the Normal view would be it. In this view (which you can see back in Figure 17.1), you do all of the editing and creating of individual slides. You enter text, apply slide transitions, add pictures—anything that can be done to a slide, you do here.

This translates, of course, into a large number of tools you can use. There are too many tools to devote a lot of words to each. To help guide you in the right direction, the following sections will highlight the main tools within the Normal view.

Standard Toolbar

In all views of Impress, only the Standard toolbar is almost always present, and it retains many of the same tools you have already seen in Writer and Calc. Only one new button is found on this toolbar, the Display Grid button, as seen in Figure 17.2. The Display Grid button displays a placement grid on the slide to assist with object and text alignment.

Display Grid

Figure 17.2
The Impress Standard toolbar.

Line and Filling Toolbar

In most of the OpenOffice.org applications, the Formatting toolbar usually appears right underneath the Standard toolbar. In Impress, however, this is not always a given. In fact, the toolbar you might be familiar with and call "Formatting" only appears when you are specifically editing text in Impress. At all other times, the Line and Filling toolbar will appear in its stead. Figure 17.3 illustrates the Line and Filling toolbar as it appears when editing most Impress objects. Table 17.2 details the functions of the buttons within the Line and Filling toolbar.

Drawing Toolbar

The Drawing toolbar is a new toolbar for those of you reading this book cover to cover. You'll find it only within the Impress and Draw components. This toolbar contains a variety of features to customize the way you edit or create slides with Impress.

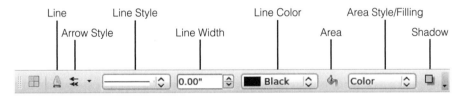

Figure 17.3
The Line and Filling toolbar.

Table 17.2 The Line and Filling Toolbar Buttons

Name	Function
Line	Opens the Line dialog box to control the attributes of a selected line.
Arrow Style	Applies arrow ends to a selected line or connector.
Line Style	Changes style of a selected line or connector.
Line Width	Changes width of a selected line or connector.
Line Color	Changes color of a selected line or connector.
Area	Opens the Area dialog box to control the attributes of a selected area.
Area Style/Filling	Two lists that control the fill type and color of a given area or background.
Shadow	Applies a shadow effect to a selected object.

In the Drawing toolbar, the buttons focus on creating text and graphic objects on the slide. Many of the icons have submenus of options, vastly increasing the number of possible tools this single toolbar possesses. Figure 17.4 highlights the buttons on the Drawing toolbar, while Table 17.3 briefly explains the function of each button.

Presentation Toolbar

The Presentation toolbar is a control unique to Impress. Appropriately, it has unique properties. Unfortunately, in the default Impress view, this powerful toolbar is sort of shoved off to one side, as you saw back in Figure 17.1. To see it more clearly, let's undock it (see Figure 17.5). Like all docked toolbars, you can undock it by clicking and dragging the toolbar handle.

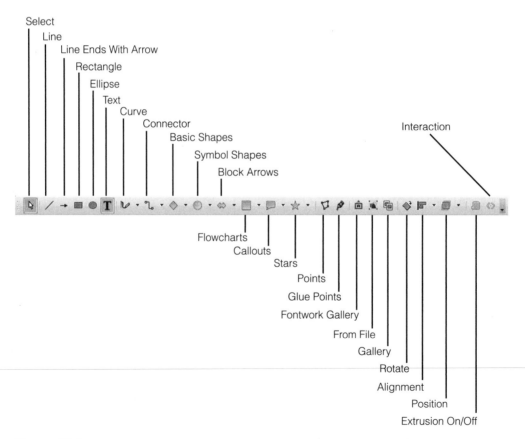

Figure 17.4
The Drawing toolbar.

Table 17.3 The Drawing Toolbar Buttons

Name	Function
Select	Activates the selection cursor.
Line	Accesses tools to create lines and filled lines in floating toolbar.
Line Ends with Arrow	Creates lines and arrows using floating toolbar.
Rectangle	Enables creation of rectangular graphic objects.
Ellipse	Enables creation of elliptical graphic objects.
Text	Activates the Text Formatting toolbar.
Curve	Enables creation of curved lines.
Connector	Enables creation of connectors between other graphic objects.
Basic Shapes	Enables creation of basic geometric shapes.
Symbol Shapes	Enables creation of symbols on slides.
Block Arrows	Enables creation of large, 2-D arrow shapes.
Flowcharts	Enables creation of standard flowchart shapes.
Callouts	Enables creation of callout shapes.
Stars	Enables creation of star shapes.
Points	Edits the control points of a selected object.
Glue Points	Edits the glue points of a selected connector.
Fontwork Gallery	Inserts stylized word-based artwork.
From File	Inserts artwork into a slide from a file.
Gallery	Activates the OpenOffice.org Gallery of images and artwork.
Rotate	Enables the rotation of a selected object.
Alignment	Aligns selected object to the slide.
Position	Directs position of object layering with other objects on the slide.
Extrusion On/Off	Activates 3-D extrusion of a selected object.
Interaction	Allows actions to be assigned to parts of the slide when clicked.

All of the buttons on the Presentation toolbar have text labels, so you can easily ascertain which button does what. Table 17.4 details the purposes of the buttons on this small toolbar.

Outline View

The Outline view in Impress facilitates the entry of clean and well-organized text within the slides. Because all of the text in the slides belongs to one big outline, this is a key view to use in Impress. The points on the screen should support and organize your presentation, not repeat it word for word.

Figure 17.5
The Presentation toolbar.

Table 17.4 The Presentation Toolbar Buttons

Name	Function
Slide	Inserts a new slide after the selected slide.
Slide Design	Allows a new slide design to be exchanged with the current slide's design.
Slide Show	Starts the Slide Show view of Impress.

The tools and interface in the Outline view are rather simple, since the Normal view handles most of the formatting and special effects. Figure 17.6 reveals a look at the Outline view.

As you can see in Figure 17.6, the Standard toolbar remains the same, and the Line and Filling, Drawing, and Presentation toolbars are not present at all—nor is the Tasks pane. In place of the Line and Filling toolbar is the Text Formatting toolbar, and the Presentation toolbar has been swapped out by the Outline toolbar.

The way the Outline view functions is simple: when one of the slide icons is selected in the Slide pane, the corresponding top-level heading in the outline is highlighted.

The toolbars in this view also provide a unique set of tools to work with.

Outline Toolbar

The number of icons on the Outline toolbar has been heavily curtailed in the Outline view. Again, this is fine, since this view only needs a simple text editor.

Figure 17.7 focuses on the Outline toolbar, and Table 17.5 details the buttons' functionality.

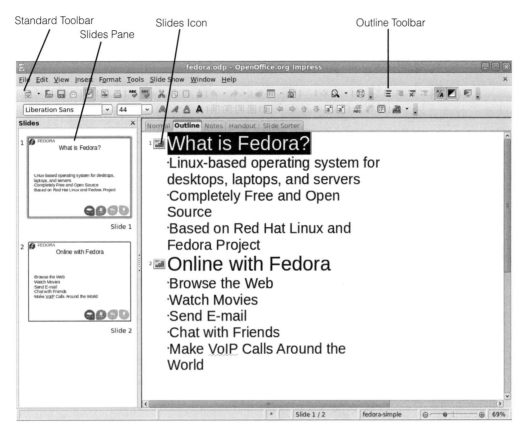

Figure 17.6
The Impress Outline view.

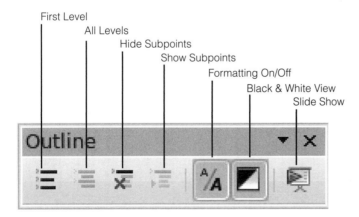

Figure 17.7
The Outline toolbar.

Table 17.5 The Outline Toolbar Buttons

Name	Function
First Level	Hides all levels in outline but first level.
All Levels	Shows all levels in outline.
Hide Subpoints	Hides any subpoints under selected outline paragraph.
Show Subpoints	Shows all subpoints under selected outline paragraph.
Formatting On/Off	Displays formatting of slide text in Outline view.
Black & White View	Displays all text in black and white, regardless of formatting.
Slide Show	Starts the Slide Show view.

Text Formatting Toolbar

As mentioned previously, in the Outline view there is no Line and Filling toolbar. Instead, the Text Formatting toolbar takes its place. This toolbar is very similar in form to the usual Formatting toolbar that appears in other OpenOffice.org applications. But it has enough new tools to warrant its own name and place in the Impress toolbar collection. As you can see in Figure 17.8, much is familiar about the Text Formatting toolbar. Table 17.6 discusses the new toolset.

Notes and Handout Views

The controls in the Notes and Handout views are nearly identical to the ones in the Normal view.

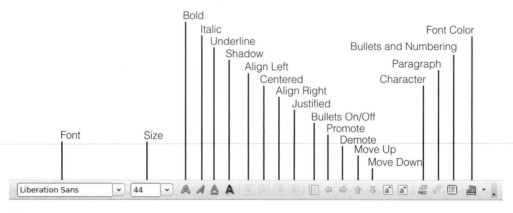

Figure 17.8
The Text Formatting toolbar.

Table 17.6 The Text Formatting Toolbar Buttons

Name	Function
Font	Changes the font of selected text.
Size	Changes the font size of selected text.
Bold	Applies the bold style to selected text.
Italic	Applies the italic style to selected text.
Underline	Underlines selected text.
Shadow	Applies a shadow effect to selected text.
Align Left	Aligns selected paragraphs to left margin.
Centered	Centers selected paragraphs on page.
Align Right	Aligns selected paragraphs to right margin.
Justified	Justifies selected paragraphs to fill all space between margins.
Bullets On/Off	Changes selected paragraphs to a bulleted list.
Promote	Promotes selected paragraph to the next highest outline level.
Demote	Demotes selected paragraph to the next lowest outline level.
Move Up	Moves selected paragraph up in the text block.
Move Down	Moves selected paragraph down in the text block.
Character	Formats selected characters.
Paragraph	Formats selected paragraphs.
Bullets and Numbering	Formats bullets and numbering of selected list.
Font Color	Single-click applies displayed color to selected text. Click and hold reveals more colors to apply.

As you can see in Figures 17.9 and 17.10, the one significant difference in the controls is the disabling of buttons in the Presentation toolbar.

The Notes view presents each slide individually on a single sheet of paper. The slide covers the top half of the sheet, and the bottom half has a note box. Within this note box, you can enter any additional points or examples beyond your outline to assist during the actual presentation.

The Handout view is the simplest view of all. It simply displays a certain number of slides on a page that you can print and give to audience members to allow them to follow along. Handouts are very useful when giving a lot of detail in a presentation.

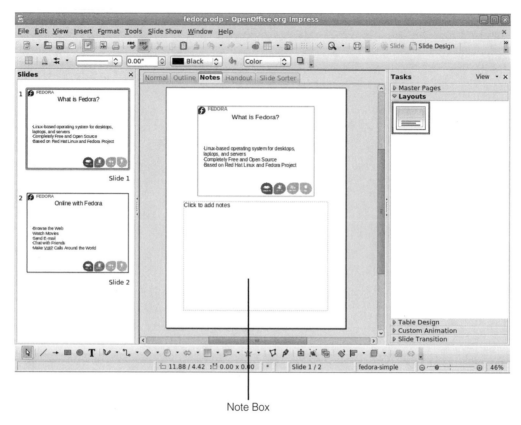

Figure 17.9
The Impress Notes view.

To change the number of slides displayed per page in the Handout view, click one of the alternative layouts displayed in the Tasks pane.

Slide Sort View

The Slide Sort view, illustrated in Figure 17.11, displays all of the slides in the presentation in miniature form. As the name suggests, this view offers an easy way to sort the order of the slides in the presentation.

The Slide View and Slide Sorter toolbars are something unique to this mode of Impress. Replacing the Line and Filling and Text Formatting toolbars, these small toolbars pack a lot of punch.

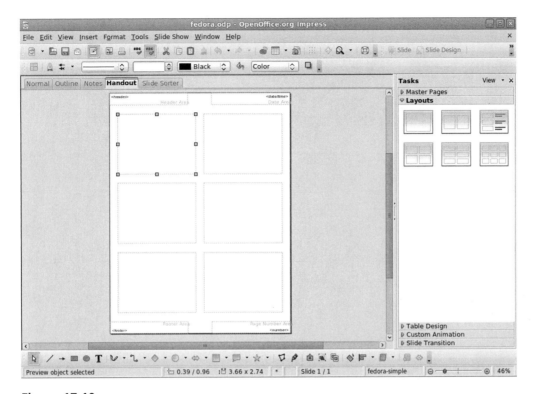

Figure 17.10
The Impress Handout view.

Back to Normal

Double-clicking any slide in the Slide Sort view opens that slide in the Normal view.

This view does more than just allow the sorting of slides. It also permits easy editing of the transitions between slides, among other things. The new Slide toolbars, which the next section examines more closely, were created to accomplish these jobs.

Slide Sorter and Slide View Toolbars

Transitions are the effects that occur when moving from one slide to another, such as the sliding of one slide over the previous one.

Transition Beginnings

When editing transitions, bear in mind that you are editing the transition that *starts* the current slide.

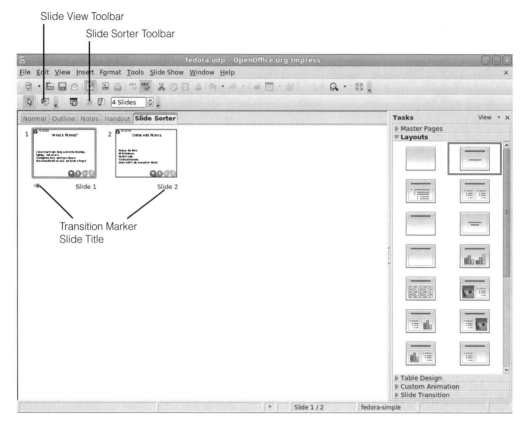

Figure 17.11
The Slide Sort view.

Figure 17.12 shows the Slide Sorter toolbar in detail, while Figure 17.13 accomplishes the same thing for the Slide View toolbar. Table 17.7 explains the functionality of both of the toolbars' buttons.

Creating a Presentation

After you have figured out what to say, there are two opposing schools of thought when beginning a new presentation in Impress:

■ Outline your presentation content first and worry about the design later.

■ Create a blank design and fill in the text later.

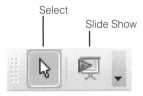

Figure 17.12
The Slide Sorter toolbar.

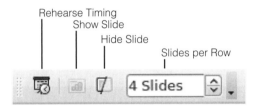

Figure 17.13
The Slide View toolbar.

Table 17.7   The Slide Sorter and View Toolbars Buttons

Name	Function
Select	Activates the selection cursor.
Slide Show	Activates the Slide Show view.
Rehearse Timing	Determines the timing for the slide by starting the Slide Show view with the addition of a timer that indicates the time to speak with this slide.
Show Slide	Shows the selected slide in the Slide Show view.
Hide Slide	Hides the selected slide in the Slide Show view.
Slides per Row	Enter the number of slides per row in this view.

There is no right way to do this, really. Each method has an equal number of pros and cons. It basically comes down to personal preferences: Do you like to organize your text first or your slides first?

If you are new to using Impress or a similar application, I recommend that you use the Wizard to get things started. It's simple and quick. Plus, it's much easier to build a base of slide design and add content as needed.

1. From any application of OpenOffice.org, choose File | Wizards | Presentation. The Presentation Wizard dialog box will open (see Figure 17.14).

2. Select the From Template radio button. A list of presentation templates will appear.

3. Select the Recommendation of a Strategy option. The template will appear in the Preview window (see Figure 17.15).

4. Click Next. The Presentation Backgrounds page will appear, as shown in Figure 17.16.

5. In the Select a Slide Design list, select the Water option.

6. Select the Screen radio button for Select an Output Medium. A preview of the style will appear in the Preview window.

7. Click Next. The Transition page will appear (see Figure 17.17).

8. Select an option in the Effect drop-down list. An animation of the transition will appear in the Preview window for every effect you choose.

9. Select a Speed option. An animation of the transition will appear in the Preview window.

10. Click Next. The Content page will appear, as shown in Figure 17.18.

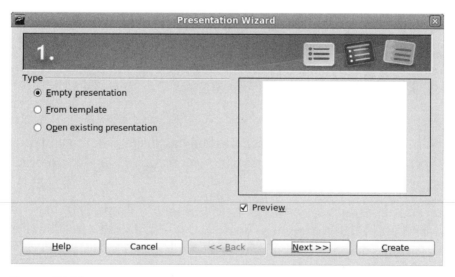

Figure 17.14
Starting the Presentation Wizard.

11. Enter the pertinent information in each field and then click Next. The Slide Selection page will appear (see Figure 17.19).

12. Use the expansion controls to see the contents of each slide. Select or clear the check boxes for the slides you do or do not need.

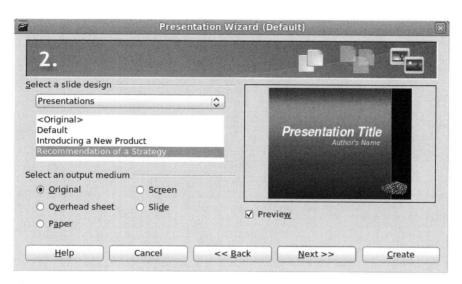

Figure 17.15
Impress has some nice templates to work with.

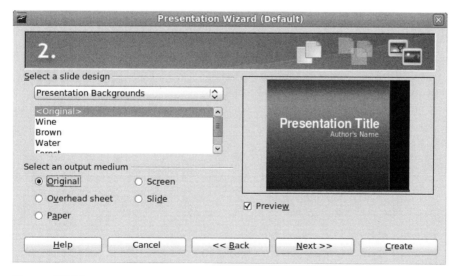

Figure 17.16
Choosing a background design.

13. Click Create. The presentation will be created and displayed in Normal view.

Figure 17.20 shows how a new presentation with placeholder slides based on the settings made in the Wizard could look.

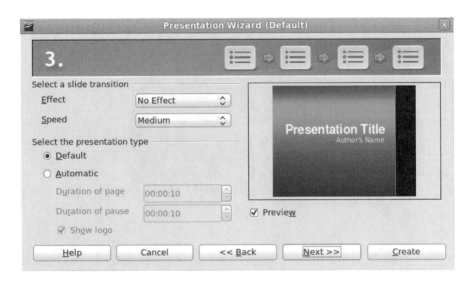

Figure 17.17
Transitions are configured here.

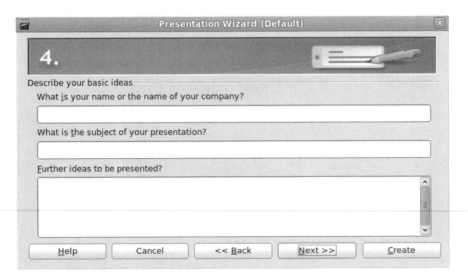

Figure 17.18
Basic content information can be entered here.

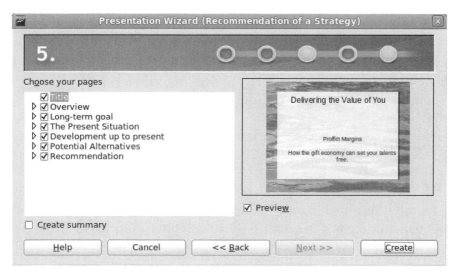

Figure 17.19
Choose the slides you want.

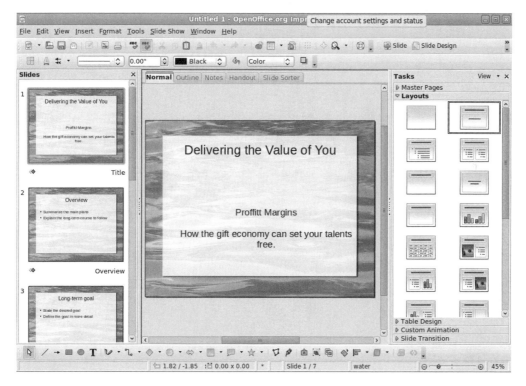

Figure 17.20
A new presentation for you to modify.

Now all you need to do is click on each slide in the Slide pane to view it and edit the slide's content in the Normal or Outline view. When your presentation is finished and saved, simply click the Slide Show icon in the Presentation toolbar to start the slide show.

Conclusion

In this chapter, you reviewed the wealth of tools contained within the Impress component.

In Chapter 18, we will take a look at one of the newest additions to the OpenOffice.org application suite, one that you will definitely be able to use in your office or even home: the aptly named database application, Base.

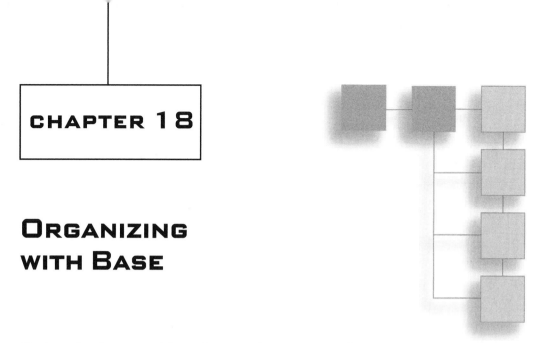

CHAPTER 18

ORGANIZING WITH BASE

Fiction: databases are big, evil, scary things. Somewhere along your professional career, you may have heard this rumor. Database administrators may be regarded with awe at your company. The simple truth is, anyone can make a database and understand how it works.

You will see for yourself in this chapter, as we explore the database component of OpenOffice.org, Base. Specifically, you will learn about:

- The basic concepts of databases

- The different components of a database

- How to use the Base interface

- How to build a database

Database Concepts

Four different types of objects comprise databases. All of these objects working together make up the database. Any of them taken separately does not have much use.

These objects are tables, forms, queries, and reports. Before examining the workings of an actual database, it will help to review the functionality of each object.

You're probably already familiar with tables. They are essentially simplified spreadsheets. A database table is simpler because the purpose of the rows and columns is set, whereas a spreadsheet has more flexibility in how you can use rows and columns. Also, spreadsheets allow cells to interact with each other, whereas database tables don't. If you need mathematical comparisons made, put your data in a spreadsheet.

In a database table, each row is a database record. A database record is a collection of related data. In a database of books, for example, one record could be:

Ivanhoe, Sir Walter Scott, New American Library, September 1987

This record has five fields: Book Title, Author, Publisher, Published Month, and Published Year. All other records in this database table use the same fields. If a record needs to have more information, then the database table needs additional fields. In database programmer lingo, this is sometimes referred to as adding columns.

A form is the interface structure between the user and the table. Though you can directly enter data into a table (and some prefer this), a form gives the user visual cues to help enter data more quickly, rather than tediously tabbing across row after row of the database table.

At the very least, a good database needs tables and forms. If the database had just a table, it would be rather dull. If it had just a form, it would only be a shell surrounding nothingness.

Queries are little programming scripts that pull specific information out of a database. Don't panic if you don't think you can program anything. You can master queries once you understand the way they are structured. And Base has a wizard to help you with this.

Once a query has gathered information, it needs to be displayed. This is done in a report, the final piece of the database puzzle. Reports are, again, similar to spreadsheets, in that they typically present data in tabular form. Reports, however, are not interactive. They simply place the data requested by a query into a read-only file, which can be printed or displayed on-screen. If data needs to be changed, it has to be done in the table (through the form).

Databases can have multiple versions of all of these objects. In a climatology database, you could have a table of known temperature highs and lows for a region and another table of rainfall amounts, each accessed by separate forms. The choices are limitless.

To start understanding databases at the day-to-day level, let's walk through the creation of a database to see how all of these components fit together.

Building Your Own Database

Databases are excellent tools to use in the business world. If you have a small business, creating a database to keep track of inventory or customers is a vital task. If you're using Fedora at home, a database could also come in handy. If you have a collection, you know how important it is to keep track of it. You may constantly acquire new items for the collection, trading with other hobbyists in order to finagle acquisition of the item you desire most.

Whether you use it for home or office, Base makes database creation simple.

To create a working database, you need to build the following items in this order:

1. Database file

2. Table

3. Form

You always need to build the database file first. You could, in theory, create the form before the table, but that would be cumbersome, and why do all the extra work?

The remainder of this chapter is devoted to the creation of a comic book collection database, which is, essentially, an inventory database. As you follow along, watch carefully and think about how you would like to build a database for your own needs.

Choosing Database Formats

OpenOffice.org is unique among office suites because of its compatibility with so many other programs. Base is no exception, having the capability to create and read databases in several formats beyond its native Base format:

- Adabas D

- dBASE

- Evolution LDAP

- Evolution Local

- Groupwise

- JDBC

- Microsoft Access

- MySQL

- ODBC

- Oracle JDBC

- Spreadsheet

- Text

Which format you choose depends on a couple of things. If you import data from another database in one of these formats, then you should select that format. You might also save a copy of the database in an alternate format if you intend to share the file with others who—heaven forbid—might not use OpenOffice.org or Fedora.

Before using Base, you will need to install it within Fedora. Using the techniques described in Chapter 6, "Installing and Updating Software," you can use PackageKit to search for and install the OpenOffice.org Base program.

The following steps show the beginning of the database construction—specifically, the first stage of creating a database in Base, which involves creating the main database file.

1. In any OpenOffice.org component, click File | New | Database. The Database Wizard will open, as shown in Figure 18.1.

2. Click the Create a New Database radio button; then click Next. The Save and Proceed page will appear (see Figure 18.2).

Database Registration

Registering a database is something that all users should do with their database files. Registering will allow other applications to access your data easily when it is called upon. For instance, if you want to create a form letter and have a registered database of contact information, you will be able to refer to the data in that database much more easily.

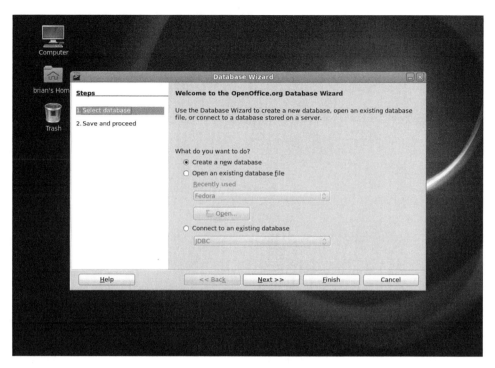

Figure 18.1
The first step in creating a database.

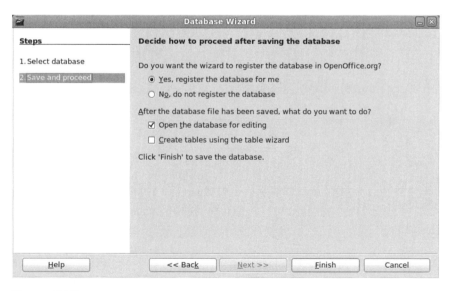

Figure 18.2
The second step in creating a database.

3. Confirm the Yes, Register the Database for Me radio button is selected.

4. Confirm the Open the Database for Editing check box is selected.

5. Click Finish. The Save dialog box will open.

6. Type in a name for your new database file in the Name field.

7. Click Save. The Save dialog box will close, and the main Base window will open (see Figure 18.3).

Before we move on to create our database, it would be a good idea to examine the streamlined interface of Base. The window is divided into three primary areas, which are illustrated in Figure 18.3: the Database, Tasks, and Database Object panes.

In that same figure, you may have noticed that the Database Object pane is actually labeled "Tables." The fluid nature of the Base interface means that as

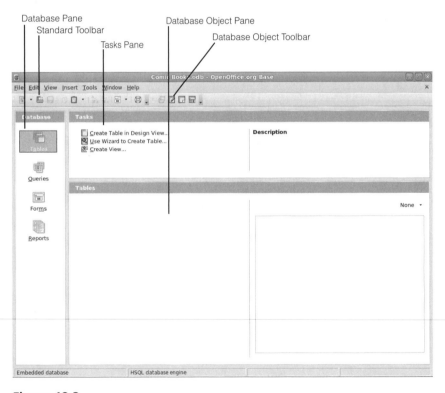

Figure 18.3
A new database, ready to begin.

certain database objects are worked with, the Database Object pane will change to reflect those objects. The Database Objects toolbar and the contents of the Tasks pane will also be altered as different objects are handled. Try clicking on the different objects to see this in action.

In the Base window, only the Standard toolbar stays immutable, as shown in Figure 18.4.

Of these tools, the only one new to OpenOffice.org users is the Form button. Clicking it will begin the process of creating a form in the Design view of Writer, the application Base borrows to enable users to build forms by hand. Clicking the Form drop-down menu reveals a variety of tools, all designed to create various database components or view them.

The Database Objects toolbar has four versions, one for each object. It also has four buttons in each version: Open Database Object, Edit, Delete, and Rename, as seen in Figure 18.5. The functionality of these buttons is pretty straightforward, so we will not delve into them much further.

As you can see, the interface of Base is very simple. This is good because, as mentioned at the beginning of the chapter, traditionally database work has been

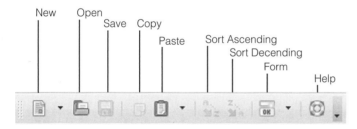

Figure 18.4
The Standard toolbar in Base.

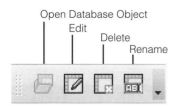

Figure 18.5
The Database Objects toolbar.

regarded as complicated. And while it is true that manipulating data can be a complex process at times, Base's tools are not going to make it more complicated. In fact, the automated wizards in Base can create any component you need, which makes it even simpler.

Creating a Table

Now that you have created the database file and poked around the interface, it's time to put something in the database file. The logical place to start is creating the container to hold the data, which is the table. Using the Table Wizard, here's how to create the database table.

1. Click the Tables object in the Database pane. The Base window will display table-oriented functions and objects.

2. Click Use Wizard to Create Table in the Tasks pane. The Table Wizard dialog box will open (see Figure 18.6).

3. In the Category section, select the Personal radio button.

4. In the drop-down list, select the Sample Tables option that most closely matches the kind of table you want to build. Don't worry if you don't see an exact match—you can modify the table in a moment. For this example, choose Library.

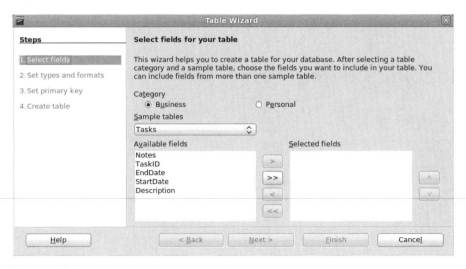

Figure 18.6
Select the table type you want to build.

5. In the Available fields box, click the Fields that most closely match those you want to use.

6. Use the arrow keys to move the fields from the Available Fields box to the Selected Fields box.

Adding New Fields

If you do not see any fields close to your desired fields, add extra placeholder fields that you can rename. For this example, select the fields Title, Publisher, EditionNumber, CopyrightYear, Rating, Genre, and Notes.

7. Click the Next button. The Set Field Types and Formats page will appear (see Figure 18.7).

8. Select EditionNumber in the Selected Fields box.

9. In the Field Name field, change EditionNumber to Volume.

10. Repeat Steps 8 and 9, changing CopyrightYear to Issue.

11. Click the Next button. The Set Primary Key page will appear (see Figure 18.8).

Figure 18.7
Modify the fields you have chosen.

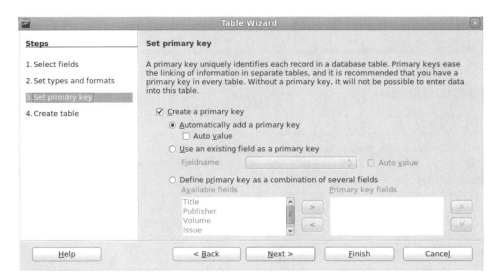

Figure 18.8
Confirming primary key selection.

12. Confirm the Create a Primary Key and Automatically Add a Primary Key radio buttons are selected and click Next. The Create Table page will appear (see Figure 18.9).

13. Type Comics into the What Do You Want to Name Your Table? field.

Figure 18.9
Putting the final touches on the table.

14. Click the Insert Data Immediately radio button and click Finish. The Table Wizard will close.

To see the table you just created, double-click the Comics table in the Tables pane. The Table window will appear, as shown in Figure 18.10.

In addition to the field names you changed in the previous steps, other properties may need to be changed as well. For instance, the CopyrightYear field had a Date format by default, but under its new name of Issue, we need to change it to a Number format.

1. Click the Comics table object in the Tables pane.

2. Click Edit in the Database Objects toolbar. The Table Design window for the Comics table will open (see Figure 18.11).

3. Select Integer from the Field Type list next to the Issue field.

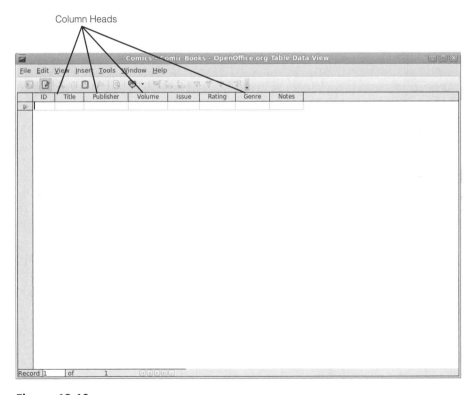

Figure 18.10
A fresh new database table.

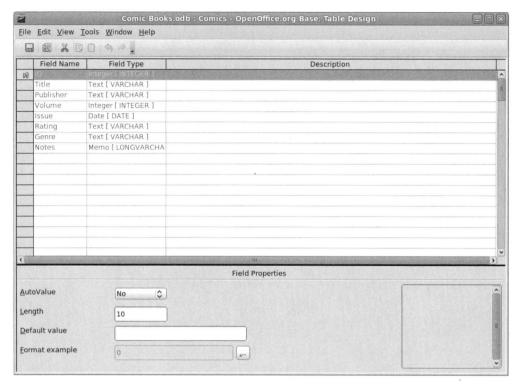

Figure 18.11
Edit and design table fields.

4. Click Save.

5. Close the Table Design window.

Forms to Fill Out

You have created the heart of the database by making the table. You could stop right now and enter data to your heart's content. But, after a while, it might become difficult to enter data in such a monotonous way.

So take the next step and create a form to enter your material.

1. Click the Forms object in the Database pane. The Base window will display form-oriented functions and objects.

2. Click Use Wizard to Create Form in the Tasks pane. The Form Wizard dialog box and the Form Design view of Writer will open (see Figure 18.12).

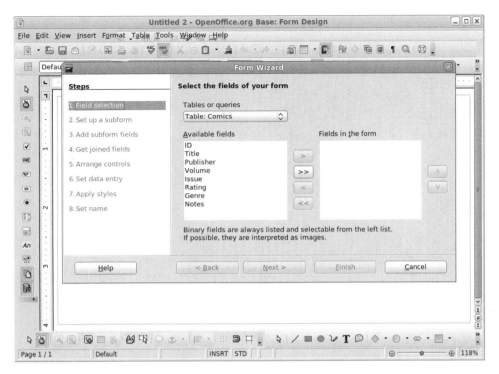

Figure 18.12
Starting the Form Wizard.

3. Confirm that the selected Tables or Queries are Table: Comics.

4. In the Available Fields box, click the fields that you want in your form.

5. Use the arrow keys to move the fields from the Available Fields box to the Fields in the Form box.

6. Click Next. The Set Up a Subform page will appear (see Figure 18.13).

Subforms and You

Subforms are used when you need to add a lot of detailed information about a particular aspect of your data, such as multiple classifications for an object. For this example, we'll forgo subforms, since managing a simple inventory does not need them.

7. Click Next. The Arrange Controls page will appear (see Figure 18.14).

8. Click the In Blocks - Labels Above option and then click Next. The Set Data Entry page will appear, as shown in Figure 18.15.

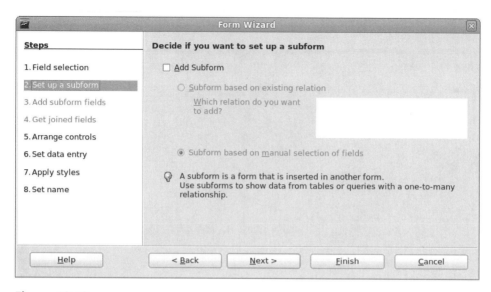

Figure 18.13
Decide to use subforms.

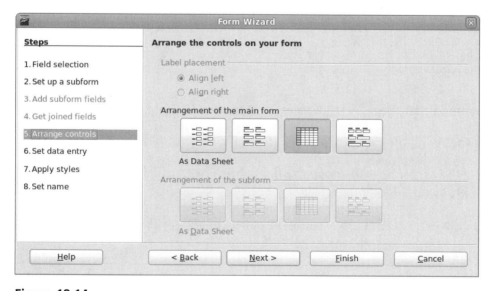

Figure 18.14
Choose the general structure of your form.

9. If you want to just enter new data in a hurry, select the This Form is To Be Used for Entering New Data Only radio button. Otherwise, leave the settings as is and click Next. The Apply Styles page will appear (see Figure 18.16).

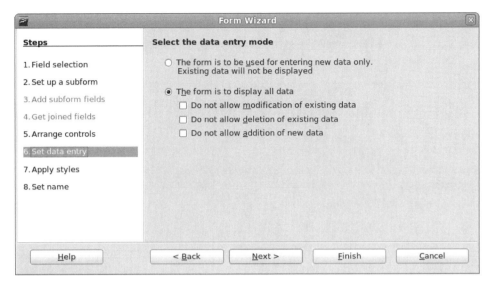

Figure 18.15
Decide how to enter data.

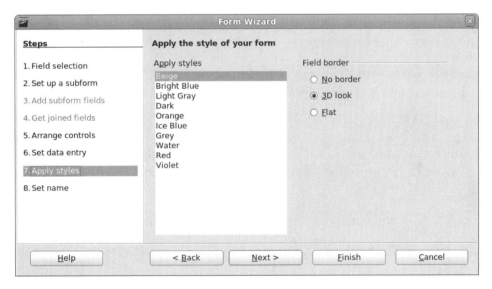

Figure 18.16
Get some style into your form.

10. Choose the Water option. The form being designed for the Form Wizard will change its color scheme.

11. Confirm the 3D Look radio button is selected and click Next. The Set Name page will appear, as seen in Figure 18.17.

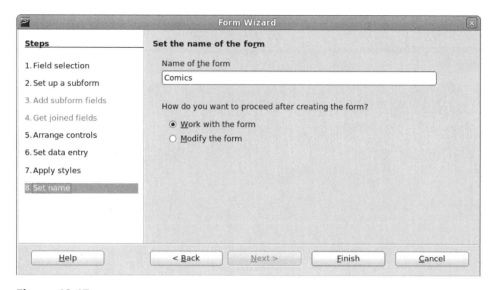

Figure 18.17
Polishing details on your form.

12. Enter a new name on the form.

13. Select the Work with the Form radio button and click Finish. The form will be displayed in a Writer window (see Figure 18.18).

14. Close the form.

The wizard does a good job of setting up a form, but it has its limitations. You can circumvent those limitations if you use the Form Design feature to tweak this form a bit.

1. Click the Comics_Form form object in the Forms pane.

2. Click Edit in the Database Objects toolbar. The Form Design window in Writer will open (see Figure 18.19).

3. Click the Notes field. An anchor and field handles will appear, as shown in Figure 18.20.

4. Right-click the Notes field. The context menu will appear.

5. Select the Group | Ungroup menu command. This will break the connection between the Notes field and its label.

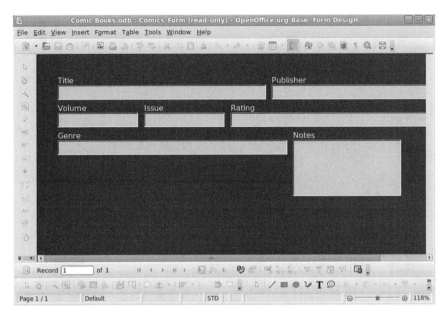

Figure 18.18
A pretty good start to a form.

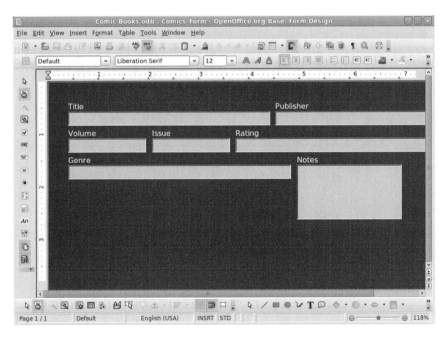

Figure 18.19
Form design is done in Writer.

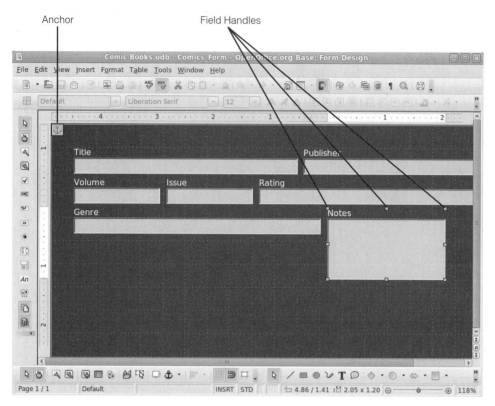

Figure 18.20
Additional elements make it clear you are in Form Design view.

Ungroup Encounter

Ungrouping fields and their labels is necessary because otherwise any resizing operation would resize both label and field, leaving you with a funny-looking form.

6. Drag the lower center field handle of the Notes field to increase the field size.

7. Right-click the field and choose Anchor | To Page from the context menu.

8. Drag the Notes field to another location on the form.

9. Drag the Notes label to an adjacent position to the Notes field.

10. Add a title to the form by clicking in the main form area and entering the text in the first paragraph of the form. Figure 18.21 shows one possible finished look to the form.

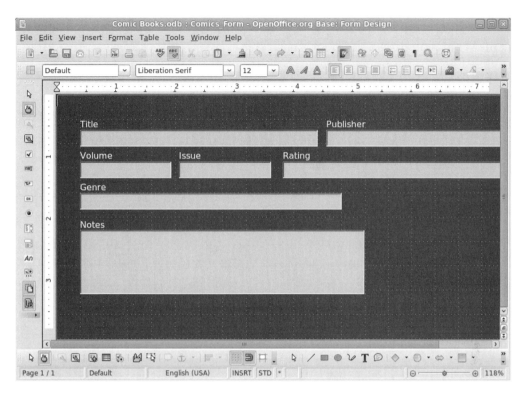

Figure 18.21
A form more customized to your needs.

11. Save your changes by clicking Save.

12. Close the Form Design window by clicking File | Close.

Queries to Ask

You enter data into the form, which in turn goes into the table. All is well and happy in the world.

Then you decide you want to know how many Spider-Man comic books you have entered so far. You can't see this in the form, and after entering so many comic books, you find it impractical to scan the table for every Spider-Man issue you have.

So what do you do? Build a query!

A query is a set of instructions that tells the database to pull out certain pieces of information and store them in a query table, which is sort of like a subtable. You can even edit records from the query table and have those changes reflected in the main database table.

Working Ahead

In this example, several comic book records have been entered into the database already.

1. Click the Queries object in the Database pane. The Base window will display query-oriented functions and objects.

2. Click Use Wizard to Create Query in the Tasks pane. The Query Wizard dialog box will open.

3. In the Available Fields dialog box, choose the fields you want to have in the query. In this example, move all but Notes to the Fields in the Query box.

4. Click Next. The Sorting Order page will appear.

5. Select Comics.Publisher in the first Sort By field.

6. Select Comics.Title in the first Then By field.

7. Click Next. The Search Conditions page will appear.

8. Select Comics.Title as the first Field value.

9. Select Equal to for the first Condition value.

10. Enter Spider in the Value field.

11. Click Next. The Detail or Summary page will appear.

12. For most queries, leave the default settings and click Next. The Aliases page will appear.

13. Again, for most queries, leave the default alias settings and click Next. The Summary page will appear.

14. Review the query selections and click Finish. The Query Wizard will close, and the Query Results window will appear.

The main database will reflect any changes made to the data in the query if you click the Refresh icon on the Database toolbar after making your edits.

Reports to Make

A query is nice for those occasions when you seek information for yourself on your Fedora PC. But, if you want to share the information with others or you want to transport the information, a report is the way to go.

A report differs from a query only in the type of output. Reports are read-only. Once information is in a report, you cannot change it there. You would have to change data in the database table and re-run the report to make changes on the report.

1. Click the Reports object in the Database pane. The Base window will display report-oriented functions and objects.

2. Click Use Wizard to Create Report in the Tasks pane. The Report Wizard dialog box and a blank Writer window will open.

3. Confirm that the selected Tables or Queries are Table: Comics.

4. In the Available Fields box, click the fields that you want in your form.

5. Use the arrow keys to move the fields from the Available Fields box to the Fields in Report box.

6. Click Next. The Labeling Fields page will appear.

7. Confirm the labels are the ones you want to use and click Next. The Grouping page will appear.

8. Click the arrow key to move desired fields to the Groupings box.

9. Click Next. The Sort Options page will appear.

10. Select Publisher in the first Sort By field.

11. Select Title in the first Then By field.

12. Click Next. The Choose Layout page will appear.

13. Choose an option in the Layout of Data field. The style will be reflected in the Writer window behind the Report Wizard.

14. Choose an option in the Layout of Headers and Footers field. The style will be reflected in the Writer window behind the Report Wizard.

15. Click Next. The Create Report page will appear.

16. Enter a name for your report, leaving all other options as is.

17. Click Finish. The report will be generated in the Writer window.

Conclusion

There is much more power to Base than just keeping track of collections, and this chapter was intended to give you a taste of this robust application. You are invited to experiment with Base on your own and create your own databases, which will help you at your job, business, or home projects.

We have come to the end of our introduction to Fedora. By now you should have a pretty good understanding of this popular operating system and be well on your way to making Fedora an integral part of your computing life. Thanks for coming along on this journey, and enjoy your Fedora!

INDEX

License Agreement/Notice of Limited Warranty

By opening the sealed disc container in this book, you agree to the following terms and conditions. If, upon reading the following license agreement and notice of limited warranty, you cannot agree to the terms and conditions set forth, return the unused book with unopened disc to the place where you purchased it for a refund.

License:

The enclosed software is copyrighted by the copyright holder(s) indicated on the software disc. You are licensed to copy the software onto a single computer for use by a single user and to a backup disc. You may not reproduce, make copies, or distribute copies or rent or lease the software in whole or in part, except with written permission of the copyright holder(s). You may transfer the enclosed disc only together with this license, and only if you destroy all other copies of the software and the transferee agrees to the terms of the license. You may not decompile, reverse assemble, or reverse engineer the software.

Notice of Limited Warranty:

The enclosed disc is warranted by Course Technology to be free of physical defects in materials and workmanship for a period of sixty (60) days from end user's purchase of the book/ disc combination. During the sixty-day term of the limited warranty, Course Technology will provide a replacement disc upon the return of a defective disc.

Limited Liability:

THE SOLE REMEDY FOR BREACH OF THIS LIMITED WARRANTY SHALL CONSIST ENTIRELY OF REPLACEMENT OF THE DEFECTIVE DISC. IN NO EVENT SHALL COURSE TECHNOLOGY OR THE AUTHOR BE LIABLE FOR ANY OTHER DAMAGES, INCLUDING LOSS OR CORRUPTION OF DATA, CHANGES IN THE FUNCTIONAL CHARACTERISTICS OF THE HARDWARE OR OPERATING SYSTEM, DELETERIOUS INTERACTION WITH OTHER SOFTWARE, OR ANY OTHER SPECIAL, INCIDENTAL, OR CONSEQUENTIAL DAMAGES THAT MAY ARISE, EVEN IF COURSE TECHNOLOGY AND/OR THE AUTHOR HAS PREVIOUSLY BEEN NOTIFIED THAT THE POSSIBILITY OF SUCH DAMAGES EXISTS.

Disclaimer of Warranties:

COURSE TECHNOLOGY AND THE AUTHOR SPECIFICALLY DISCLAIM ANY AND ALL OTHER WARRANTIES, EITHER EXPRESS OR IMPLIED, INCLUDING WARRANTIES OF MERCHANTABILITY, SUITABILITY TO A PARTICULAR TASK OR PURPOSE, OR FREEDOM FROM ERRORS. SOME STATES DO NOT ALLOW FOR EXCLUSION OF IMPLIED WARRANTIES OR LIMITATION OF INCIDENTAL OR CONSEQUENTIAL DAMAGES, SO THESE LIMITATIONS MIGHT NOT APPLY TO YOU.

Other:

This Agreement is governed by the laws of the State of Massachusetts without regard to choice of law principles. The United Convention of Contracts for the International Sale of Goods is specifically disclaimed. This Agreement constitutes the entire agreement between you and Course Technology regarding use of the software.